LEADERSHIP

*Communication and Social Influence
in Personal and Professional Contexts*

Ralph A. Gigliotti

Brent D. Ruben

Christine Goldthwaite

Kendall Hunt
publishing company

DEDICATION

Dedicated to a future generation of leaders:

Landon Gigliotti
Adeline Gigliotti

*   *   *

Robbi and Matt Urm
Rebecca Urm
Nathan Urm
Nicholas Urm
Marc and Larissa Ruben

*   *   *

Ben Goldthwaite
Will Goldthwaite

ACKNOWLEDGEMENTS

It is with sincere appreciation that we recognize the following individuals and groups for their direct and indirect contributions to this volume.

- To Paul Carty, Director of Publishing Partnerships at Kendall Hunt Publishing Company, for his enthusiastic support of this book project and for encouraging us to complete the manuscript in a timely manner.
- To Angela Willenbring, Senior Developmental Editor at Kendall Hunt Publishing Company, for guiding us through the numerous phases of the publication process with careful attention to many details.
- To Barbara Lee, Senior Vice President for Academic Affairs at Rutgers University, for her genuine commitment to our leadership development efforts in the Center for Organizational Development and Leadership.
- To Richard De Lisi, University Professor and Senior Fellow for the Center for Organizational Development and Leadership at Rutgers University, for introducing many of the concepts and themes raised in this book through our previous collaborations and for the many insights that he continues to offer through his role in our Center.
- To our colleagues in the Center for Organizational Development and Leadership, including Sherrie Tromp, Barbara Corso, and Kimberly Davis, for supporting us with numerous aspects of this book project and for the care, compassion, and collegiality that they demonstrate in our collaborative work.
- To our colleagues and students in the Department of Communication within the School of Communication and Information at Rutgers University, with whom we have discussed many of the ideas presented in this book and whose interest in leadership communication has inspired the development of this book.
- To Rick Dool, Teaching Professor and Director of the Master of Communication and Media Program in the School of Communication and Information at Rutgers University, for his excellent contributions to the chapter on Teams and Conflict in this volume.
- To Martha Lansing, Associate Professor and Vice Chair of Family Medicine and Community Health, and Carol Terregino, Senior Associate Dean for Education, Associate Dean for Admissions, and Professor of Medicine at Rutgers Robert Wood

Johnson Medical School, for their collaboration in the Distinction in Leadership in Academic Healthcare program and for helping us think through a number of general leadership and communication topics that would be of interest to medical students in our collaborative leadership development program.

■ To Denis Hamilton, Assistant Professor of Professional Practice and Director of Management Education at the Rutgers Business School, for his careful review of many chapters in this volume and for encouraging us to pursue additional topics in this text that could be of use for students enrolled in undergraduate and graduate business programs.

■ To the participants involved in our various Center for Organizational Development and Leadership programs who motivated us to pursue a project of this nature and who led us to identify many of the ideas, strategies, and insights offered in this text.

■ To Ralph's former colleagues, teachers, and students from Villanova University and Duquesne University who provided him with the opportunity to both study and practice leadership and who inspired him to pursue this topic as an area of scholarly interest.

■ To Brent's colleagues, students, and friends, and to Rutgers leaders who have been so generous in supporting and recognizing his scholarly and professional contributions in his years as a member of the Department of Communication, the School of Communication and Information, and the University.

■ To Christine's professors, colleagues, and friends in the School of Communication and Information at Rutgers University, as well as classmates and faculty in the Pre-Doctoral Leadership Institute including fellow authors of this book, who have created an encouraging, supportive, and motivating scholarly community to which she is grateful to belong.

BRIEF CONTENTS

CONTENTS

ABOUT THE AUTHORS

Ralph A. Gigliotti (Ph.D., Rutgers University) is Assistant Director for Leadership Programs of the Center for Organizational Development and Leadership at Rutgers University, where he oversees a number of faculty and staff leadership development

Courtesy of Albert Chau

initiatives and leads several research projects related to leadership and communication in higher education. He serves as the co-director of the Rutgers Leadership Academy, co-director of the Distinction in Leadership in Academic Healthcare Program, and part-time lecturer in the Department of Communication. His research explores the intersection of organizational communication, leadership, and crisis communication, particularly in the context of higher education. Ralph's research appears in numerous books and journals, including the *Journal of Leadership and Organizational Studies, Journal of Applied Research in Higher Education, Journal of Leadership Education,* and *Atlantic Journal of Communication.* Ralph is also the co-author of *A Guide for Leaders in Higher Education: Core Concepts, Competencies, and Tools* (with B. Ruben and R. De Lisi).

Brent D. Ruben (Ph.D., University of Iowa) is a distinguished professor, and executive director of the Center for Organizational Development and Leadership at Rutgers

Courtesy of Nat Clymer

University. He is also a member of the faculties of the Rutgers Ph.D. Program in Higher Education and the Robert Wood Johnson School of Medicine. Brent's academic interests include interpersonal, health, and cross-cultural communication, and organizational leadership, planning, assessment, and change. He is author of numerous publications including *Excellence in Higher Education Guide, What Leaders Need to Know and Do, Communication and Human Behavior* (with L. Stewart), and *A Guide for Leaders in Higher Education: Core Concepts, Competencies, and Tools* (with R. De Lisi and R. Gigliotti). Brent was a founder of the Rutgers Department of Communication. He is a Rutgers liaison to the Big Ten Academic Alliance leadership programs and he serves as an adviser to colleges and universities nationally and internationally.

Christine Goldthwaite (MCIS, Rutgers University) is a Doctoral Candidate in the School of Communication & Information (SC&I) at Rutgers University studying organizational and mediated communication. She was a 2012–2014 fellow in the PreDoctoral

Courtesy of Ben Goldthwaite

Leadership Development Institute (PLDI), and currently serves as the graduate coordinator for leadership programs at the Rutgers Center for Organizational Development and Leadership. She is also an adjunct professor at Rutgers where she teaches leadership in digital contexts for the Digital Communication, Information, and Media Minor (DCIM) program. Her primary research interests include communication design relative to creative and innovative activities and is currently working on her dissertation investigating organizing for interdisciplinary research. Christine has presented at state and international conferences such as the New Jersey Communication Association, the National Association of Communication, and the International Communication Association annual conferences, as well as the Organizational Communication Mini-Conference. Before beginning her career in academia, Christine worked in advertising and business-to-business communications.

PART ONE:

Foundational Leadership Theories and Concepts

CHAPTER 1

UNDERSTANDING LEADERSHIP: AN INTRODUCTION TO STUDY AND PRACTICE

> ⚠️ **Guiding Questions:**
>
> 1) What is leadership?
> 2) What makes the study of leadership both important and challenging?
> 3) What is the purpose of this book and who are the intended audiences?
> 4) In what ways can you exert influence in personal and professional settings?

Leadership matters, and it is for this reason that the topic is widely discussed in popular and professional writing and remains a focus of study by scholars in a number of fields. There is broad consensus that leadership is extremely important to the dynamics that occur in social settings at all levels—within families, work groups, teams, organizations, and communities of all kinds, and in national and international affairs.

For all the interest and attention that leadership receives, we might assume that there is an agreed upon understanding of what leadership is, how it operates, and how one goes about developing the knowledge and skills necessary to become competent in the various informal and formal settings where leadership dynamics are important. However, as this book explains, no single or shared understanding exists. Because leadership is studied and practiced in so many different disciplines and settings, the numerous perspectives on leadership often do not fully align with one another. While all these theories and concepts are useful for highlighting various facets of leadership, they do not provide a prescription for action that guarantees the success of one's leadership efforts.

Another consideration that adds complexity to the study and practice of leadership has to do with the tendency to glamorize the role and potential influence of leaders. This "romanticization" of leadership sometimes leads observers and critics to reduce the complexities of organizational life, and to attribute all successes and failures of systems to a single factor that focuses on the leader (Meindl & Ehrlich, 1987). In so doing, one can fail to adequately describe the role of context, history, followers, and any number of other factors that may be involved. It should also be noted that the term "leadership" is often used as a convenient label for integrating a number of different competencies, any of which may be important in their own right. One writer has gone so far as to refer to this preoccupation with the topic as a "dangerous leadership obsession" (Rothman, 2016), and scholar Jeffrey Pfeffer (2015) challenges the leadership development industry not to overstate the influence of leaders in his book, *Leadership BS*. In an article entitled "Why Are American Colleges Obsessed with 'Leadership'?" Burton (2014) discusses the growing emphasis on cultivating leadership skills during one's collegiate experience. As she suggests, "in valorizing 'leadership' as a quality, we risk overlooking other—less obvious—qualities," such as the need for and contributions of good followers, an important point about which we will have more to say in the pages ahead.

These important cautions regarding the risks of adopting an exaggerated view of leadership should not be taken to imply that leadership knowledge or skill is unimportant. When groups, organizations, communities, or nations encounter setbacks, the issue is often traced back to a failure in leadership. A growing chorus of critics point to the "leadership deficit" in our society, and urge colleges and universities to focus on leadership education and development inside and outside of the classroom. Unquestionably, leadership skills are in very high demand by employers, and a growing number of business, non-profit, public sector, and educational organizations. A survey conducted by the National Association of Colleges and Employers (2015) found that more than 80% of responding employers seek to recruit candidates with evidence of leadership experience and skill on their resume. Leadership is also an important (and expensive) focus of training and development initiatives, with recent statistics from the Association for Talent Development (2015) suggesting that nearly $20 billion of the approximately $160 billion spent on employee learning and development was spent on leadership education and development.

Our primary focus in this book is on formal and informal leadership in groups and organizations. That said, we believe that most, if not all, of the concepts and ideas discussed in this book have applicability across settings—in families, clubs, teams, communities, and society more broadly. Furthermore, in an effort to strengthen the effectiveness of leadership development efforts, we believe that the focus on communication and social influence offered in this book can provide a more productive, nuanced, and realistic way to think about the dynamics of leadership.

© Rawpixel.com/Shutterstock.com

COMPETING PERSPECTIVES ON LEADERSHIP

There are a number of well-developed theories about the nature of leadership, and we will discuss these extensively in the pages ahead. It seems appropriate to begin a textbook on leadership, however, with an explanation of what we mean by "leadership," as we will be using the term in this book. We view leadership as the process of social influence—a process that takes place through communication (Ruben, De Lisi, & Gigliotti, 2017). Leadership can be planned and unplanned, formal and informal, and used for purposes that may be "good" or "evil." As indicated above, there are a number of ways to think about leadership, and the perspective one adopts in doing so and the elements one chooses as the focus of discussion matter. For example, leadership can be understood in terms of position, person, process, and result—each of which raises different questions, considerations, and expectations (Grint, 2010). The way individuals approach leadership will shape how they think about the operation of influence in group, team, organizational, and community settings, and more generally, how they make sense of the dynamics of social life. On a personal level, an individual's perspective on leadership has implications for how one understands his or her own contributions to leading others and to being led by others in a variety of contexts, including work, home, school, and the community. Finally, an individual's understanding of leadership may shape both the particular goals that are established and the strategies adopted to achieve these goals. Thus, the conceptualization of leadership informs both the study *and* practice of leadership.

Given the popularity of the term leadership, it is not surprising that there are many "folk theories" related to the topic. On the one hand, these signal the importance attached to understanding leadership, yet they also reveal and contribute to what are often overly simplistic theories of leadership dynamics and practices. One such notion is the belief that some individuals are natural leaders while others are not. This view is sometimes accompanied by the presumption that leadership traits are an inherent part of an individual's personality or personal makeup rather than the product of experiences and skill development. Those who adopt this perspective might be less willing to try to develop the skills necessary to become a more adept leader or support others in their leadership development. While this idea was quite common in early theoretical conceptions, the general view now is that a person's natural leadership capacities are honed through experience, and that any of us can acquire enhanced leadership capability if we dedicate ourselves to that goal (Northouse, 2015; Parks, 2005; Velsor, McCauley, & Ruderman, 2010).

Another common notion is that in order to be influential one must be outgoing and highly verbal. There are certainly instances where this style is associated with those in highly visible leadership positions, and it is not difficult to see how these skills can be helpful in many settings. However, there are also instances where these behaviors are associated with the tendency to be overpowering and domineering, thereby causing a backlash and increasing resistance to intended outcomes and, over time, diminishing the respect and influence the leader may enjoy. You can probably think of group projects or team experiences where one outspoken individual had a disruptive impact on the dynamics of the group. Conversely, being skilled at restrained communicative engagement and careful decision making about with whom and when to assert one's views can be a very important leadership quality in a range of situations. For example, there are moments where silence or withheld communication may be the more advantageous strategy in group settings. This idea echoes Cain's (2013) description of the potential influence of introverts in her book, *Quiet: The Power of Introverts in a World that Can't Stop Talking.*

The term "leadership" is often associated with formal positions or titles, and we assume that those who occupy these roles represent the essence of what is meant by leadership. While this is certainly a familiar and understandable way of thinking, it is also true that informal roles afford excellent opportunities for leadership influence, as will be discussed in Chapter 4. For example, one of the authors of this book raised the following question with a group of undergraduates who were participating in a co-curricular leadership program: "How many of you identify yourselves as being leaders?" Very few students raised their hands, which is particularly interesting given the program's central emphasis on leadership development. After some probing, it became clear that many of the students in attendance—particularly those first-year students—failed to identify themselves as leaders because of their new status at the university and because they failed to consider the wide range of circumstances in which they have likely served as informal leaders in the past. We want to challenge this way of thinking in this book. Regardless of formal title or leadership position, we want to encourage you to consider the wide array of formal and informal contexts where you can exert positive social influence. Think less about "being a leader" (i.e., having a title) and more about pursuing opportunities for "doing leadership" (i.e., being influential).

Another topic that provokes much debate is whether or not there exists one or more leadership skills or competencies that, if possessed and applied, will lead to consistently positive outcomes across a broad range of settings, situations, and cultures. We examine this topic at greater length later, but suffice it to say here that some universal leadership capabilities transcend circumstances and settings in their import and impact. But as various leadership theories and models demonstrate, there are also situation- and context-specific knowledge and skill sets that can be vital to producing desired outcomes, such that there is no simple or single profile of *the* successful leadership approach. Perhaps the greatest challenge, as noted later in this text, is to know which cross-cutting capabilities are most essential, and which setting- and position-specific knowledge and skills are critical, as well as how to determine and apply the appropriate leadership approach given the needs and expectations of those around you and the unique circumstances of a particular context.

LEADERSHIP: A COMMUNICATION-CENTERED APPROACH

© Rawpixel.com/Shutterstock.com

Clearly, the diversity of theories, approaches, models, and guides that offer insight and advice for leadership thinking and practice is both expansive and expanding. For those wishing to better understand and become more competent in leadership, the multiplicity of perspectives and relevant issues present quite a challenge, but the richness and diversity of perspectives is also very much an asset. Our goal in this book is to provide a kind of GPS to help readers navigate through the complexity associated with the topic in order to develop an integrated and useful understanding of leadership dynamics. In doing so, we provide an overview of core concepts that are central to the traditions of leadership, but our emphasis is on communication and social influence, and the central role that both play in the study and practice of leadership.

As described earlier, we view leadership as the process of social influence—a process that takes place through communication (Ruben et al., 2017). From the perspective of communication, the nature of the relationships and dynamics that develop between leaders and followers is central, and as we shall see, when we view leadership in this way, it becomes clear that the outcomes of social influence are defined as much by followers as by leaders. Similar to others who approach leadership as a process (Northouse, 2015), leadership is not a static act or event, although it may appear that way to a casual observer; nor is it limited to one individual or position in group or organizational settings. Suggesting that leadership is a process implies that any single observed leadership event or action has a history that precedes it, which creates the conditions one needs to understand to fully make sense of any "leadership moment." Relevant to understanding a "leadership moment" are a number of "historical" elements, including the history of a leader and the development and evolution of his or her leadership knowledge and skills, the history of the followers and their reasons for being engaged in the situation, and the history of the relationships between a leader and his or her followers—all of which we will have more to say about later in the book. The idea of process also underscores the reciprocal nature of the leader-follower relationship and influence that is often characteristic of leader-follower exchanges. Thus, to define leadership as a process is to imply that it is dynamic and involves multiple steps, actions, and reactions, and that the conditions necessary for leadership and social influence and its consequences evolve over time through communication and interaction between leaders and followers, rather than being a static or single event.

By approaching the topic of leadership as a process of social influence, we hope you are able to make connections to opportunities for social influence in your personal and professional lives, regardless of your formal leadership titles, your institutional or organizational affiliations, or your past experiences with leading those around you. Furthermore, the view offered in this book can complement other disciplinary perspectives on leadership. We believe that a communication-centered approach is particularly helpful in providing a framework for understanding the dynamics of leadership-in-action. Because of this focus on a process of mutual and reciprocal influence exerted by leaders *and* followers, we believe that the communication perspective presented in this book will help you integrate and apply leadership insights across a variety of settings including communities, organizations, groups, and families, as well as the college or university campus. Finally, unlike other approaches that present communication solely as a tool or technique for accomplishing leadership, the perspective taken in this book goes beyond this view to explore the fundamental role that communication plays in social influence and in creating the situations in which leadership influence take place. The concepts and examples presented in this book are intended to challenge and encourage readers—undergraduate and graduate students, leadership education and development professionals, and any individuals with an interest in leadership theory and practice—to understand and exercise leadership in both personal and professional settings.

IN PURSUIT OF "POSITIVE" SOCIAL INFLUENCE

One additional issue deserves mention. There is frequently a blurring of distinction between "good" or "effective" leadership practices, on the one hand, and "good" or "effective" outcomes, on the other. Clearly, an individual can exercise what would be considered successful leadership, whether in professional or personal settings, even when the outcomes of those social influence efforts may be seen as negative or undesirable, either by intention or default. There is no shortage of historical or contemporary examples, such as Adolf Hitler, Pol Pot, and Jim Jones—individuals who were extremely influential, but whose efforts led to outcomes that were both negative and destructive.

Quite aside from the ethical issues these situations raise, when the goal is to learn about leadership, it is important to differentiate between how we value leaders' intentions, strategies, and practices, and how we value the outcomes of their efforts. We can often learn a great deal about leadership from those who are successful in achieving outcomes—regardless of how we might feel about the value or appropriateness of those outcomes or their motives. By the same token, much can be learned from those whose aims are worthy and desirable, but whose efforts to achieve these ends are not successful or admirable.

Not everyone will have the same idea as to what constitutes "positive" social influence, which is also one of the great challenges in leadership study and practice. Nonetheless, we advocate for positive social influence throughout this text, as discussed in more detail in Chapter 6. We believe that leaders should aspire to enrich the lives of those around them, but we also recognize that there is often a range of opinions about how one thinks about "enrichment." In a world full of discord, the time for positive social influence has perhaps never been greater.

WHAT MAKES A GREAT LEADER?

One's success as a leader is generally based on the assessment by others of the positive role a leader has played in relation to a group, team, organization, and/or society. These results are attributed to the leaders' influence based on a wide array of considerations, including, but not limited to, one's decisions, actions, personal characteristics, context, resources, persuasiveness, or communication skills—as well as the actions and reactions of followers.

© Rawpixel.com/Shutterstock.com

There is no single formula for successful leadership. Libraries are filled with the biographies and narratives of individuals who were outgoing and others who were very shy, those born into wealth and others born into poverty, yet all found a way to leave an enduring legacy. There also exist a number of individuals who seem to excel as leaders based on their credentials, attitude, and position in the organization, yet are criticized by many for their leadership failures or inadequacies. In some instances, a particular critical incident and highly visible leadership moment may create a leadership impression that becomes emblematic of the legacy an individual leader leaves. One's legacy, for example, may include something tangible such as the development of a new student-run club that supports a local charity, or something less tangible and less visible, such as playing an informal, but influential and supportive role within one's work group or organization.

What then are the necessary qualities of a great leader? A traits perspective, as discussed in more detail in the next chapter, would lead us to consider the following attributes that are typically associated with effective leadership, and certainly other qualities could be added to this list:

- Natural ability
- Experience
- Perseverence
- Knowledge of theory and concepts
- Being in the right position or role
- Skilled at personal relationships and networking
- Good at leveraging the talents of others
- Persuasiveness
- Good learner and able to adapt quickly to a situation

A number of scholars have addressed the important question of "What makes a great leader?" One prominent author, Warren Bennis (2007, p. 5), for example, offers the following view of the actions related to effective leadership: Great leaders. . .

- create a sense of mission
- motivate others to join them on that mission
- create an adaptive social architecture for their followers
- generate trust and optimism
- develop other leaders
- get results

Similarly, in his synthesis of the common leadership definitions, Brent Ruben (2012) captures the following characteristics associated with effective leadership as presented in the existing literature:

- Attracting people (Maxwell, 1999)
- Building community (DePree, 1999)
- Creating and sustaining culture (Schein, 1999)
- Change management (Kanter, 1983)

- Pursuit of mutually beneficial purposes (Hackman & Johnson, 2013)
- Influencing individual or group behavior (Hersey, 1984; DuBrin, 2004)
- Problem solving (Luke, 1998)
- Vision plus action (Useem, 1998)
- Vision plus strategy (Ruben, 2006)

Considering these characteristics and modeling your behaviors after those leaders whom you admire is an important component of leadership development. Some of these views of leadership focus on the characteristics and actions of the individual leader; others, such as those proposed by Maxwell (1999) and Bennis (2007), make clear reference not only to the attributes of leaders, but also to the importance of followers and the relationship formed between leaders and followers—a perspective that is underscored by the communication perspective presented in this book.

© Dmitrijs Kaminskis/Shutterstock.com

A ROADMAP FOR THIS BOOK

There is a craving for effective leadership across society that demands our attention. This book serves as an invitation for the reader to think through the notion of social influence in personal and professional contexts. The following chapters blend theory and practice, provide guiding questions and inventories for self-reflection, and offer specific tools, strategies, and models for applied engagement with these leadership topics. Thus, using communication as the primary lens, this text serves as a point of entry into the study of leadership theory and practice. These chapters provide an overview of the existing leadership literature and we hope you take the time to further explore the cited references for more detailed explorations into each of these relevant topics of inquiry.

Part One: Foundational Leadership Theories and Concepts highlights a variety of theoretical concepts that inform our approach to leadership communication throughout the book. This broad synthesis of the existing literature will allow you to better understand the evolution of leadership scholarship and equip you with a host of theoretical lenses for analyzing the many leadership encounters that you face in your personal and professional life. Chapter 2: Evolving Views of Leadership: An Overview of Classical, Contemporary, and Competency Theories presents an introductory summary of the evolution of leadership thinking, focusing primarily on the diverse array of classical, contemporary, and competency theories. An understanding of leadership theory can inform your approach to leadership practice, and can also help you to better explain, understand, and analyze the leadership decisions and challenges in your environment. Building upon these central theories, Chapter 3: Leadership Communication Theories and Strategies introduces the concepts and behaviors most germane to the study and practice of leadership communication. In this chapter, we make the case for adopting a communication-centered understanding of leadership, and we explore a number of actions and behaviors that can enhance one's ability to influence others in a variety of situations. In Chapter 4: Formal and Informal Leadership, we differentiate formal and informal occasions for leadership from one another and we highlight the central dynamics associated with social influence in both settings. The final chapter of this first section, Chapter 5: Understanding Culture in Groups, Teams, and Organizations: The Leader as Cross-Cultural Communicator and Organizational Ethnographer, explores the importance of culture as a central concept for leadership. An understanding of culture, along with an appreciation for intercultural differences, is critical for effective leadership. It is often the case that tensions in organizations and interpersonal relationships are the result of leaders who are ill-equipped for dealing with intercultural differences, or lack understanding of the broader and deeper cultural norms and expectations that shape and influence processes. For this reason, we present a number of helpful strategies in this chapter for enhancing your intercultural competence as a leader.

Part Two: Your Personal Approach to Leadership provides key considerations for thinking through your personal approach to leadership, particularly in light of the many challenges and ethical tensions that you may encounter. For example, in Chapter 6: Leadership in Everyday Encounters: Ethics, Values, and Integrity, we explore the importance of ethics, values, and integrity as central pillars for effective leadership. In particular, you will have an opportunity to reflect on the core values and guiding principles that motivate you to lead in personal and professional contexts. In Chapter 7: The Foundations of Personal and Professional Leadership: Philosophy, Passion, and Goals, we explore a variety of topics to help you consider your philosophy of leadership and followership. By reflecting on your goals for leadership, you can ultimately gain a better understanding of your motivations, expectations, preferences, and desired outcomes—all of which are essential to formal and informal leadership effectiveness. Finally, Chapter 8: Becoming a Better Leader: Personal Assessment and Leadership Development, offers a variety of methods and models for cultivating your leadership skills and developing a more informed understanding of your strengths and areas for improvement.

Part Three: Applied Leadership Communication in Personal and Professional Settings outlines a number of strategies, tools, and focused topics on leadership communication that are rooted in communication theory. These applied tools and tactics distill key insights for effective leadership communication practice and will contribute to your growing toolkit of skills and competencies for positive social influence in groups, teams, and organizations. There are three applied domains that we find to be especially relevant for effective formal and informal leadership—planning and change, the use of assessment and metrics, and teams and conflict. Chapter 9: Planning and Change: Principles and Practices, Chapter 10: Defining and Pursuing a Vision of Excellence: A Framework for Groups, Clubs, and Organizations, and Chapter 11: Teamwork and Conflict in Organizations: Leadership Trends and Implications address each of these domains respectively, with the hope that you will be able to use these tools in navigating these complex areas for leadership influence. Finally, to round out our exploration of leadership concepts and tools, the role of technology must be considered. Technology has certainly contributed to an interconnected—yet increasingly complex—global environment, and in Chapter 12: The Digital World: Leadership in an Interconnected Society, we describe a number of relevant insights, tools, and concepts to consider as you think through the role of technology in leading others, along with the influence of technology on your personal and professional reputation.

CONCLUSION

Leadership in everyday encounters is a key theme that runs throughout this book. Multiple contexts provide a venue for social influence. These contexts cut across your personal and professional experiences and may include your encounters with family members, friends, roommates, classmates, members of student clubs and organizations, teachers, employers, co-workers, and members of the community. We believe that the classroom, the workplace, and democratic society more broadly all provide a space for you to demonstrate positive and constructive social influence. Regardless of your formal leadership title or informal status in a club or organization, academic major, or your desired career path, the focus on leadership and communication is a relevant one for all. We hope you find the following chapters to be useful as you interrogate what leadership means and why it matters, and focus attention on the ways you can improve your leadership effectiveness—all of which involve a deeper, more nuanced, and greater appreciation for communication.

As noted at the outset of this chapter, leadership is a vitally important topic, and we believe this book can be a useful guide as you pursue personal and professional opportunities for social influence and engage followers in a mutually beneficial pursuit of shared values and goals.

CHAPTER 2

EVOLVING VIEWS OF LEADERSHIP: AN OVERVIEW OF CLASSICAL, CONTEMPORARY, AND COMPETENCY THEORIES

⚠️ **Guiding Questions:**

1) Why is there such a diverse array of views about leadership and leadership practice?
2) What are the major concepts, approaches, and theories of leadership?
3) How can leadership theory provide a useful foundation for leadership practice?
4) What are the differences between the vertical and horizontal approaches to leadership competence, and in what ways does the proposed two-dimensional competency model help to explain leadership development and practice?

As discussed in the previous chapter, the study of leadership has historically attracted a great deal of interest from scholars and practitioners alike (Bass, 1990; Northouse, 2015; Yukl, 2012). Despite the voluminous literature on the subject, leadership remains an exceedingly complex phenomenon (Burns, 1978). Leadership is difficult to describe, let alone define with enough flexibility to take account of the many interpretations, examples, and dynamics at play in any given moment. The aim of this chapter is to provide a broad overview of classical, contemporary, and competency theories for understanding leadership as a topic of scholarly investigation and applied practice.

© Rawpixel.com/Shutterstock.com

ALTERNATIVE WAYS OF UNDERSTANDING THE NATURE OF LEADERSHIP

Prior to describing some of the more popular leadership theories, it is important to first acknowledge the difficulty associated with disentangling these various theories, approaches, and areas of emphasis in the leadership literature. Often, the distinct and alternative foci offer competing—even contradictory—ways of thinking about leadership. For example, some scholars and practitioners highlight the importance of "understanding leadership *theory*," whereas others emphasize the importance of "applying leadership *skills*." Contrasting views of leadership such as these are often presented as "dichotomies," which Merriam-Webster (2017) defines as "a division into two especially mutually exclusive or contradictory groups or entities." These dichotomies present contrasting, but not always mutually exclusive, views of leadership. Rather, they represent alternative ways of thinking about leadership, and point to "tensions" that shape and enrich how we think about the nature of leadership. We believe a review and discussion of some of these dichotomies can help to introduce the range of leadership perspectives that both complicate and enrich the study and practice of leadership. Below is an initial list of the dichotomies currently found in the literature:

- Theory or Practice
- Management or Leadership
- Transparent or Opaque
- Authentic or Calculating
- Planning or Execution
- Servant or Master
- Incremental or Strategic
- Formal or Informal
- Directing or Role Modeling
- Transactional or Transformational
- Leadership as Decision Making or Leadership as Process Facilitation
- Context Specific or Context General

We will focus on three of these dichotomies in greater detail here and others will be discussed further throughout the book. First, let us consider the alternative views of leadership suggested by those who differentiate leadership from management. The leadership literature tends to identify the manager's role in maintaining order and consistency through the demonstration and accomplishment of activities and routines. Leaders, on the other hand, are typically responsible for articulating a vision for the future that both privileges and produces change (Bennis & Nanus; 1985; Kotter, 2012; Rost, 1993; Zaleznik, 1992). As summarized by Galsworth (2016), "Management is about stabilization. Leadership is about growth. Management creates short-term safety and a knowable future. Leadership creates short-term risk and future expansion" (para 4). This separation between leadership and management presents a helpful dichotomy for high-lighting differences and for building parsimonious theories or models about one or both of these topics. However, in so doing, this way of thinking risks depicting leadership as the more glamorous role, suggesting that attention to detail and routine work are not required for effective leadership performance. Although this dichotomy is useful in some ways, "leadership" and "management" are not mutually exclusive activities in practice. A closer examination reveals that the presumed work of a leader and that of a manager are blurred in many respects—leaders often have many management respon-sibilities and vice versa.

The distinction between leader and follower is a second dichotomy that is com-monly identified in the leadership literature. Much of the literature presents a clear distinction between *leaders*—those who exercise power (make critical decisions, super-vise, influence, create vision, direct activities, manage resources, etc.) and *followers*—those who are led (carry out the directions of leaders, receive guidance and supervision, "report to," etc.). While it seems reasonable to use the term "leader" to refer to activities associated with initiating personal, professional, and task-oriented relationships, as we discuss in the next chapter, leadership and followership—and the distinction between them—can be quite fuzzy and fluid. Despite the implied power and importance ascribed to leaders, individuals have no ability to lead unless there are others who are willing to follow. Moreover, as with the distinction between leaders and managers discussed pre-viously, in practice, leaders often follow and followers often lead. In fact, in the ongoing subtleties of group and organizational life, it may be quite difficult to discern who is leading and who is following at any moment in time, and the roles are often dynamic. Recent scholarship stresses the inseparability of leader and follower, by suggesting that leadership itself is co-constructed through interactions between leaders and followers via communication (Barge & Fairhurst, 2008; Ruben, 2006; Smircich & Morgan, 1982; Witherspoon, 1997), a topic for further discussion. Unless there are those who follow, the concept of leader has little or no value.

The third dichotomy that we will discuss relates to our view that leadership lies at the intersection of science and art. From a scientific or scholarly perspective, there exist a number of generalizable theories and concepts that are useful to both the thinking and practice of leadership. We might also consider the "art" associated with leadership application and implementation, whereby leadership is recognized as a personal, subjec-tive, and creative activity that is greatly influenced by individual strengths, weaknesses, and idiosyncrasies that are in play as scientific and scholarly theories are translated into practice (Grint, 2001). Both science and art have an important role to play in the implementation of leadership, and by prioritizing one over the other, we run the risk of adopting an incomplete view of leadership. With the dichotomies discussed thus far, and many others listed above that will be referred to in later discussion, each pair of terms identifies a contrasting view. However, these views are not necessarily mutually exclu-sive, and it is the tension between the two perspectives that adds richness to leadership study and practice.

AN INTRODUCTION TO LEADERSHIP THEORIES

© Login/Shutterstock.com

Theories are lenses through which we see and understand our world. As Ruben and Stewart (2016) suggest, theories are building blocks of understanding, and as noted by Popper (2002), theories are the "net[s] that we throw out to catch the world—to rationalize, explain, and dominate it" (pp. 37, 38). Theories help us to explain phenomena, and particularly in the social sciences, theories offer explanations for often complex and unpredictable behavior.

As society has evolved, so too have the definitions, models, and approaches to leadership theory and practice (Stogdill, 1974). Witherspoon (1997) explains that "Theories are a product of the sociopolitical and historical context in which their creators live" (p. 11). Trends in the workplace and organizational life more broadly have contributed to a shift in our thinking about leadership from the primary focus on individuals perceived to exercise extreme power over others, to perspectives that place an increased emphasis on the interactions between leaders and followers. For our purposes here, leadership theories can be organized into four broad categories (Ruben et al., 2017). These include:

- **Classical approaches**—traditional approaches to the study of leadership that include the following theories: trait (Bass, 1990; Jago, 1982), skills (Katz, 1955), style (Blake & McCanse, 1991; Lewin, Lippitt, & White 1939), situational (Hersey, 1984; Hersey & Blanchard, 1969), and path-goal (House, 1971, 1996; House & Mitchell, 1974)
- **Contemporary approaches**—modern approaches to the study of leadership theory and practice, including transformational (Bass & Avolio, 1994; Diaz-Saenz, 2011), authentic (Avolio & Gardner, 2005; George, 2003); and servant leadership (Greenleaf, 1977; Sendjaya & Sarros, 2002)

- **Competency approaches**—approaches to leadership that focus on the ability of successful leaders to acquire a portfolio of knowledge and skills that they can apply strategically in their formal and informal leadership roles (Goleman, 1995, 1998; Kotter, 2012; Pfeffer & Sutton, 2000; Ruben, 2012; Salovey & Mayer, 1990; Smith, 2007; Wisniewski, 1999)
- **Communication approaches**—approaches to leadership that illustrate the inseparable relationship between communication and leadership, and that foreground the role of communication theory in understanding the dynamics of leadership and social influence (Barge & Fairhurst, 2008; Fairhurst, 2007; Fairhurst & Connaughton, 2014a, 2014b; Fairhurst & Sarr, 1996; Ruben & Gigliotti, 2016, 2017; Ruben et al., 2017; Witherspoon, 1997)

Many of the ideas within the classical, contemporary, competency, and communication approaches to leadership overlap with one another, yet we believe it is important for students of leadership to be aware of this useful taxonomy of the primary perspectives. The following section provides a high-level overview of several of the theories included in this taxonomy.

OVERVIEW OF POPULAR LEADERSHIP THEORIES

© Rawpixel.com/Shutterstock.com

The following section provides an overview of major classical and contemporary leadership theories based on the seminal work by Peter Northouse (2015), as also summarized in Ruben et al. (2017). For each, we offer a summary that includes an overview of key concepts advanced by the theory and a brief discussion of key strengths and criticisms associated with each theoretical perspective.[1] As you read through each of the descriptions below, consider how you might apply the theories to your own leadership

---

1 The summary of theories was initially created by Immordino and Gigliotti, based on the framework provided by Northouse (2015). The overview of theoretical perspectives, including the summary of strengths and critiques, reflects many of the central ideas from Northouse's work.

in everyday personal and professional contexts. Which of the theories are most useful for how you think about the nature of leadership and social influence? Additionally, if every way of seeing is also a way of not seeing, which aspects of leadership do the following theories tend to highlight and which aspects of leadership do the theories tend to ignore?

Trait Approach

This approach to leadership captures the thinking of many of the early classical theories, including the Great Man and so-called trait theories. In this perspective, leaders are viewed as possessing innate leadership qualities that differentiate them from non-leaders (e.g., intelligence, self-confidence, determination, integrity, and sociability) (Northouse, 2015). Historically, this approach has been appealing because of its simplicity and the substantial body of research that it has generated. The perspective suggests that specific traits, such as agreeableness, extraversion, or openness, may be measured and matched to specific jobs. A major strength was the attention given to leadership and to the personal characteristics of individuals serving in leadership roles. On the other hand, this focus set the stage for a primary—sometimes exclusive—focus on the nature of the individual leader in explaining the dynamics of leader-follower dynamics. Another significant weakness of this approach is its assumption that only individuals with particular fixed traits will be effective leaders.

The implication of this way of thinking is that individuals who possess specific traits should be selected for leadership roles. A further implication is that these traits are naturally occurring in some individuals, suggesting that it is unlikely that someone without these ideal traits could learn or develop the competencies necessary to become an effective leader. This approach has been very influential and has been the focus of extensive research. However, an exclusive list of traits that would differentiate leaders from non-leaders has not been identified, and gradually, the initial popularity of the trait approach has waned, leading to the emergence of other ways of thinking.

Skills Approach

The skills approach to understanding leadership reflects a shift in focus from innate and generally fixed traits to an emphasis on individual leader skills that are cultivated and developed over time (Northouse, 2015). Various taxonomies of leadership skills have been presented, including the three-skill approach, which highlights the technical, human, and conceptual skills required for effective leadership (Katz, 1955). This leader-centered model indicates that leadership skills are accessible to all and suggests that anyone can learn the necessary skills for influencing others.

Thus, unlike the classical trait approach, a skills perspective suggests that key leadership skills can be learned. A critical implication is that efforts to identify potentially effective leaders need not exclusively focus on an individual's personality traits, but rather these efforts could emphasize one's current skills and the likelihood that he or she could develop additional skills that would enhance one's capability as a leader. A key limitation of this approach, however, is its lack of predictive value. For example, research based on this approach has not been successful in explaining how variations in particular skills have an impact on overall leadership performance or effectiveness.

Style Approach

A style approach to leadership focuses on common leadership behaviors in a variety of contexts. Unlike the previous two approaches to leadership, a style approach considers the needs of followers in determining one's leadership effectiveness (Northouse, 2015). Seminal studies conducted at The Ohio State University and the University of Michigan point to the various leadership styles that leaders may typically exhibit, distinguishing task-oriented behaviors from more relationship-oriented behaviors. Building upon this way of thinking, scholars and practitioners utilized these concepts to identify and develop the approach that leaders take to consider both tasks and relationships. Blake and McCanse's (1991) Leadership Grid (formerly Blake and Mouton's Managerial Grid) is one of many tools developed and widely used to enable potential individuals to self-assess, change, and improve upon their leadership style. Another benefit of this approach is its emphasis on leadership behavior in a broad range of situations and contexts. As with the skills approach, however, no consistent link has been identified between task and relationship behaviors and outcomes, and thus the approach has not been shown to be particularly helpful in identifying a single "best" leadership style.

Situational Approach

One explanation for why other approaches have not been successful in identifying a "best" leadership style relates to the dynamic and evolving context in which leadership occurs. Taking account of the uniqueness of each context, the situational approach, based on research by Hersey and Blanchard (1969), suggests that the traits needed for effective leadership vary based on the circumstances. This approach calls attention to the need for leaders to have an awareness of the nature of the situation in which they are leading and to adapt their behaviors accordingly. Different situations call for different approaches to leadership, including directing, coaching, supporting, and delegating. According to this perspective, a leader must adapt his or her style to adequately meet the demands of the situation (Northouse, 2015).

An implication of this approach is the importance of the match between an individual's approach to leadership and the nature of the situation in which he or she will provide leadership. A further implication is that the emphasis should be placed on selecting individuals whose leadership capabilities align with the needs of a given situation, and alternatively—or perhaps additionally—to prepare individuals with the ability to observe, analyze, and adjust their actions to the needs of a unique setting. Despite the intuitive appeal of this way of thinking, there is an absence of a strong body of empirical research to support this model.

Contingency Theory

An extension of the situational approach—contingency theory—also focuses on the match between a leader's preferred style and the context in which that person is leading (Northouse, 2015). Contingency theory identifies specific styles of leadership, such as task-oriented or relationship-oriented, while also focusing on the specific organizational context and leader-member relationship. The approach endeavors to identify what may be best or worst for a specific organizational context. For example, Fiedler's (1967) contingency model offers a series of preferred leadership styles based on the leader-member relations, task structure, and position of power in a given situation. Unlike the situational approach that stresses the ways in which a leader should adapt to the situation, contingency theorists tend to suggest that the behaviors of leaders are naturally fixed, and that in order to change the ways in which a situation is handled, the leader must be changed in order to match the needs and demands of the situation (Northouse, 2015).

Acknowledging the many factors that come into play in leadership situations, this framework gives more detailed attention to factors that could affect a leader's success in a specific context. Perhaps because of its greater complexity and the broader array of factors considered, this theory is supported by empirical research and allows for predictions to be made whereby it is possible to determine the probability of success for an individual style in a given situation. A key criticism of this approach, however, is that it is cumbersome to apply in real-world settings. Moreover, it lacks explanatory power regarding why certain styles are more effective in some situations than others.

Path-Goal Theory

The path-goal theory seeks to explain the ways in which a leader motivates followers to accomplish desired goals (House, 1971, 1996; House & Mitchell, 1974). Based on this theory, subordinates will be motivated if they think they are capable of performing the work, if they believe efforts will result in a beneficial outcome, and if they trust that the payoffs for doing the work are worthwhile. Leaders can motivate followers by clearing the path to the goal (House, 1971, 1996; House & Mitchell, 1974; Northouse, 2015). This theory deals directly with motivation in a way that other theories do not.

An implication of this approach is that leaders should select an appropriate style based on the demands of the task and the goals of those they wish to motivate. Path-goal theory is often criticized for being overly complex and for the lack of conclusive research findings. Additionally, this theory can be criticized for treating leadership influence as a one-way event—directly controllable by the leader—and for failing to fully recognize the significance of the abilities of followers.

Leader-Member Exchange Theory

Unlike previous theories that tend to emphasize the individual leader or the situation in which they lead, leader-member exchange theory regards leadership as a process, paying particular attention to the interaction between leaders and followers. According to Graen and Uhl-Bien (1995), the quality of a leader-member exchange is related to positive outcomes for leaders, followers, groups, and the organization in general. One classification to emerge from this theory is the distinction between in-group and out-group leader-member relationships, whereby managers sort team members (often unintentionally) into one of these two groups (Northouse, 2015). In-group members maintain the trust of the leader and often receive both challenging and meaningful work, unlike the out-group members who have limited access to the leader and are often restricted to less challenging work responsibilities.

According to leader-member exchange theory, this approach explores how leaders engage some subordinates more effectively than others to accomplish goals. From this perspective, leaders play a significant role in identifying and developing followers with potential (Graen & Canedo, 2016). The leader-member relationship is the focal point of this approach, yet some suggest that this approach gives insufficient attention to the role of followers in shaping outcomes. Furthermore, the theory does not adequately explain how leaders might go about creating high-quality exchanges with followers.

Transformational Leadership

A more contemporary approach to leadership, transformational leadership focuses on the ability of leaders to create positive change in the lives of those they lead. The origin of this approach is credited to James MacGregor Burns (1978). Burns viewed transformational leadership as a process through which "leaders and followers help each other to advance to a higher level of morale and motivation" (p. 20). A concern with the collective good is central to this leadership approach (Northouse, 2015). As described in the framework, transformational leaders demonstrate an exceptional influence that moves followers to accomplish more than would normally be expected of them. Four factors of transformational leadership include idealized influence, inspirational motivation, intellectual stimulation, and individualized consideration (Bass & Avolio, 1994; Bass, 1990).

This approach is intuitively appealing because it is possible to identify a number of noted leaders who embody this approach. It also provides an expansive view of leadership that demonstrates utility across a variety of situations, and it emphasizes the moral purpose and social value of leadership. An implication of this perspective is that leaders should focus their efforts on significant change that elevate the aspirations and achievements of individuals and the group or organization. Despite the wealth of research on this approach, it has been criticized for its breadth and lack of conceptual clarity.

Furthermore, by focusing so heavily on individual leaders and their impact, some see the approach as elitist and unduly marginalizing of the role of followers.

Servant Leadership

According to the individual who coined the term, Robert Greenleaf (1977), servant leadership "begins with the natural feeling that one wants to serve, to serve first. Then conscious choice brings one to aspire to lead" (p. 13). This approach to leadership suggests that servant leaders are those who place the good of followers ahead of their own self-interest. Servant leadership extends beyond the act of "doing" and reflects a specific way of "being" (Sendjaya & Sarros, 2002). One model of servant leadership outlines a series of antecedent conditions, behaviors, and outcomes associated with this other-oriented approach to leadership (Liden, Wayne, Zhao, & Henderson, 2008). Servant leadership is unique in making altruism the central component of the leadership process and it presents a provocative, counterintuitive approach to the use of power and influence (Northouse, 2015).

The clear implication for leaders is that individuals should seek to serve the needs of others, rather than to pursue their own personal aims. Some criticisms of this approach include the sense that this approach may be applicable in a limited range of situations, the perceived moralistic tone of this approach, the lack of a consistent theoretical framework, and the contradictions between principles of servant leadership and other traditional principles of leadership.

Authentic Leadership

Authentic leadership calls for an approach to leadership "that is consistent with our personality and character" (George, 2003). In an exploration of whether leadership is genuine or real, authentic leadership consists of four components: self-awareness, internalized moral perspective, balanced processing, and transparency in relationships. A more practical approach to authentic leadership identifies the following characteristics: purpose, values, relationships, self-discipline, and heart (George, 2003). Similar to servant leadership, authentic leadership calls for leaders to do what is right and good for both followers and society. Being true to oneself and forthright with others is fundamental to this approach. Trustworthiness is understood to be critical for effective leadership. Some of the other concepts of authentic leadership, including the moral component, lack empirical research, and the specific connections between authentic leadership and positive organizational outcomes remain unclear (Northouse, 2015).

This perspective emphasizes the idea that "knowing thyself" and behaving in a way that is consistent with one's true self is a positive aspect of social influence. Authentic leaders have a clear sense of who they are—and their behaviors reflect this self-perception. Yet, in her article on the "authenticity paradox," Herminia Ibarra (2015a) casts authenticity in a different light. She notes that all of us have multiple identities and approaches, potentially calling into question the existence of one, true authentic self. Being preoccupied with a single authentic identity as a leader can create an inflexibility and "can be a recipe for staying stuck in the past" (p. 59). Fear of acting in an inauthentic manner serves as an "excuse for sticking with what's comfortable" (p. 54). Ibarra points to the value of recognizing and experimenting with multiple identities and different leadership styles and behaviors. In the course of a leader's daily responsibilities, a number of situations present themselves where candor, disclosure, and transparency are appropriate and highly valued; but there are also circumstances involving personnel or human resource matters where one is obligated to maintain confidentiality and where the commitment to transparency and authenticity can present challenges for all involved.

Team Leadership

A team leadership model explores the ways in which interdependent members of groups coordinate activities and accomplish shared goals (Northouse, 2015). The leader of the team is responsible for the effectiveness of the group, which demands behavioral flexibility whereby a leader matches his or her behavior to the complexity of a particular situation. Team leaders, according to McGrath (1962), play a critical role in diagnosing group deficiencies, taking remedial action, forecasting environmental changes, and preventing deleterious changes. As an increasing amount of work is accomplished in teams, this approach to leadership strikes a relevant chord for leadership scholars and practitioners. Furthermore, it addresses the dynamic and evolving roles of leader and follower in a team setting.

As will be discussed in greater detail in Chapter 11, the emphasis on the development and maintenance of a team of individuals who share a common purpose and approach seems quite useful for a broad range of contemporary group and organizational leadership situations. One criticism of the approach, however, is that the list of skills needed for effective team leadership is somewhat limited and may fail to fully address the specific problems associated with the realities of team dynamics.

Leadership Theory Summary

The ongoing research on these theoretical perspectives is expansive, and the brief summaries offered above are inherently limited and cursory.[2] Each theoretical approach has strengths and weaknesses and as noted at the outset of this section, each is a way of seeing and *not* seeing. By understanding and utilizing a number of theoretical lenses, one may gain a more thorough understanding of leadership and the factors that are important to leadership outcomes in practice. As Hackman and Johnson (2013) suggest, "Sometimes the approaches overlap; other times they contradict one another. No single approach provides a universal explanation of leadership behavior, but each provides

2 For a more comprehensive treatment of many of these theories, we would encourage you to review the work by Bass (1990), Gill (2012), Hackman and Johnson (2013), Northouse (2015), Rost (1991), and Yukl (2012).

useful insights" (p. 73). The process of analyzing individuals and situations through these multiple leadership theories can be a useful exercise for more fully understanding the dynamics of leadership.

A COMPETENCY APPROACH TO UNDERSTANDING LEADERSHIP

© Alexander Supertramp/Shutterstock.com

As is apparent from the foregoing review, approaches to leadership have evolved from those focused solely on the individual's inherent capabilities to those that acknowledge the importance of developing and acquiring leadership capabilities over time. In the evolution of leadership theories, an increasing emphasis has been placed on the choices leaders are able to make, and the importance of situation, timing, goals, followers, and the interactions between and among these factors in explaining the success and failure of a particular leader.

A competency approach to understanding leadership builds upon the existing classical and contemporary theories and focuses on the ability of successful leaders to acquire a portfolio of knowledge and skills that they can apply strategically in a given situation. This section describes three examples of research that explore the diverse, non-sector-specific competencies needed for effective leadership; however, one could draw on many additional leadership studies that reflect this approach.

One noteworthy example is provided by John Maxwell (1993), who offers 10 leadership competencies that distinguish leaders from managers. These characteristics include the following:

1. Creating positive influence
2. Setting the right priorities
3. Modeling integrity
4. Creating positive change

5. Problem solving
6. Having the right positive attitude
7. Developing people
8. Charting the vision
9. Practicing self-discipline
10. Developing staff

According to Maxwell, these 10 qualities—or what we would characterize as leadership competencies—may be learned and cultivated over time. For example, consider the ways in which you have learned to effectively prioritize responsibilities or solve problems as a result of your experiences inside and outside of the classroom.

A second approach to leadership is provided in the ongoing work on emotional intelligence. A number of scholars have contributed to current thinking about emotional intelligence, many building upon the work by Salovey and Mayer (1990) and Goleman (1995, 1998, 2000) in this area. According to Goleman, emotional intelligence is understood to be "The capacity for recognizing our own feelings and those of others, for motivating ourselves, and for managing emotions well in ourselves and in our relationships" (p. 317). Emotional intelligence, according to Mayer, Salovey, & Caruso (2000), involves "the ability to perceive and express emotion, assimilate emotion in thought, understand and reason with emotion, and regulate emotion in the self and others" (p. 396). Or as Gignac (2010) suggests, emotional intelligence involves "The ability to purposively adapt, shape, and select environments through the use of emotionally relevant processes" (p. 132).

Emotional intelligence is seen as an important competency for leaders in a variety of organizational settings—a competency that can be learned and developed over time (Goleman, 2004). In his writing on the topic, Cherniss (2010) acknowledges that success in work and life is often dependent upon more than one's cognitive abilities. As he indicates, "it also depends on a number of personal qualities that involve the perception, understanding, and regulation of emotion" (p. 184). Related to the process of social influence, Goleman (1998) describes emotional intelligence as "the sine qua non of leadership. Without it, a person can have the best training in the world, an incisive, analytical mind, and an endless supply of smart ideas, but he still won't make a great leader" (p. 5). Intellect alone will not predict effective leadership.

A third competency approach is provided by Ruben's (2012) Leadership Competency Framework, which is the result of a review and thematic analysis of approximately 100 academic and professional writings on the topic of leadership. In his research, Ruben (2012) differentiates vertical competencies from horizontal competencies. Vertical competencies are understood to be the specific type of knowledge and skills that directly correspond with particular positions, types of work, work settings, organizations, or sectors. For example, an understanding of college or university governance would be important for success in a campus leadership role. Thinking beyond a college or university, an understanding of accounting principles is critical to the work of leading an accounting firm, the knowledge of the broader athletic landscape is important for leaders in the field of sports management, and effective leadership of a team in the non-profit sector demands an understanding of the unique mission of the organization. These vertical competencies represent the deep knowledge- and skill-set that are important for leadership excellence in a specific unit, department, organization, or sector. Horizontal competencies, on the other hand, involve more general approaches to understanding leadership. Based on a horizontal view, effective leadership requires general knowledge and skills that transcend specific contexts, such as student clubs or organizations, athletic teams, professional fields, technical disciplines, or communities.

Ruben created a competency framework and scorecard that identifies five thematic areas, or leadership competency clusters, each composed of a number of other competencies. The five competency areas and the sub-competencies illustrated in Figure 2.1 are of importance to leadership effectiveness across multiple sectors and organizations. These competencies have *both* a knowledge and a skill component. Knowledge refers to leaders' understanding of a concept. Skill refers to leaders' effectiveness in operationalizing the knowledge they possess and their strategic ability to effectively act on this information (Ruben, 2012). Both an understanding of the competency and a proficiency associated with the "doing" of the competency are important.

LCS 2.0: Five Major Competency Themes, Each Including a Number of Specific Competency Areas				
Analytic	**Personal**	**Organizational**	**Positional**	**Communication**
Self-Assessment	Character, Personal Values, and Ethics	Vision-Setting, Strategy Development, Goal-Setting	Education	Credibility and Trust
Problem-Definition	Cognitive Ability and Creativity	Management and Supervision	Experience	Influence and Persuasion
Stakeholder Analysis	Enthusiasm	Information/Knowledge Management and Boundary Spanning	Expertise	Interpersonal and Group Relations, and Team Building
Systems/Organizational Analysis	High Standards	Technological Capability	Knowledge of Sector	Listening, Attention, Questioning, and Learning
Analysis of Technology to Support Leadership	Personal Conviction and Persistence	Collaborative Decision Making and Empowerment	Knowledge of Organization	Writing and Public Speaking
Problem-Solving	Self-Discipline and Self-Confidence	Teaching and Coaching	Familiarity with Work	Diversity and Intercultural Relations
Review and Analysis of Results	Role Modeling	Change, Risk, and Crisis Management	Professional Involvement	Facilitation, Negotiation, and Conflict Resolution

Figure 2.1: Five Major Competency Themes (Ruben, 2012)

PROPOSED TWO-DIMENSIONAL LEADERSHIP COMPETENCY FRAMEWORK

When appropriately analyzed, interpreted, and applied, the knowledge from vertically oriented perspectives can provide extremely useful insights into the work associated with specific roles and positions. However, the many studies that focus on the more generic and cross-cutting capabilities required for leadership effectiveness, including the leadership competencies framework (Ruben, 2012) and emotional intelligence (Cherniss, 2010; Gignac, 2010; Goleman, 1995, 1998; Mayer, Salovey, & Caruso, 2000), also offer a valuable perspective into the types of broader competencies needed to excel, no matter the field or professional domain you pursue in the future. Given that there are advantages associated with developing both vertical and horizontal competencies, we propose a two-dimensional leadership competency framework, as illustrated in Figure 2.2. The proposed framework may be useful for your leadership pursuits at your college or university and in your career. The two-dimensional framework acknowledges the importance of both the knowledge and skills that are uniquely important within a particular sector or specific position, while simultaneously recognizing the value of cross-cutting competencies that are associated with leadership across diverse sectors and positions. The framework illustrates the need to learn from within your unique sector, and also underscores the value of looking at competencies that are considered to be important in sectors other than your own, as well.

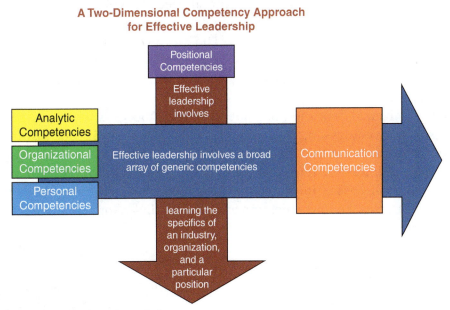

Figure 2.2: Two-Dimensional Model

CONCLUSION

© Rawpixel.com/Shutterstock.com

The theories and approaches discussed in this chapter raise a number of interesting questions for our pursuit of leadership in this book. In what ways do these theories and approaches influence how we understand leadership in everyday encounters? Furthermore, how do the theories that we use influence our behaviors as individuals with an interest in leadership? We believe that each of the aforementioned perspectives provide a particular way of thinking about what leadership is, and by implication, what a leader does—or should do. Reviewing the concepts and approaches presented in this chapter offers a reminder of the range of ways of enacting leadership roles, the potential strengths and limitations of various approaches, and the potential match or mismatch of these approaches to the particular context and needs to which a leader responds.

These theories are lenses—ways of seeing and thinking about the nature of leadership and the roles and practices of leaders. The more we understand their underlying assumptions and can see their principles in action, the broader will be the array of insights and choices available to make sense of and address the full range of leadership challenges that arise.

Although a universal definition of leadership is not necessary, or perhaps even possible (Alvesson & Sveningsson, 2003; Barker, 1997; Rost, 1993), our synthesis of the vast amount of research on this topic has led us to identify the nature of leadership as a process of social influence that is accomplished through communication (Ruben & Gigliotti, 2016), as discussed in Chapter 1. This definition highlights the complex and intimate linkage between communication and leadership—a topic that will be discussed further in the next chapter.

CHAPTER 3

LEADERSHIP COMMUNICATION THEORIES AND STRATEGIES

⚠️ **Guiding Questions:**

1) In what ways does the study of communication intersect with the study of leadership?
2) Which communication concepts are particularly important to the study and practice of leadership?
3) What is the distinction between the "informational" and "relational" dimensions of communication and why is this distinction important?
4) What insights, principles, and tactics related to strategic communication and influence are most relevant for leaders?

As noted at the outset of this book, our approach to the study and practice of leadership is very much informed by communication concepts. To be human is to communicate—and perhaps even more relevant to this book, to *lead* is to communicate. This chapter will explore ways of thinking about the process of communication and its contribution to leadership knowledge and practice. We will highlight three models for understanding leadership communication and a number of communication-oriented concepts that are particularly important to the study and practice of leadership. Finally, the chapter will conclude with a strategic communication framework that you might use in your leadership pursuits in any setting—with family and friends, on campus, in the community, or in the workplace.

WHAT IS COMMUNICATION?

Communication, a "universal human experience," is critical to social behavior, yet familiar enough for it to be taken for granted (Thayer, 1968, 2003). In much the same way that we easily take for granted the dynamics of breathing, and assume

© Rawpixel.com/Shutterstock.com

that we understand how the process works, so too, it is easy to assume we under-stand the nature of communication. As Watzlawick, Bavelas, and Jackson (1967) sug-gest, "all behavior, not only speech, is communication, and all communication—even the communicational clues in an impersonal context—affects behavior" (p. 22). Two definitions may be helpful as we further explore the connections between leader-ship and communication. First, Ruben and Stewart (2016) define communication as "the process through which individuals in relationships, groups, organizations, and societies create and respond to messages in order to relate to the environment and one another" (p. 16). Similarly, Beebe, Beebe, and Ivy (2013) present another useful definition of communication "as the process of making sense out of the world and sharing that sense with others by creating meaning through the use of verbal and nonverbal messages" (p. 5).

The extensive research on the topic of human communication, and the two afore-mentioned definitions, reflect a number of fundamental concepts. Communication is a process that occurs over time. It involves both the creation and interpretation of mes-sages, and it is through this process that individuals adapt to people and their environ-ment (Ruben & Stewart, 2016). The message itself may be intentional or unintentional, planned or unplanned. Additionally, as acknowledged by Watzlawick, Bavelas, and Jack-son (1967) in their widely cited axiom of human communication, "one cannot *not* com-municate" (p. 49). The study of communication extends beyond talk-in-interaction and must also consider that which is *not* said. For example, you might consider the message communicated by a friend who fails to respond to your phone call or text message, or the message created by a leader who remains silent when encountering conflict in a group, organization, or community setting. While many of the messages that are vital to our lives are verbal—spoken or written—perhaps even more are non-verbal. Non-verbal messages may be in the form of actions, gestures, posture, facial expressions, and dress, for example.

Finally, the process of communication is multi-dimensional. Both the content (what is communicated) and relationship (who is communicating) dimensions of communication have the potential to influence the interpretation of messages in any communicative transaction (Watzlawick, Bavelas, & Jackson, 1967). This is an especially important concept to consider as we think about the content and relationships embedded in leader-follower interactions, as discussed in the next section.

LEADERSHIP-COMMUNICATION CONNECTIONS

© Rawpixel.com/Shutterstock.com

Conceiving of communication as the creation and interpretation of messages is very helpful in understanding the dynamics of leadership and social influence. Simply put, everything that a leader says or does is a potential source of communication in that it creates a message about both content and relationships that may be of significance to others (Barge, 2014; Bateson, 1972). Witherspoon (1997) makes the point this way: "leadership is first and foremost a communication process, or set of processes. Every leadership behavior is enacted through communication" (p. 2). In her analysis of leadership, Fairhurst (2007) echoes this idea by illustrating the ways in which leadership is constituted in and through discourse, including both verbal and non-verbal interactions between leaders and followers (Ruben & Gigliotti, 2016, 2017). Obvious examples of leadership behaviors that are communicative include the use of an agenda that outlines the main discussion items for a meeting, the type of formal language that the leader uses in a public presentation, or an "open-door" policy that one might adopt in his or her formal leadership role. Less obvious examples include an email request for a meeting to discuss one's job performance to which a supervisor does not respond, a pattern of arriving late to meetings, or one's choice of dress to be worn to a weekend social event with work colleagues. A communication-oriented way of thinking about leadership focuses attention on the role of communication involved in social influence—influence that may be immediate, but also influence that occurs over time among members of a group, organization, or community.

LEADERSHIP COMMUNICATION: CLASSICAL LINEAR, INTERACTIONAL, AND SYSTEMS MODELS

In this section, we discuss three ways of thinking about how communication works and how each contributes to an understanding of leadership (Ruben & Gigliotti, 2016, 2017; Ruben, et al., 2017).

Classical Linear Model

In classical writings on the subject, leadership is described in terms of the intentional creation and transmission of messages with particular influence outcomes in mind. As portrayed in Figure 3.1, this implies that a leader begins with a goal, and then he or she creates and transmits messages designed to achieve the desired goal among those he or she wishes to influence. This familiar way of thinking about leadership communication views the process as linear (one-way) and quite predictable, beginning with a leader and one's intentions and ending with a follower having received and interpreted the message as intended. A simple example would be the case of a leader who announces a change to a work procedure in an email or memo, expecting employees to accept and embrace the change.

Essentially, such a view reflects a one-way, cause-and-effect-oriented characterization of the communication and influence process, which assumes that the message initiator—the leader—is able to have a strong effect on the outcome of the communication and influence process. But the reality is that seldom does message sent = message received (Ruben & Stewart, 2016). Neither communication nor social influence operates in such a predictable manner. As much as the "transmission," "exchange," or "sharing" of information is a familiar and customary way of describing and thinking about communication, this portrayal oversimplifies and actually obscures some critical dimensions of the process. While this model sometimes seems to provide a helpful explanation for how leader-follower influence works, in many more instances, it fails to be helpful—as in the numerous situations where a leader's intended

The Classical Linear Perspective

Implications for Conceptualizing Leadership...
Classical models describe communication as consisting of a source/sender conveying a message to a receiver through a one-way process that results in the receiver being influenced. This paradigm provides a view of how leadership communication works, how leaders bring about influence, and more generally, what leadership is and how it works.

Figure 3.1: The Classical Linear Perspective

messages seem to be ignored, distorted, and not acted upon appropriately. In these circumstances, it becomes apparent that the simple linear model provides an incomplete explanation of the communication dynamics associated with social influence.

Interactional Model

An interactional perspective, such as that depicted in Figure 3.2, attempts to capture more of the complexity and two-way influence between a leader and follower. The interactional perspective recognizes that communication is not a one-way process, but rather is best understood as multi-directional, with no distinguishable beginning or end (Ruben, 2003). This way of thinking about communication does not imply that influence is controlled by the leader and his or her messages, but rather that it is the result of interactions between leaders *and* followers.

This more contemporary understanding of communication reminds us that only a fraction of the influence that occurs in communication situations is the outcome of direct, purposeful, and intentional leader-controlled words and actions, as depicted in Figure 3.2. Instead, it suggests that a multiplicity of factors is at play in even the most basic situation, and the result is that the communication process associated with influence is far more complex and unpredictable than suggested by the classic one-way model. Indeed, many of the messages that make a difference in communication and influence situations are unplanned and unpredicted, non-verbal as well as very verbal—and the product of ongoing dynamics, rather than a single message-sending/message-receiving event. These key points are not well-captured by the linear classic model. Unlike the limited one-way linear model, the interactional model expands the focus to a more complex two-way interchange between sender(s) and receiver(s). This model explains why the leadership behaviors of an individual may not be received or reacted to as intended, and why outcomes can be very unpredictable.

Despite the more expansive focus of the interactional model, the focus is still on the intentional exchange of messages and the model tends to characterize

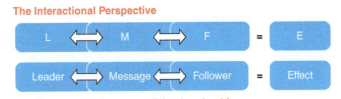

The Interactional Perspective

Implications for Conceptualizing Leadership...
Interactional models describe communication as consisting of an ongoing process of negotiation between sources and receivers through messages. Influence is understood to result from interaction and the negotiation of meanings, providing the basis for a more collaborative view of what leadership is and how leadership functions.

Figure 3.2: The Interactional Perspective

communication and influence in terms of the exchange, sharing, or transmission of information. Even with added nuances of the interactional model, the complexity of communication and the critical issues for understanding the dynamics of leadership and influence are not fully explored.

Systems Model

A systems view of communication, as depicted in Figure 3.3, overcomes many limitations of these models and, in our opinion, more adequately captures the complexity of leadership communication and social influence. This view of communication focuses directly on the way people create, convey, select, and interpret the messages that inform and shape their lived experiences—viewing communication as a basic life process rather than an exchange of information or meaning between people (Ruben & Stewart, 2016). This perspective recognizes that some of these messages are intentionally created, while others are produced accidentally. Some messages are constructed to achieve specific influence goals or intentions, while others may be unconsciously created by their initiator with no specific purpose in mind. Some messages are created in the moment in face-to-face settings, while others occur at remote times and places and are conveyed via print or electronic media (Ruben & Stewart, 2016). The model also allows for consideration of messages that can be influential for communication outcomes that have inanimate sources, such as a rained-out campaign event or a regional natural disaster—either of which could cause the delay of planned leadership events.

This view of communication takes into account the fact that throughout any message-sending/message-receiving process, followers and leaders bring their own

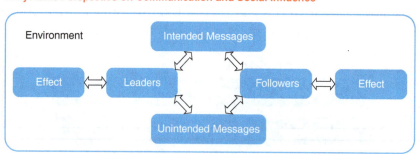

A Systems Perspective on Communication and Social Influence

Implications for Conceptualizing Leadership…
A multiplicity of factors are at play in even the most basic situation, and the result is that the communication process associated with influence is multi-dimensional, multi-directional, and extremely complex—involving some messages created and sent intentionally, and others that are unintentional.

Figure 3.3: A Systems Perspective on Communication and Social Influence

unique "maps" and "personal luggage" to the interaction. Each individual has his or her own unique needs, values, attitudes, goals, aspirations, styles, education, cultures, physical and emotional abilities and disabilities, life history, and present life circumstances that influence one's interpretation of messages that make up the communication process. These "belongings," or what some may refer to as "mental models," travel with an individual and influence every aspect of the way messages are created (or not), made sense of (or not), and reacted to (or not). As Thayer (1968) describes the process, "needs, values, expectations, attitudes, and goals are brought to every communication encounter. These predispositions, susceptibilities, and take-into-account-abilities influence the outcome of the interaction and are equivalent to our individual make-meaningful-abilities" (p. 36). Often the communication "luggage" of one individual does not align all that well with the expectations, attributes, outlooks, and orientations of others with whom they are engaging. Generally speaking, the greater the extent of mismatch, the less the likelihood that message-sent will equal message-received (Ruben, 2015; Ruben & Stewart, 2016). For example, the use of phrases such as "outstanding leader," "mission alignment," and "the pursuit of excellence," will be interpreted differently based on individual experiences and expectations, and it is important for leaders to recognize these diverse perspectives and interpretations.

This view of communication underscores the limitations of the linear and meaning-transmission or information-exchange views of communication and reminds us that single messages and single message-sending events seldom yield momentous message-reception outcomes. Rather, communication and social influence are parts of an ongoing process through which messages wash over individuals—somewhat analogous to waves repeatedly washing upon the shore. Over time, these messages shape the sensibilities and responses of receivers, much as waves shape a shoreline. The exceptions to this subtle process are those rare, life-changing messages that can have a tsunami-like impact on message reception, such as the doctor sharing a serious diagnosis with a patient or a boss sharing a termination letter with an employee.

Perhaps most importantly, this view of the influence process suggests that leaders and followers engage together in creating the situation through which interaction and the potential for influence take place. Each brings his or her own intentions, perspectives, needs, understandings, and goals, and each takes away one's own interpretations and understandings. The idea that leaders and followers co-create and co-control the outcomes—that are often attributed solely to the behaviors of leaders—is a particularly significant contribution of this model. This insight challenges the dominant tendency to romanticize the leader's role, as discussed in Chapter 1. It also helps to explain why it is also often the case that a leader cannot be held solely responsible for leader-follower outcomes, because in fact, the leader does not have control over many important components of the communication and influence process. The implications of these ideas will be discussed more fully in subsequent sections of the book.

USEFUL LEADERSHIP COMMUNICATION CONCEPTS

Building upon the previous perspectives on leadership and communication, the following section highlights three distinct areas of communication scholarship that are very much related to leadership practice. These three communication-oriented concepts are sensemaking and sensegiving, the management of meaning and framing, and attention and agenda-setting.

Sensemaking and Sensegiving

As suggested in the systems model discussed previously, humans live in a world of uncertainty and try to shape the interpretations of individuals and groups they hope to influence (Dervin, 1992, 1998). It is through the act of sensemaking that human actors "structure the unknown" (Waterman, 1990, p. 41) as a way of constructing experiences which then become sensible to those whom one leads (Weick, 1995). An underlying point of significance is that all of us are confronted with the need to make sense of our environments and the people and circumstances we encounter (Berger & Luckmann, 1966). Within this context, we may think of leadership as the effort to actively share our sensemaking activities with others—and in effect, to create understandings with and for others.

The process of sensemaking involves more than interpretation. According to Weick (1995), as sensemakers, we are both the authors and interpreters—we create as well as discover reality. An emphasis on sensemaking must also consider the role of communication and context in understanding the actions and behaviors of leaders (Fairhurst, 2009; Weick, 1979, 1995; Weick, Sutcliffe, & Obstfeld, 2005). Thayer (1988) suggests that a leader's communicative roles include both sensemaker and sensegiver:

> [A leader is] one who alters or guides the manner in which his followers "mind" the world by giving it a compelling "face." A leader at work is one who gives others a different sense of the meaning of that which they do by recreating it in a different

form, a different "face," in the same way that a pivotal painter or sculptor or poet gives those who follow him (or her) a different way of "seeing"—and therefore saying and doing and knowing in the world. A leader does not tell it "as it is"; he tells it as it might be, giving what "is" thereby a different "face" . . . The leader is a sense-giver. The leader always embodies the possibilities of escape from what might otherwise appear to us to be incomprehensible, or from what might otherwise appear to us to be a chaotic, indifferent, or incorrigible world—one over which we have no ultimate control. (pp. 250, 254)

This extended passage captures the leader's dual role as sensemaker and sensegiver. Gioia and Chittipeddi (1991) clarify this further in suggesting that sensemaking is associated with understanding, while sensegiving is associated with influencing others. Leaders, through communication, interpret the environment (sensemaking) and share this interpretation (sensegiving) with those whom they lead. The sensemaking or sensegiving process is especially critical for leaders during times of organizational uncertainty, change, or crisis. It is during these moments that leaders must build trust and goodwill by offering a sound explanation or interpretation of the uncertain environment—yet once again, this trust and goodwill depends as much on the followers as it does the leader.

The Management of Meaning and Framing

As noted earlier, the transmission model of human communication devotes insufficient attention to the complexities of communication and influence—and particularly those associated with how individuals attach meaning to the messages they send and receive (Axley, 1984). More contemporary views of communication focus far more attention on these issues, and some scholars have, in fact, described leadership as the "management of meaning" (Smircich & Morgan, 1982). This meaning-centered view of communication envisions leadership outcomes as a product, result, or outcome of collective meaning making (Barge, 2007; Barge & Fairhurst, 2008; Parker, 2005). According to Smircich and Morgan (1982), "In understanding the way leadership actions attempt to shape and interpret situations to guide organizational members into a common interpretation of reality, we are able to understand how leadership works to create an important foundation for organized activity" (p. 260). According to this process, leaders contribute to how others understand and experience their "reality"; yet, at the same time, followers play an active role in accepting and taking on this proposed interpretation of a given situation.

Related to the management of meaning, the work done on "framing" is also a communication-centered concept that is very much relevant to the process of leadership. Drawing upon the work of Pondy (1978), Entman (1993), and Weick (1979); Fairhurst and Sarr (1996) define framing as:

the ability to shape the meaning of a subject, to judge its character and significance. To hold the frame of a subject is to choose one particular meaning (or set of meanings) over another. When we share our frames with others (the process of framing), we manage meaning because we assert that our interpretations should be taken as real over other possible interpretations (p. 3).

According to Fairhurst and Sarr (1996), "Leaders operate in uncertain, sometimes chaotic environments that are partly of their own creation: while leaders do not control events, they do influence how events are seen and understood" (p. xi). Leaders are seen as having the ability to co-create the contexts, situations, and opportunities to which they and others must respond (Fairhurst, 2009). Framing has the potential to encourage others to accept one meaning or interpretation over another. During unprecedented and chaotic moments of organizational disruption, for example, it is often the leader's role to frame the situation in a way that resonates with their followers to build trust, confidence, and hope.

Not only is "talk" the way in which leaders accomplish many specific tasks (Gronn, 1983), but it is through communication—and framing, more specifically—that leaders are able to construct reality with and for those whom one leads (Fairhurst & Sarr, 1996). For example, when leaders make public statements in response to a crisis or when introducing significant changes that have the potential to invite criticism, the leader frames the situation in an attempt to maintain some control of its interpretation, all the while recognizing that the interpretation is very much shaped and co-constructed by one's followers.

Attention and Agenda-Setting

Organizational leaders play an important role in influencing those items that receive attention, a phenomenon also known as agenda-setting. In their seminal work on the subject, McCombs and Shaw (1972) studied the role of the mass media during the 1968 presidential election. As the authors hypothesized, "the mass media set the agenda for each political campaign, influencing the salience of attitudes toward the political issues" (p. 177). From this perspective, the news plays an important role in not only influencing *what* audiences pay attention to, but also *how* to think about these items (McCombs & Shaw, 1993).

As you have likely experienced as a member of a group working on a project for class or a student club, or as a member of a work organization, there are often a myriad of messages competing for attention at any moment in time. Some of these messages may relate directly to the situation at hand, while others could have to do with personal or professional concerns that are unrelated to the immediate situation. This presents an initial challenge for the formal or informal leader of the group who is trying to guide followers toward the achievement of shared objectives. Further, the identification of a problem in the group or organization does not necessarily imply the possibility of or need for immediate action. As suggested in the public policy literature, while recognizing a problem is important to attract significant attention, recognition alone is not enough to place an item on the political agenda (Kingdon, 1984). In order for an issue to receive attention that leads to constructive action, three streams of influence including a recognition of the problem, a proposed solution, and the political will, must converge to create a "window of opportunity" (Kingdon, 1984). As these three components come together in the political sphere, a "window of opportunity" opens for individuals to act upon a problem with widespread consensus. Effective leaders are able to identify the shifting "windows of opportunity" in their group or organization, and thus are able to determine when and how particular issues will resonate with others in order to advance items to respective agendas, and to promote their intended influence in the ways others think about particular agenda items. This same principle applies more generally in other group, organizational, or community situations, where consensus or some level of agreement is required for action. In all such situations, a leader is well-served by his or her efforts to identify the ways in which issues may best be presented so that they mesh with the needs, goals, and appetites of those individuals whom the leader hopes to influence.

These three interconnected and communication-oriented concepts—sensemaking and sensegiving, the management of meaning and framing, and attention and agenda-setting—describe processes through which leader-follower social influence occurs. In each instance, the influence that may occur hinges very much on the expectations, needs, interests, and values of those individuals who are being led. The three concepts all benefit from an acknowledgment that the leadership communication process is not unidirectional; rather, as indicated by the systems model, the ways that people create, convey, select, and interpret the messages that inform and shape their lives are much more complex, dynamic, and unpredictable (Ruben & Stewart, 2016).

COMMUNICATION AND STRATEGIC LEADERSHIP

© Monkey Business Images/Shutterstock.com

As we have seen, communication theory can contribute in fundamental ways to an understanding of leadership-follower dynamics and the nature of social influence. Communication theory also provides the basis for a number of strategies and tactics that prove useful for navigating challenging leadership situations. Strategic communication refers to deliberate, intentional, purposeful, thoughtful, and future-oriented communication. A general theme underlying this section of the chapter is that effective leadership is not solely about being authentic, intuitive, acting instinctively, or simply "being yourself." No matter how small, all of the many critical leadership moments and challenges matter—and there is an element of strategy that becomes critical to one's leadership during these moments and challenges. The way you handle each situation makes a statement about who you are and what matters to you. Each action creates precedents, strengthens or diminishes the quality of relationships, and shapes the history and legacy upon which future actions will be judged.

Strategic leadership involves the formulation and implementation of effective strategies that simultaneously consider the perspectives of the leader and his or her colleagues, the communication history of a group or organization, and the informational and relational dynamics associated with human communication (Watzlawick, Bavelas, & Jackson, 1967). Asking yourself "what to say" is basic; additionally, a leader must also consider "how to say it," "when to say it," "to whom to say it," "in what setting to say it"—and the answers to all of these questions need to reflect an understanding of the present circumstances and history of communication among those involved (Ruben & Gigliotti, 2016, 2017). These additional questions serve as a reminder that the interpretation, and hence the impact, of leadership messages are fundamentally shaped, molded, and impacted by the recipient(s) of those messages.

What often makes leadership so challenging is the need to listen to and balance the expectations, goals, and needs of diverse constituents, stakeholders, or followers[1] and to deliver messages that will resonate in the intended ways with a large and diverse group. At the same time, leaders are often called to lead with the goal of pursuing any number of personal agendas that are hopefully consistent with the mission and values of the group or organization. Given the complexity of leadership and the importance of communication, we see great value in pursuing strategic leadership opportunities where leaders analyze situations, clarify goals, share information, cultivate relationships, and analyze intended audiences all in an effort to shape an increasingly cohesive and cooperative group of individuals that are capable of realizing their fullest aspirations.

A GENERAL APPROACH TO STRATEGIC LEADERSHIP AND PROBLEM SOLVING

All leaders encounter a number of challenging circumstances on a daily basis; some are complex and nuanced, others may be more routine and easily addressed. Fortunately, each leadership situation affords an opportunity to apply, test, and further refine one's

---

1 In order to accommodate the wide array of possible interpretations, we use a number of interchangeable labels to refer to "followers" throughout this book, including subordinates, constituents, stakeholders, and organizational members.

skills. Thinking and acting strategically eventually become leadership habits—habits that greatly enhance one's effectiveness across a variety of situations.

The following rubric for strategic leadership outlines five critical steps that can be extremely helpful in dealing with the multiplicity of challenges associated with any leadership role. In a way, this rubric serves as a formal framework for leadership sensemaking:

1. Analyze the situation
2. Define the audience(s)
3. Clarify goal(s)
4. Select and implement a plan of action
5. Debrief

These steps offer a model for thinking through strategic communication decisions in personal and professional situations—decisions that require conscious and thoughtful analysis and choice, yet, without consciously making them a focus of attention, can very easily be acted upon in a careless, detached, and arbitrary manner. You may move through these steps, especially the first four, in any order based on the needs of the circumstance.

1. Analyze the situation

The first step involves a careful assessment of the situation facing a leader and his or her group, team, department, or organization. The critical question one must ask is: What is at stake in this situation, recognizing that the most mundane and most tumultuous situations can shape the legacy of an individual and/or organization?

- *What is at stake for the group, team, or organization?*
  - ❐ Solving a specific problem?
  - ❐ Clarifying purposes and/or aspirations?
  - ❐ Upholding foundational values or principles?
  - ❐ Establishing a precedent?
  - ❐ Maintaining consistent and equitable practices?
  - ❐ Conforming to regulations and/or policies?
  - ❐ Assuring fair and equitable treatment?
  - ❐ Establishing and upholding standards?

- *What is at stake for you as a leader?*
  - ❐ Clarifying your role?
  - ❐ Establishing your voice?
  - ❐ Upholding personal values or principles?
  - ❐ Setting or maintaining a precedent?
  - ❐ Building your credibility?

- ❑ Defining your personal/leadership style?
- ❑ Establishing and/or maintaining your reputation?
- ❑ Demonstrating consistency in how you treat colleagues, students, or problems?

2. Define the audience(s)

The next step allows the leader to determine his or her intended audience(s). It is far too easy to omit careful consideration of whom you need to reach with a specific message, thereby missing an important stage of the strategic communication process. The guiding questions at this particular stage are twofold:

- ■ Who needs to know?
- ■ To whom should responses be directed?

Recall that the communication message may be verbal or non-verbal (e.g., an email, text message, or public website announcement). The intended audiences, along with the previously identified goals, will help to determine the most appropriate medium for disseminating a specific message.

3. Clarify goal(s)

The third step calls for one to clarify his or her goals in addressing the situation. Building upon the assessment of the situation, it becomes important to consider exactly what one wants, needs, or intends to accomplish—and to define messages and methods based on these predetermined goals. Recognize that it is impossible to determine what would be an effective or ineffective strategy without knowing the goal. There may exist a myriad of communication goals, including, but not limited to, any of the following:

- ■ Provide input?
- ■ Solicit input?
- ■ Clarify facts?
- ■ Demonstrate interest/concern?
- ■ Persuade or influence?
- ■ Demonstrate your expertise?
- ■ Assure that your position, reaction, and perspective is clear?
- ■ Be on the record?

4. Select and implement a plan of action

The fourth step involves reviewing options and selecting a plan of action. At this point in the process, one must consider whether it makes sense to respond to the situation at hand. Strategic leaders intentionally identify the potential costs, benefits, barriers, and sources of resistance, and then select a course of action, accordingly. This stage is often where leaders are inclined to begin, but it should be apparent why moving to action without first being clear about what is at stake, who the appropriate audience is, and precisely what the goals should be is a mistake.

It is during this fourth stage that leaders engage in the communication action determined to be most effective, such as the following:

- Respond immediately (why?)
  - ❐ To whom would you direct your response?
  - ❐ Who else would you inform (e.g., using a "cc" or "bcc" on an email, and why?)
  - ❐ What communication channel would you use (e.g., email, phone, schedule an in-person meeting, "spontaneous" hallway conversation, and why?)
- Do nothing (e.g., not much at stake, benefit versus costs of response not clear, the problem will likely take care of itself)
- Delay response (e.g., the matter further thought, and then revisit options above)

This decision should reflect a thoughtful awareness of the situation and a careful analysis of the goals, options, and audiences.

5. Debrief

The final stage of this process, and perhaps the most overlooked, relates to our previous discussions of self-awareness and reflection. This debriefing stage leads one to consider how well the plan and execution worked, seeking and using feedback where available. The following questions can be useful during this stage:

- What outcome was achieved? Was this the intended outcome?
- What would you do differently in the future to prevent this kind of problem? (e.g., set clear expectations, stay closer to the process, request periodic progress reports, assign several people to collaborate on the task)
- What might you do differently in the future to address this kind of problem if it were to occur?
- Have you derived any personal and/or professional leadership lessons from the situation?
- Is further follow up needed?
- How would others involved in the process describe how things went?

It is far too easy to react in a casual and spontaneous way to a situation as a leader, particularly when the stakes do not initially appear to be so high. However, the decision to address a specific situation often carries enormous consequences, some of which are not realized until a later time. This rubric points to the importance of, when possible, moving through the first four stages prior to designing and delivering a message or initiating an action.

As a way of summarizing these six stages, take note of the following synthesis of questions to consider as they relate to communication strategy:

- Who are your intended recipients?
- What are your communication goals?
- What message do you want to convey?
- Who should deliver this message?
- Through what channels, at what time, and in what setting (e.g., email, face-to-face, at work, over lunch) should the message be delivered?
- What barriers and resistance do you anticipate, and how will you deal with these if they occur?
- How will you follow up to assure that you have been successful and your goal has been achieved?

The model and sets of questions provide the outline of a very basic approach for leadership communication. Clearly, their application in any situation is a matter of subtlety and nuance, but the basic stages and their purposes remain constant; and as highlighted throughout this chapter, leadership communication must always take into account the active role followers play in making leadership possible.

CONCLUSION

© Digital Storm/Shutterstock.com

Human communication is messy. A great number of disruptions in interpersonal relationships and encounters in groups, organizations, and communities are attributed to failures in communication. At any moment in time, we are situated in an environment full of an infinite number of messages and distractions. As highlighted in this chapter, individuals involved in any communication encounter are engaged in a process of co-creation. In an environment where many individuals are attempting to influence others, leaders who strive to be successful must learn to carefully assess their prospective followers and present their messages in ways that have the potential to attract, resonate with, and engage others whom they seek to influence. The leader's role is only meaningful if individuals are willing to listen, learn, and be led, and it is important for any leader to consider the appetites, interests, and motivations of others whom an individual hopes to lead (Ruben & Gigliotti, 2016, 2017).

Many factors both within and beyond the leader's control affect the impact of a leader's influence efforts. For all of these reasons, the value of strategic leadership cannot be underestimated. An understanding of the nuances of communication theory proves useful for enacting leadership in all sectors, and as discussed in the following chapters, it will also help when navigating formal and informal leadership opportunities across different cultures of any group, team, organization, or community.

CHAPTER 4

FORMAL AND INFORMAL LEADERSHIP

> ⚠️ **Guiding Questions:**
>
> 1) What distinguishes formal leadership from informal leadership?
> 2) What are some of the benefits and limitations associated with each type of leadership?
> 3) What specific competencies are critical for formal and informal leadership, and do these differ for the two types of leadership?
> 4) What particular opportunities for influence are available to informal leaders?

Most often when we hear the term *leadership*, what comes to mind are formal positions—such as president, vice president, dean, director, chairman, coach, or coordinator—and the related activities of the individuals who have these titles. Consistent with this way of thinking, when we are asked about our past leadership experience, we generally assume that what is being requested is a listing of titled positions or roles which we have occupied in social, work, or civic settings.

Clearly, these kinds of titled positions are fundamental to any discussion of the theory and practice of leadership. However, when formal leadership is the sole focus of such discussions, important facets of group, organizational, and community leadership are overlooked. In addition to the activities engaged in by individuals in titled roles, it is also the case that leadership takes place in a wide range of settings, through the actions of individuals who may not occupy formal positions nor have designated leadership titles.

Because of the visibility and significance of formal leadership roles, it is easy to ignore the importance and impact of informal leaders, which can be every bit as consequential as that of formal leaders. In this chapter, we will discuss both formal and informal leadership, describe some of the differences between them, identify several benefits and limitations associated with each type of leadership role, and offer practical suggestions for becoming more successful as a formal and informal leader.

FORMAL LEADERSHIP ROLES

© Mima Antic/Shutterstock.com

Formal leadership positions have designated titles, and they generally come with well-defined expectations. Depending on the group, team, or organization, these responsibilities and expectations may be detailed in official job descriptions, memos of understanding, or bylaws. Descriptions of formal leadership positions may include details as to who is eligible to serve in particular roles, what qualifications are required or desired, and in some cases, the manner in which and length of time the leader will serve. Consider any formal leadership roles that you currently hold. For each, there is quite likely to be a handbook or constitution that one could consult for a description of the official duties associated with the defined leadership roles.

In most cases, individuals are selected for formal leadership roles through a structured process that is likely to include a detailed application procedure, an extensive set of interviews, or an election—and sometimes through a combination of these. For those selected or elected, clear documentation is typically provided that highlights the responsibilities for formal leaders, the areas and functions for which they are responsible, and in some cases, the methods and frequency with which their performance will be evaluated. This documentation may offer extensive details indicating the kinds of decisions for which the leader has authority. For example, these may range from a list of the major areas of decision making for which a leader is responsible, to specific communication duties associated with the position, such as holding meetings at specified intervals and distributing monthly or annual reports, and other such activities. The relationships between various formal leadership roles are generally depicted in an organizational chart. Typically, these charts are hierarchical, and indicate to whom each leader "reports to" and who "reports to them."

The extent to which these expectations are specified and documented varies, of course, from one setting to another. Predictably, greater detail is provided in some groups or organizations as a function of the nature of the group or organization's activities, the size of the group, and the scope of responsibilities associated with the position. An important point to keep in mind is that while the characteristics and requirements of formal leadership positions vary widely, what they share in common is the fact that the nature of the role, and the major duties associated with it, will be specified, defined, documented, and largely determined by the group or organization rather than the individual leader.

APPROACHES TO DECISION MAKING AND PROBLEM SOLVING IN FORMAL LEADERSHIP POSITIONS

© A Lot Of People/Shutterstock.com

In considering leadership in group and organizational settings, distinctions are often drawn between *autocratic, democratic,* and *laissez-faire* approaches (Lewin et al., 1939). The term *autocratic* refers to leadership approaches that are leader-centric, highly directive, and top down, often following formal lines of authority. When this approach is enacted, the leader essentially uses his or her formal authority to issue directives or mandates, with minimal engagement or participation in areas such as planning the agenda of the group or organization, allocating resources, making decisions, or problem solving. Although many perceive this style to be generally undesirable, directive leadership can certainly prove useful when time is limited for decision making and action, such as during times of crisis or widespread disruption in a group, organization, or community.

When leadership authority is broadly shared, the approach is described as *participatory* or *democratic*. Leaders who broadly engage colleagues or team members in planning, decision making, and problem solving are often well-regarded for their use of this democratic approach to leadership. However, this method is less desirable in situations where time is limited.

The phrase *laissez-faire* refers to a very loose and non-directive leadership style. Where this style is employed, a leader may choose neither to be directive nor to systematically encourage or facilitate democratic decision making. Rather, leadership functions are widely distributed and unpredictable, potentially leading to creative and evolving processes, but also to a high degree of ambiguity and potential frustration—and sometimes chaos—among members of the group or organization. For these reasons, the laissez-faire approach has been characterized as the "non-leadership style."

In actual practice, these approaches are not necessarily mutually exclusive, nor do they need to be applied consistently across all contexts by a leader. That is, a leader could employ a style that blends aspects of these approaches, utilizing highly directive approaches for some decisions, in some areas and at some times, and a highly participative approach in other instances. The formal delegation of authority to others within a group or organization can be viewed as an example of a blend of these two approaches. For example, the decision to delegate specific responsibilities to a person selected by the leader can be seen as highly directive; but once that delegation has taken place, the designated leader may have the opportunity to be quite participatory in his or her approach, and the designated individual may choose to solicit advice and engage others in decision making and in the implementation of solutions. Ideally, a formal leader would have the ability to operate using a purposeful blending of these approaches, depending on the setting, individuals involved, and perhaps most importantly, based on a careful analysis of what is at stake—as discussed in the problem solving model presented in the previous chapter.

Differences in communication are generally quite distinct depending on which approach is used by a formal leader. Generally speaking, authoritative leadership is associated with top-down communication, whereas participatory styles make use of multi-directional communication to facilitate collaborative planning and decision making. For example, communicative behaviors associated with autocratic leadership are primarily uni-directional, such as giving orders, outlining procedures, and announcing the outcomes of decisions, whereas the communicative behaviors of participatory leaders are multi-directional, and might include asking questions, sharing information, and seeking the ideas and opinions of others. Finally, the communicative behaviors of laissez-faire leadership are more difficult to identify, but can be "non-committal and superficial." For example, a leader may say "we need to do this" as a general request for an unspecified person other than the leader to take action (Nowicki & Summers, 2008).

INFORMAL LEADERSHIP ROLES

Informal leadership tends to be emergent rather than predetermined, as is the case with formal leadership roles. For example, through specific behaviors such as suggesting alternative courses of action, motivating others, or influencing the beliefs of group members, the informal leader emerges naturally.

Generally, informal leadership opportunities do not come with specified expectations, terms of tenure, or modes of accountability. While expectations for these roles may evolve, these are emergent rather than formally prescribed by the group or organization. For these reasons, informal leadership affords far more flexibility for individuals adopting these roles than formal leadership. Not only does one have the

opportunity to choose whether or not to become an informal leader, but he or she can also select the ways in which to serve, as well as how long to occupy the role.

By way of contrast with formal leadership positions, informal roles have no specific titles, nor are they associated with group-specific or organization-specific leadership responsibilities, expectations, or duties. Usually, these roles arise out of an unfilled need perceived by individual members of the group or organization. Informal leaders, to a large extent, invent their positions and the array of associated responsibilities that accompany them. One may simply choose to be a member of a social network, club, or work team—with no designated leadership role or obligation. In such situations, individuals have a wide range of options as to whether and how they may choose to participate and exercise social influence. At one extreme, an individual may take on the informal leadership role of "supportive follower." This decision may mean that the individual will exercise his or her influence by encouraging, recognizing, or supporting the work of the titled leader in his or her role, or offer or promote complementary, supplementary, or even alternative plans or actions. At the other extreme, he or she may create or assume the position as an active and vocal opinion leader or advocate for alternative points of view.

Informal leadership is not fundamentally about taking charge or dominating conversations, although these behaviors sometimes occur. In thinking about the characteristics and communication practices associated with informal leadership, it is helpful to think about the way these dynamics can and do operate in the clubs, teams, or workgroups to which you currently belong. In what ways is informal leadership manifested in this particular group? Do informal leaders tend to exercise social influence in a way that is intended to support—or detract from—the goals of the formal leader and other group members?

Broadly speaking, informal leadership is present in any social situation where decisions are being made, issues are being discussed, or problems are being addressed—in essence, whenever and wherever social influence is occurring. Such situations are routinely present throughout the day, such as in family, friendship, social, and occupational exchanges. In these settings, whether an individual is consciously planning to

Table 4.1. Characteristics of Formal and Informal Leadership

Formal Leadership	Informal Leadership
Organizationally defined; carries a title. Officially designated position with specified responsibilities and authority.	Behaviorally defined; no official title. Emerges through credibility and respect in the context of interpersonal relationships.
Part of the hierarchy within the organization.	Typically exercised among peers within committees or interpersonal networks.
Accountable to higher levels of authority; must ensure that routine administrative tasks are completed.	Does not carry specific responsibilities or administrative duties; no specific accountability.*
Controls tangible and intangible resources; can use carrots and sticks as means of influence.	Does not control tangible or intangible resources; influence is embedded within peer networks, interpersonal rewards, and sanctions.

Table 4.1 "Characteristics of Formal and Informal Leadership" from *A Guide for Leaders in Higher Education: Core Concepts, Competencies, and Tools, 8/e* by B. D. Ruben, R. De Lisi, and R. A. Gigliotti. Copyright © 2017 by Stylus Publishing, LLC. Reprinted by permission of Stylus Publishing, LLC.

* Informal leaders might serve as chairs of committees or task forces and therefore have a committee chair title and the responsibility to work with others to complete a specific charge. In this case, committee chair roles have elements of both informal and formal leadership.

influence others or not, leadership functions may still be occurring. Whether the topic of a conversation deals with where to go to dinner, when to go shopping, or who should drive to an event, leadership dynamics associated with social influence are at play as options are presented and decisions are considered and made. The fact that leadership in these situations is often unplanned and sometimes unnoticed, even to those exercising influence, makes them interesting circumstances to examine and reflect upon. Indeed, these simple settings can be useful "laboratory sites" for studying and understanding the fundamentals of social influence and informal leadership dynamics, as well as the leadership behaviors of specific individuals, and most especially, oneself. As we discuss in more detail later, such situations provide ideal opportunities for individuals to become more self-reflective and analytic, both of which are critical for effective formal and informal leadership. See Table 4.1 for an overview of characteristics associated with both formal and informal leadership.

NOT ALWAYS A CLEAR DISTINCTION

While the distinction between formal and informal leadership is quite clear in the abstract, there are some cases where the positions that individuals occupy in groups and organizations blur this distinction. This is most likely to occur in situations involving larger groups or organizations. While there may well be titled leaders in these situations—chair, coordinator, or convener, for example—a "member" of a group or a committee can also be viewed as a title, and depending on the group or organization, the role of "member" may come with some defined responsibilities, including attendance, voting, or other forms of participation or service. Another similar example involves the role of "citizen" within a community—a position that carries both responsibilities and significant opportunities for influence in democratic societies. Examples such as these highlight the blurring of the distinction between formal and informal leadership. In both examples, while there may be some formal designation and specific responsibilities for attendees or members, it is generally the case that individuals in these roles have a wide range of options they may exercise involving whether and in what ways to participate.

FUNCTIONS SERVED BY FORMAL AND INFORMAL LEADERS

It is important to recognize that despite the major differences between formal and informal leadership roles, a number of the same functions can be served by individuals serving in either capacity. Two types of leadership activities are most often associated with these roles, as noted in Baird and Weinberg (1981). The first approach, *task-oriented* leadership, includes the most familiar and generally, the most obvious types of leadership activities. Task-oriented leadership relates to productivity and "getting the job done." These activities are associated with analyzing situations, conveying information, making decisions, solving problems, and completing tasks or assignments. Specific leadership behaviors that fall into this category include actions associated with:

- Informing
- Planning
- Orienting
- Integrating
- Representing
- Coordinating
- Clarifying
- Evaluating

Typically, the explicit requirements associated with formal leadership roles focus on task-oriented aspects of a position. Indeed, these are likely the most common behaviors that come to mind when one thinks of what a leader should do. And, in many situations, particularly when time and productivity pressures are present, emphasizing behaviors that relate to task completion is a very reasonable focus of activity.

The second and less familiar of the important leadership behaviors are those *relationship-oriented* activities that involve encouraging engagement, participation, motivation, positive morale, and to promoting high standards, mutual respect, and teamwork within the group or organization. Traditionally, these dimensions of leadership are given less attention and sometimes less value than task-oriented behaviors, and they are seldom listed among formal responsibilities in titled position descriptions. As noted previously, actions associated with "getting the job done" tend to become the priority for formal leaders, in part, because their performance related to these tasks is often the primary focus for evaluating their leadership effectiveness.

Relationship-oriented leadership behaviors associated with team building and cultivating positive morale and engagement are, nonetheless, just as vital for a group or an organization, both because of their inherent value and because over the long term these behaviors contribute to member commitment, personal investment, and often the quality of the work. So, while task achievement functions are certainly necessary and important, so too are behaviors related to the creation of a participative and engaging environment—an environment characterized by a positive communication climate, meaningful commitment to the work of a group or an organization, and support for all members of the group or organization, including its leaders. It is important to indicate once again that leadership in these important areas is an option available for both formal and informal leaders.

Specific behaviors that contribute to relationship-oriented leadership include:

- Promoting participation
- Regulating interaction
- Promoting the satisfaction of member needs
- Promoting cooperation
- Protecting individual rights
- Role modeling
- Assuming responsibility for failures
- Promoting group or organizational development

Both productivity and cohesiveness are important in most settings, and task and relational behaviors are therefore essential. Both depend on the culture of the group or organization as well as the leader's personal style. Leaders in formal and informal positions would ideally attend to both of these functions, but few leaders are equally focused on, or adept at, addressing each of these needs. Other individuals who serve as members of a group, team, club, or organization can make extremely useful contributions by adopting informal roles that emphasize areas where gaps are present—either because a formal leader's attention is directed elsewhere, or due to the emergence of particular needs or priorities within the dynamics of ongoing activity which others are not addressing.

POWER AND INFLUENCE

© Vladimir Gjorgiev/Shutterstock.com

As summarized by Spector (2016), "Power resides in the capacity of one or more individuals to impact the behavior of others. It is a force without which leaders simply cannot lead" (p. 70). Power is embedded in both formal and informal leadership roles, and there are interesting similarities and important differences between formal and informal roles as it relates to issues of power and influence. With the array of formalized responsibilities and documented expectations associated with formal leadership comes *positional power*. Individuals who hold formal leadership positions have authority over any number of functions and activities, and this authority provides a basis for influence. In addition, formal leaders may also have influence and credibility that derives from their knowledge and experience. This authority may be talked about in varying ways depending on the setting, size, type, and complexity of the group or organization. Individuals in titled positions may be described in terms of "the person in charge," and "the person to whom one reports," or more informally, as the "leader of the team." Regardless of the language used, operating in a setting where others "look to you" as the leader has numerous benefits related to one's ability to influence the direction of others' activities and actions, and it also affords some degree of autonomy in setting those directions for oneself and others. That said, serving in a titled position does not guarantee that others will follow the guidance a leader provides. And, even in cases where followers say they will comply with the leader's wishes, there is no guarantee they will wholeheartedly support the directions when he or she is out of sight or out of mind. The level of commitment followers bring to a leadership situation has an impact on one's ability to lead, and to some extent this commitment can be cultivated by the approach and style a leader employs.

Turning to the issues of power, authority, and influence as they relate to informal leadership, a complicated picture emerges. In any group or organization there are unlimited opportunities for individuals to be influential—the loose and emergent nature of informal leadership can be a great asset. Nevertheless, while informal leadership roles allow you to pursue the goals and work you care about, others have no clear incentive to follow an informal leader (Lawrence & De Lisi, 2017). Therefore, to be effective, individuals must understand follower interests and needs, find ways to enact behaviors that resonate with these needs, and earn the acceptance of others through positive actions—and they must do this without the benefit of structurally defined expectations and formally sanctioned authority. While formal leaders enjoy the benefits of positional power, informal leaders must rely on personal or situational power and influence that begins with understanding the needs or issues that are salient for others. As with formal leaders, informal leaders may have credibility that derives from their personal knowledge and experience. To a considerable degree, however, the influence of informal leaders depends on the personal power they acquire and exercise, which is often a direct consequence of specific behaviors that result in the granting of respect and credibility by followers.

If interested in developing personal influence in any situation, a number of strategies exist, some of which are quite obvious and others often overlooked. Fundamentally, these include showing up at appropriate times, meeting expectations, becoming knowledgeable on topics and issues under consideration, volunteering to take on support roles, being seen as sincerely interested in the activities and successes of the group, communicating effectively and respectfully with colleagues, and exhibiting other leadership competencies discussed in previous chapters. De Lisi and Lawrence (2017) identify several additional strategies that contribute to this form of influence, many of which you might currently draw upon in your various formal and informal leadership roles:

- Earn a reputation for integrity, discretion, genuine interest, helpfulness, and reliability.
- Follow through on promises, big and small.
- Model hard work and dedication to the common good.
- Become an asset to those above and an assistant to those below. Cultivate the support of the people doing the day-to-day on-the-ground implementation and get the support of whomever the various implementers and stakeholders report to.
- Develop a broad network across rank, role, status, and culture.
- Express gratitude: thank people for their contributions and be genuinely appreciative. It can be especially powerful to recognize those contributions that many others overlook. Praising those who contribute to others, particularly to their formal leaders, earns loyal friends.
- Know your peers and cultivate good will among them.
- Know the relevant formal and informal leaders and their views and cultivate their support.
- Make the lives of formal leaders easier by getting buy-in from those that report to them, so that your project is not their problem.

- Always show up prepared and provide appropriate information.
- Ask strategic questions and ask questions that "reframe" the issue.
- Volunteer for tasks and follow-through.
- Frame the debate by introducing drafts or other materials to use as starting points for discussion; this makes following your lead easy.
- View the situation from other participants' points of view and in light of their various interests.
- Be open to other views, accept suggestions that improve the outcome, and compromise when it will get to "the good," even if not to "the perfect."
- Share the credit. Be more concerned with getting good ideas adopted and/or the task completed than receiving credit for it. Patience may be required. Often, you are planting seeds that may take a while to germinate.
- Mentor, and be mentored.
- Be humble and have a sense of humor.

It is important to recognize that successful leaders—formal and informal—can make use of the same strategies and tools. Achieving support and commitment—beyond simple compliance—involves many of the same competencies and skills as does effectiveness in informal leadership. So, while there may appear to be a major difference between the affordances of formal leadership roles as compared to informal roles, in practice, leadership effectiveness, particularly over the long term, nearly always depends on the competencies of informal leadership—those deriving not from *positional*, but rather from *personal* power.

INFLUENCE TACTICS

Leadership scholars (Yukl, 2001; Yukl, Seifert, & Chavez, 2008) have identified and defined various tactics that leaders and managers use to influence the behaviors of others. Such tactics can be useful in both formal and informal leadership requests, but must be used thoughtfully and in an ethical manner. Important to note, however, is that the desired outcome of any attempt to influence another is never guaranteed—possible outcomes range from commitment, compliance, or to resistance (Falbe & Yukl, 1992). Once again, as discussed throughout the book, the outcome of an effort to lead others is highly dependent on the willingness of others to follow. Commitment occurs when an individual agrees with an appeal and willingly carries out a request; compliance occurs when an individual carries out a request, but does not necessarily agree with the reasoning or rationale offered in the appeal; and resistance or rejection occurs when an individual is actively opposed to an appeal and fails to comply with a request.

Research on these topics demonstrates that some communication and influence tactics are more effective than others (Falbe & Yukl, 1992). For example, Yukl (2013) proposes that the following influence tactics are most likely to elicit commitment: using rational persuasion in the form of logical arguments and credible evidence, seeking advice or suggestions, appealing to values and ideals, and providing assistance and support in exchange for agreement. Other influence tactics such as explaining how an individual will benefit, using praise, asking for personal favors, offering an exchange, asserting authority, threatening or badgering, or developing a coalition of supporters are less effective tactics and, at the most, may result only in outward compliance. Research has shown that while consultation and inspirational appeals are typically the most effective, influence tactics are often more effective when used in combination. For example, rational persuasion appears to be more effective when used along with consultation, inspirational appeals, or ingratiation. The least effective influence tactics appear to be pressure tactics, coalition building, and asserting authority, but these same tactics are somewhat effective in gaining compliance when used with rational persuasion. Exchange was also found to be effective, but must be carefully used so as to be manipulative (Falbe & Yukl, 1992).

Building upon these earlier concepts, Yukl (2010) suggests a number of strategies for improving the effectiveness of one's influence strategies. These include:

- Dedicating sufficient time to developing an influence strategy, especially when requests are unusual or likely perceived as risky
- Increasing knowledge and skill by reflecting on the outcomes of influence attempts
- Seeking feedback from others or participating in training programs to gain insight into your own influence behaviors

FORMAL AND INFORMAL LEADERSHIP OPPORTUNITIES ABOUND

Whether one thinks in terms of formal or informal leadership positions, there are many opportunities for influence that are easily overlooked. These include influence

by serving as teachers, ambassadors, stewards, and change agents, each of which is discussed below.

Teachers.   Regardless of our responsibilities or positions, we may serve as teachers in our groups or organizations. We often do not consciously choose this role. Rather, by virtue of our presence and behaviors, we take on the role of teacher and role model, and thereby act as sources of social influence. From this perspective, each choice we make in what we say or do in our interactions helps to shape the culture and socialization processes of others with whom we communicate. We may not be used to thinking of this as a leadership role; but with some reflection, it becomes clear how significant our capacity for influence is in this regard.

Ambassadors.   When we engage with others outside of the groups or organizations in which we are members, we function as representatives or ambassadors. Our behaviors, the values we display, and our ways of handling situations and ourselves serve as a source of potential influence for others—shaping their views not only of us, but also of the groups and organizations in which we currently belong. Given this role as "ambassador," we must continually think about the impact that our decisions and behaviors might have within and outside of the group, team, or organization.

Stewards.   Whether we have formal titled roles or not, we are stewards of the culture and resources of the groups and organizations of which we are a part. Again, this occurs whether we plan to serve as leaders in this way or not. As we carry out the array of activities associated with our participation in a group, team, organization, or community, we have responsibilities for contributing to the well-being of these personal and professional entities. It is also the case that our decisions and actions are on display and potentially a source of social influence to others.

Change Agents. Each of us can be an agent of change or source of positive influence in our groups, organizations, or communities. This potential is present for informal as well as formal leaders, representing an important opportunity available to each of us for constructive and positive contributions.

CONCLUSION

Through the discussion in this chapter, and indeed throughout the book thus far, we have emphasized the characteristics of formal leadership. We have also provided insights into the nature of informal leadership and the important role one can play when serving in this capacity. Informal leadership comes with few defined responsibilities, but also great opportunities for making a difference in ways that matter to the leader and his or her group or organization. In some instances, it affords mechanisms for social influence that are not accessible through formal roles.

We have also emphasized the point that many, if not most, of the leadership competencies required for effectiveness as an informal leader may also benefit formal leaders. Finally, we want to underscore the value of treating informal leadership situations as laboratories for developing, testing, and enhancing one's leadership skills. Take advantage of informal leadership opportunities that have the potential to enrich your knowledge and skill. These opportunities may also significantly increase your ability for being noticed and selected to serve in formal leadership roles now and in the future.

CHAPTER 5

UNDERSTANDING CULTURE IN GROUPS, TEAMS, AND ORGANIZATIONS: THE LEADER AS CROSS-CULTURAL COMMUNICATOR AND ORGANIZATIONAL ETHNOGRAPHER

⚠️ **Guiding Questions:**

1) What is culture and why is an understanding of diversity, difference, and cultural identity important for effective leadership?
2) What is a group or organizational culture, and why is an examination of these cultures important for leadership?
3) How do differences between cultures and subcultures lead to predictable "intercultural tensions"?
4) What does it mean to become a cross-cultural leader and what competencies are helpful for becoming a culturally competent leader?

In this chapter, we make the case that successful leader-follower interactions benefit greatly from a comprehensive understanding of culture. By knowing the various dimensions of culture and the influence it has on individuals, groups, organizations, and communities, you can better understand your own worldview and develop a greater appreciation of others' perspectives as well. In this chapter, we explain how culture functions at various levels within families, groups, organizations, communities, and societies, and how an appreciation of culture can be essential to effective leadership.

CULTURE AND CULTURAL IDENTITY

© Rawpixel.com/Shutterstock.com

According to Spencer-Oatey (2008), "Culture is notoriously difficult to define," with at least 164 different definitions in the discipline of anthropology alone (p. 3). Despite this challenge, it is important to identify some of the more critical aspects of culture that are most relevant for our purposes. Given the approach of this book, it is particularly important to understand the relationship between culture and communication. Simply stated, culture is the product of communication processes that occur over time as individuals interact with one another in varying settings. It is composed of a complex and interconnected web of language patterns, stories, norms of behavior, rules, traditions, customs, and preferred practices (Ruben & Stewart, 2016). Culture is manifested in symbols that represent the beliefs and values of a group, and that serve as a guide to its members as they make sense of their environment. Recall the idea presented in Chapter 3 that we all need to interpret the circumstances that confront us as human beings, and it is through this fundamental act of sensemaking that we are able to adapt to our surroundings and the people and events we encounter (Berger & Luckmann, 1966). This process involves the creation and interpretation not only of the spoken and written messages of others, but also of the various symbols we encounter which, in turn, become central elements of our culture. For example, important symbols in the United States include the flag, our national anthem, and the Statue of Liberty. A university also has many cultural symbols including its school colors, team mascot, and notable campus structures, statues, and buildings.

As implied in the foregoing discussion, culture is not something that individuals are born with; rather, we are born into particular cultures, and through repeated interactions with others, we learn and come to share the beliefs, values, and norms of behavior practiced by a majority of its members. Cultures are often taken for granted by members of a cultural group and accepted without question. Each culture has its own traditions and customs, and its own assumptions about the preferred ways to behave, and these seem quite natural to us as they are mirrored and reinforced by others with whom we interact (Ruben & Stewart, 2016). It is important to note that cultures are not static; rather they can change over time due to the multiple, and sometimes competing, perspectives, life experiences, and goals that individuals bring to them.

We all have multiple cultural identities and the many groups, organizations, and communities of which we are members influence the personal identity and core beliefs that we learn and display to the world. For instance, we develop identities as an American or an Egyptian, a professor or a student, a physician or a salesperson, and we reflect a blend of the teachings of the various cultures and subcultures to others through our thoughts, communication styles, dress, and actions. Although our individual cultural identities are not rigid, nor wholly predictable, they are nonetheless important in understanding who we are, how we think about the world, and how we act. Perhaps not surprisingly, research has shown that we are more likely to affiliate with people we perceive as sharing a similar identity and with groups we perceive to be prestigious or beneficial to us in some way (Ashforth & Mael, 1989; Hogg & Terry, 2000).

CULTURAL DIVERSITY IN SOCIETY

© DGLimages/Shutterstock.com

Cultures develop when people share a common geography, race or ethnicity, age, gender, socioeconomic status, and education. Most societies are composed of a dominant culture, one that is most widespread and influential, as well as multiple other subcultures. The United States is an increasingly diverse place, and we are likely to interact with others who have cultures that are different from our own in personal, educational, work, and community settings. Metaphors such as "melting pot" or "kaleidoscope" are often used to describe the diverse ethnic, racial, and social groups that make up the U.S. population. As the country becomes more diverse, functioning effectively as a member of society requires us to develop sensitivity to, and an appreciation for, cultures that we perceive as different from our own.

Nationalities as subcultures.   Nationality refers to a person's place of birth or heritage. An individual's nationality is influential in the development of culture. Consider the ways in which people from Zimbabwe have cultures that are distinct from those born in New Zealand. The language, food, customs, symbols, and rituals all influence behaviors. These national cultures influence our behavior in general ways, and also have an influence on our workplace behavior, as we will discuss later in the chapter.

Ethnic and racial groups as subcultures.   In the United States, a majority culture developed primarily through the importation of various cultural practices by immigrants from the United Kingdom and Europe beginning in the 1500s. While non-Hispanic whites remain the largest racial group in the United States today, we are seeing an increase in the populations of other racial and ethnic groups. According to 2010 census data, nearly one-third of the U.S. population identified as being a member of a minority group, with Hispanics representing 16%, blacks or African-Americans representing 13%, and Asians representing 5% of the total population. Additionally, approximately 3% of the total population say they belong to more than one racial or ethnic category. According to a July 2016 Pew Research report, young Americans—those under the age of five—are a "majority minority" (Gao, 2016), in that the 2015 census reports that 50.2% of children younger than one year were members of racial or ethnic minorities (Cohn, 2016).

Generations as subcultures.   Delineated in the popular press as *Traditionalists* (born before 1946), *Baby Boomers* (1946–1964), *Generation X* (1965–1976), *Millennials* (1977–1997), and *Generation 2020* (born after 1997), each group shares life experiences that have shaped the beliefs and values of a generation, and these are distinct in some ways from other generations. Members of an age cohort often share a somewhat common worldview influenced by defining events such as WWII for the *Traditionalists*, or 9/11 for *Millennials*. Because U.S. citizens, for the most part, are living longer and working longer, today's workforce includes five generations of workers (Meister & Willyerd, 2009), each of whom bring a somewhat unique cultural identity to their work and other personal and professional activities.

Gender groups as subcultures.   Traditionally, gender was understood to be a category assigned to a person at birth based on anatomical features consistent with being male or female—gender divisions that resulted in discernable masculine and feminine cultures. For example, an all-male military platoon would have been described as having a masculine culture, while an all-female sorority would have been described as having a feminine culture. However, gender identities are increasingly recognized in contemporary society as being strongly influenced by socialization processes. In an effort to clarify these issues, the World Health Organization has defined sex (male or female) as "the biological and physiological characteristics that define men and women" and gender (masculine or feminine) as "the socially constructed roles, behaviors, activities, and attributes that a given society considers appropriate for men and women" (World

Health Organization, 2015). The changing ways that individuals identify according to their gender preference has resulted in changes in gender-related cultures and subcultures, and, vice versa, and these changes create additional cultural variation that can add complexity to the dynamics within teams, groups, organizations, and communities more generally.

Cultural Stereotypes and Tensions

In thinking about cultural identities, it is critical to keep in mind that there is a great deal of variation and diversity between and within each of these cultural groups—and generalizations about cultural identities are often oversimplifications. Not all members of an ethnic, racial, age, gender, or sexual orientation group share the same beliefs, attitudes, and values or communicate or behave in the same manner. Every cultural group is made up of unique individuals who carry with them multiple overlapping cultural identities.

When we describe cultural groups and subcultures in broad and simplistic terms, we run the risk of engaging in stereotyping. Stereotyping occurs when we overgeneralize the assumptions and perceptions we have relative to those we perceive as different—and assume that our generalizations apply to all members of a cultural group.

Social psychology research offers insight into how group membership can influence our beliefs and behaviors. Research has demonstrated a general tendency for individuals to categorize themselves as well as others according to real and sometimes imagined categories (Tajfel & Turner, 1979). While membership in a group provides benefits such as a sense of pride or higher self-esteem, individuals typically explain the uniqueness of their group by comparing it to other groups. Research conducted by Tajfel and Turner (1986) showed that in order to increase the prestige of one's own group (the in-group), groups demonstrated a natural tendency to characterize other groups (the out-group) in negative ways. An "us-versus-them" mindset can develop when members focus intently on in-group member similarities while highlighting the ways in which out-group members are different. This process sometimes is apparent in the ways individuals with particular religious or political views think about or behave toward those with differing orientations—particularly when those differences are less common. Extreme examples of these tendencies are evident in racist, xenophobic, or sexist language that reflects negative attitudes towards various cultural groups. The American social scientist, William Graham Sumner (1906), coined the term ethnocentrism, which he defined as "the view of things in which one's own group is the center of everything, and all others are scaled and rated with reference to it" (p. 13). Sumner went on to explain that there is an inherent tendency for individuals to perceive their own group as superior to others.

Whether positive or negative, stereotypes tend to obscure or overlook significant differences between individuals that leaders must take account of if they are to be successful. Whenever we reduce the essence of a complex human being to a simplistic statement or image, we limit our ability to see a person's true abilities and the value he or she brings to a group or organization. Furthermore, the ways that we see and understand the other often influences how we act toward him or her.

The critical point to keep in mind in this regard is that each of us is influenced by the cultures into which we have been socialized and of which we are a part. Our cultural identities can be extremely important factors in the ongoing dynamics of teams, groups, organizations, and communities—and they represent an important source of opportunity but also challenge when it comes to leadership.

ORGANIZATIONAL CULTURE

© Monkey Business Images/Shutterstock.com

In the same way that various groups in society at large can be characterized based on shared cultural characteristics, so too, organizations—as well as teams, committees, and groups—have distinctive cultures. Similar to the broader definition of culture presented above, management scholar Edgar Schein (1996) describes organizational culture as the tacit assumptions shared by a group of individuals that shape their perceptions, thoughts, feelings, and, to some degree, their overt behaviors. Just as your understanding of national, ethnic, age, and gender-based cultures are important to the practice of leadership, this is equally true when it comes to an understanding of the influence of organizational culture. Cultures develop in groups and organizations of all kinds, and are influenced by shared occupations, geographic regions, tenure, or professional identity that are unique in some ways and differ from the dominant organizational culture. To illustrate this point, within any given healthcare facility, the nursing, administrator, and physician subcultures may each be distinct even though all are working within the same hospital. Adding further complexity is the fact that the subcultures of nurses, doctors, or administrators, while differing substantially from one another within any one organization, may have a good deal in common with others in those same professional groups in other health care organizations. What follows are three distinct ways of understanding the manifestation of culture in organizational settings, each of which raises a number of implications for the nature of leadership (Martin, 1992).

Culture as integrated.   This perspective emphasizes commonalities in organizations that unite members and create a common identity. This view downplays the fact that any organization, or culture for that matter, can be rife with uncertainty and dissent. The integration perspective highlights the view that values and basic assumptions are consistently shared by nearly all organization members and interpreted consistently across all manifestations of culture.

Culture as differentiated.   This perspective highlights the fact that organizations are made up of various subcultures that co-exist in fluctuating states of agreement, conflict, or apathy. A differentiation perspective recognizes that subcultures hold a different interpretation of reality, downplaying the notion that organizational cultures are stable, consistent, and predictable across all members of that culture. Furthermore, the perspective highlights the idea that although members of a subculture might have a degree of shared interpretation, total consensus—if it were possible—would be a liability.

Culture as fragmented.   This perspective highlights the growing complexity of organizational culture based on a number of factors such as an increasing dependence on the use of communication technologies, a diverse and mobile workforce, and high degrees of physical and temporal distance between organizational members. The boundaries between subcultures are therefore increasingly permeable and fluctuating, implying that consensus around a shared cultural identity becomes impossible.

THE LEADER AS ORGANIZATIONAL ETHNOGRAPHER

According to Schein (2010), "Cultural forces are powerful because they operate outside of our awareness. We need to understand them not only because of their power, but also because they help to explain many of our puzzling and frustrating experiences in social and organizational life" (p. 7). Schein's words remind us that successful relationships between leaders and followers require a deep understanding of another's culture as well as a high degree of self-reflexivity in order to uncover our own biases and hidden assumptions with regard to those who are different. In this sense, leaders need to become ethnographers—observers and analysts of the groups, organizations, and communities in which they are members.

Ethnography is a research technique that requires close observation and detailed descriptions of a group of people to better understand their culture. Anthropologists and sociologists, in particular, use ethnographic research methods to gain a comprehensive understanding of a culture informed by the viewpoint of its members. The practice requires deep immersion in a culture to capture "thick descriptions" of behaviors as well as the broader context and the meanings these have for members (Geertz, 1973). This enables those outside of the culture to gain a more comprehensive understanding of how customs, norms, and everyday practices shape behaviors within communities, groups, and organizations. By observing, listening to, and analyzing the behaviors and communication practices of those around you, you are better able to identify and cultivate the sources of enthusiasm, inspiration, and pride as well as understand and manage factors that lead to resistance, drama, disengagement, and anger (Ruben et al., 2017).

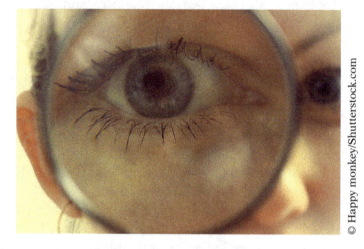

© Happy monkey/Shutterstock.com

Organizational cultures have the power to either help or hinder the ability of groups and organizations to effectively work together. The extent to which leaders can understand, analyze, and utilize their insights in their work will be a primary determinant of whether culture is seen as a facilitator or inhibitor of the work of groups and organizations. We feel strongly that positive social influence requires leaders who understand and appreciate the multiple dimensions and manifestations of organizational culture. As Biz Stone, the co-founder of Twitter, aptly stated, "A culture is going to form whether you like it or not, and if you pay attention to it, you can craft something that makes the company stronger" (Stone, 2015, p. 41). With an understanding of the forces that shape culture, leaders are better able to create the conditions for the development of cultures that inspire and excite members to participate, and to change cultures that contribute to dysfunctional groups and organizations (Schein, 2010). Unquestionably, adopting the posture of an ethnographic researcher can be a very useful strategy for leaders, particularly in circumstances where a leader is new to the group, organization, or community.

Observing Organizational Culture

Aspects of culture vary in the degree to which they are overt and visible to members and others outside of the group. For example, imagine you have just arrived at Google Headquarters (aka the Googleplex) in Mountain View, California. As you approach the visitors' center, you notice a large collection of identical bicycles in the parking lot, freely available for anyone to use to travel around the vast complex. Nearby, is a Google conference bicycle that allows groups of seven to hold a meeting while riding together. Once inside, the sleek office design and colorful accents capture your attention as you notice casually dressed employees lounging, reading, working, or collaborating with others in the brightly colored public spaces. Your host for this visit takes you on a tour where you learn about the multiple restaurants and cafés across the campus that provide free food for all employees, along with other amenities such as day care for employees' children, doctors, dry cleaning, laundry, a gym, and basketball and volleyball courts. By now, you might be drawing conclusions about Google's organizational culture based on the artifacts you have observed. These are just a few examples of the most visible manifestations of an organization's culture. While these artifacts may begin to offer the basis for some insight into Google's unique culture, many of the most important dimensions of culture are found below the level of observation.

Schein (2010) presents a three-tiered model that identifies levels of culture—artifacts, espoused beliefs and values, and underlying assumptions—arranged according to visibility. If we think of culture as an iceberg, as depicted in Figure 5.1, artifacts are found at the top and are clearly visible above the water line. Directly below the waterline are espoused beliefs and values, still somewhat visible, but increasingly murky. At the very bottom of the iceberg, deep below the surface, are the underlying assumptions—positioned so far beneath the water that they remain hidden to the observer. This metaphor highlights the difficulty in identifying and ultimately understanding the multiple dimensions of culture, particularly those aspects that are influential but nevertheless hidden well below the surface. Below is a description of additional components associated with the culture of a group, an organization, or a community.

Artifacts.   The first and most visible level corresponds to the Google example above—"all the phenomena that you would see, hear, and feel when you encounter a new group with an unfamiliar culture" (Schein, 2010, p. 23). Artifacts include both material objects

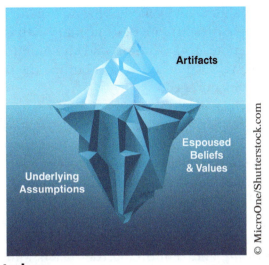

© MicroOne/Shutterstock.com

Figure 5.1: Culture as an Iceberg

such as architecture and office design, technologies, the way people dress, as well as visible social practices such as what stories or jokes are told, or what types of rituals or ceremonies are practiced. These artifacts may be easy to see and describe, but their meanings are not always evident to outsiders. A sleek and modern office design might well be an indication of an innovative culture, an office filled with all of the latest technologies and gadgets might reflect a high-tech culture, or casually dressed employees might reflect a relaxed culture. However, unless we investigate the meanings these artifacts hold for the members of that culture, our understanding is limited and we can be misled in our assumptions.

Rituals.   Rituals also help to define and shape organizational culture. For example, an annual family picnic promotes one kind of culture, whereas a weekly Friday night happy hour communicates another. Social practices also shape culture. For example, an organization where members address each other on a first name basis communicates a culture that is starkly different from one in which leaders must be addressed by their formal title. Business practices such as how decisions are made also provide insight into culture—an organization where only the formal leaders make decisions will differ from one in which all members of the group participate in decision making.

Espoused beliefs and values.   Espoused beliefs and values are less visible than artifacts, but have a powerful influence nonetheless. These reflect the group's ideals, goals, values, aspirations, ideologies, and rationalizations for behaviors. Beliefs and values reveal what is regarded to be important in a community, how things should operate, and how people should behave. Espoused beliefs and values are most evident in organizational vision, mission, and value statements. A vision statement is typically a short and inspirational declaration that outlines an organization's (or individual's) desired end-state or long-term goal. In essence, what does the individual, organization, or community, strive to be? A mission statement explains what an organization (or individual) does to support the vision through a description of its primary activities. In order to articulate the type of culture they promote, organizations and communities are increasingly developing value statements, as well. Value statements outline the underlying principles and types of behaviors that are encouraged.

Other examples of how espoused beliefs and values are communicated by leaders and group members include the frequent use of words such as "teamwork" or phrases such as "family business," "work hard, play hard," or "one for all, all for one" to name a few. An organization's espoused beliefs do not always align with the beliefs of all members, as noted by the "culture as differentiated" perspective described earlier. Although there might be evidence of what the organization wants its members to value and believe (i.e., vision, mission, and value statements), these documents are not likely to accurately or fully describe the values of everyone in the team or group. Because leaders are charged with communicating and reinforcing the beliefs and values of a community or organization, there is a need for alignment between organizational practices and

Table 5.1. The Nature Conservancy's, Vision, Mission, and Values Statement

The Nature Conservancy (https://www.nature.org/about-us/vision-mission/index.htm)	
Vision (where the organization wants to go)	Our vision is a world where the diversity of life thrives, and people act to conserve nature for its own sake and its ability to fulfill our needs and enrich our lives.
Mission (how the organization will get there)	The mission of The Nature Conservancy is to conserve the lands and waters on which all life depends
Values (the values that shape all actions)	(1) Integrity beyond reproach; (2) Respect for people, communities, and cultures; (3) Commitment to diversity; (4) One conservancy; (5) Tangible, lasting results

Table 5.1   The Nature Conservancy's vision, mission and value statement, http://www.nature.org/. Copyright © 2017 The Nature Conservancy. Reprinted with permission.

stated values and aspirations; otherwise, these values are met with increasing cynicism and may come to be disregarded by members of the organization. For example, a leader who suggests that the organization values "innovation" but then fails to provide adequate resources and support for innovative activity or worse, penalizes employees who take risks and fail, will not appear authentic. Valuing innovation, in this case, becomes a mere talking point and will have little influence on behavior.

Underlying assumptions.   Underlying assumptions exist below the surface and can be the most powerful drivers of group and organizational culture. Such assumptions can be very difficult for leaders to manage and/or change because they are not easily recognized and they become deeply embedded in groups over time. These are the taken-for-granted beliefs and values that subconsciously shape thoughts, feelings, perceptions, and behaviors of group members. According to Schein (2010), these basic assumptions "tend to be nonconfrontable and nondebatable, and hence are extremely difficult to change" (p. 28). Groups, teams, organizations, and communities do not necessarily share the same underlying assumptions, and therefore different or conflicting latent beliefs often lead to tensions. Consider, for example, an ethnographic study of a community symphony by Ruud (2000), who discovered and described the two distinctive and competing underlying sets of assumptions within the organization that caused conflict. In examining the communication patterns of the two dominant groups—musicians and managers—it became apparent how each group held opposing perspectives and talked in very different ways about the organization. The musicians embraced values consistent with an artistic approach, while the managers embraced values associated with business. Through discourse, each culture competed with one another for organizational prominence, which in turn resulted in a tense communication climate for all members of the organization. In this case, the language of the business perspective and the language of the artistic perspective each reflected an adherence to different beliefs, attitudes, and values, illustrating the ways in which culture is embedded in and sustained through communication, with the potential to have a far-reaching impact on leader-follower dynamics.

The communication climate of a group, team, organization, or community is the atmosphere one encounters as a member. Cultures shape climate. For example, a climate might be one that establishes and reinforces expectations relating to communication practices such as who speaks to whom, the types of topics that can be discussed, or the expected degree of formality or informalty—all of which are tangible manifestations of core cultural values. Consider an organization where employees are sequestered in isolated cubicles for most of the day and where the only sound heard is the tapping of computer keys. An organization such as this, one where informal talk and interruptions are discouraged, would stand in contrast to an organization where employees operate in a communal workspace and informal conversations fill the room. These two scenarios illustrate vastly different communication climates that reflect distinct organizational cultures.

INTERSECTION OF NATIONAL CULTURE AND ORGANIZATIONAL CULTURE

© Artistic Photo/Shutterstock.com

The increasing diversity of the contemporary classroom, workplace, and community presents a need for better understanding the ways in which national culture intersects with organizational cultures and climate. Geert Hofstede's (2001) extensive examination of national cultures revealed distinct differences in workplace values across more than 70 countries represented in his dataset.[1] His analysis identified five dimensions where national cultures differ, from one another, including values related to power, individualism versus collectivism, masculinity versus femininity, orientations toward uncertainty, and long-

1 For a more comprehensive understanding of Geert Hofstede's work and a list of the countries in his study, visit https://geert-hofstede.com.

versus short-term perspectives. These differences in national culture can have important implications for leader-follower dynamics in multicultural groups, organizations, and communities. In these situations, cultural differences can create significant obstacles to communication and collaboration which require leadership insight and skill to diagnose and accommodate.

Power distance.   Power distance refers to the degree to which members of a national culture expect power to be distributed unequally across a population. In a high power distance culture, such as Malaysia, people expect formal authority and hierarchy and defer to the wishes of those in power. In low power distance countries, such as the United States, people prefer power to be more equally distributed and expect to have a voice and participate in decision making.

Individualism versus collectivism.   The distinction between individualism and collectivism refers to the degree to which members of a national culture emphasize individuality to a greater extent than common values and perspectives. In individualistic cultures, such as the United States, the connections among individuals are relatively loose, with the expectation being that each person is ultimately responsible for his or her own life and well-being. In collectivistic cultures, such as South Korea, people are expected to remain in cohesive groups for their entire lives and to act in ways that serve the community over their individual preferences.

Masculinity versus femininity.   These cultural differences suggest whether a national culture embraces traditionally masculine traits, such as assertiveness and competition, as compared to traditionally feminine traits, such as modesty and cooperation. In countries where masculinity is a more dominant value, such as Austria, individuals are more likely to value competition, success, and material rewards over a concern for community. In countries where more feminine values predominate, a greater commitment to values such as cooperation and concern for others are common among both men and women.

Uncertainty avoidance.   Uncertainty avoidance refers to the degree to which members of a society are typically more comfortable with ambiguity and uncertainty than are individuals in other cultures. In countries that rank high on uncertainty avoidance, such as Greece, individuals generally prefer predictability, are less tolerant of unstructured situations, and demonstrate a preference for clear guidelines and rules for action. In countries that are lower on this scale, such as Singapore, there is greater tolerance for ambiguous situations and greater comfort with unanticipated changes.

Long-term versus short-term orientation.   The final dimension of Hofstede's research on culture is a distinction between long-term versus short-term orientation based on the degree to which individuals focus on future rewards. In countries with a long-term orientation, such as China, there is more attention to saving for the future, being persistent, and adapting to changing circumstance. In countries such as Nigeria, with a more short-term orientation, there is a greater emphasis on past traditions and present circumstances, a concern for social obligations, and a desire to maintain dignity and preserve reputation.

Each of these dimensions has the potential to influence group dynamics and communication among members of a group, a team, an organization, or a community, particularly when there is a high degree of national diversity, such as is the case in global virtual teams. As you will read in Chapter 12, the rise of globalization and the increased reliance on technologies to communicate has enabled people from around the globe to work together to accomplish goals. However, a high degree of national diversity can contribute to conflicting communication practices, and in some cases, weakened team or group identification (Gibson & Gibbs, 2006). For example, an individual from a country characterized as measuring high in power distance, such as Albania with a score of 90, might have very different expectations about who has the authority to provide input or make decisions, compared to an individual from Austria with a low score of 11 on the power distance scale. These differences, if not recognized and managed effectively by leaders, can create or heighten tensions and weaken group cohesion and shared identity.

LEADERSHIP AND INTERCULTURAL COMMUNICATION COMPETENCE

© Uber Images/Shutterstock.com

Group, organizational, and national cultures raise a number of important challenges and opportunities for formal and informal leaders. Referring back to the metaphor of the ethnographer presented earlier, leadership effectiveness requires the ability of one to understand, appreciate, and navigate these distinct cultures with both a deep level of awareness and a general sensitivity to the nuances of different cultures. Thus, as discussed in the book, leadership involves more than knowing oneself, one's role(s), and the needs and expectations of the follower(s). Leadership, as a communicative and co-constructed process, also requires one to understand, appreciate, and navigate the diversity of cultures represented in whatever context one chooses to lead.

As will be discussed in greater detail in Chapter 11, the increased diversity in teams, groups, and organizations, creates a rich opportunity for individuals with different backgrounds, interests, and areas of expertise to create, innovate, and solve complex problems. Leadership requires attention to tasks as well as relationships, with the goal of encouraging cooperation, coordination, and productive interactions (Mischel & Northcraft, 1997). Furthermore, in light of the cultural nuances presented in this chapter, leaders must be mindful of the various—and often competing—subcultures present in any team, group, organization, or community.

One of the most significant challenges for leaders results from the fact that cultural differences of various kinds can be a significant contributor to quality outcomes in groups and organizations. At the same time, as suggested earlier, research on teams has shown that individuals favor interacting with those whom they share similar beliefs and values (Carton & Cummings, 2012). Thus, while cultural differences of various kinds among team members can be an asset, cultural and subcultural differences such as those related to position, tenure, knowledge, political orientation, and national identity can be sources of conflict (Jehn, Northcraft, & Neale, 1999). Left unmanaged, culturally diverse teams can become fragmented into multiple subgroups, which may lead to reduced communication or restricted knowledge sharing across groups. High levels of conflict, as discussed further in Chapter 11, can weaken group cohesion and team identity (Carton & Cummings, 2012; Phillips, Mannix, Neale, & Gruenfeld, 2004).

The role of effective leadership as it relates to diversity and cultural differences cannot be overstated. For example, when leaders demonstrate support for and a commitment to the benefits of team diversity, subgroup divisions appear to be less problematic (Schölmerich, Schermuly, & Deller, 2016). Leaders can take a number of actions to help lessen cultural tensions in groups or teams, including the following:

- Having an awareness of the subgroups in any situation
- Appreciating differences among cultural groups and subgroups
- Treating members as individuals and not token representatives of subgroups
- Encouraging relational communication across subgroups
- Modeling the practices of inclusive leadership that values giving voice to all team, group, organization, and community stakeholders
- Responding to cultural tensions with sensitivity, sincerity, and seriousness

The discussion of culture is critical for leaders who understand the various characteristics associated with culture, appreciate the differences found in various cultures, subcultures and climates, and demonstrate proficiency in intercultural communication.

Allow us to conclude this chapter with a brief overview of what we mean by inter-cultural communication competence. Whereas interpersonal communication competence involves the ability to communicate appropriately across different contexts (Spitzberg & Cupach, 1984), intercultural communication competence is the ability to communicate effectively with members of another culture. As previously noted, individual members of a group, a community, and an organization carry with them their own multiple cultural identities according to ethnicity, nationality, age, gender, physical ability, education, socioeconomic background, roles, political orientations, or professional identities, and these forces shape how individuals make sense of their world and interact with others. These differences might not always be obvious to us when we share the same language or the same professional or group identity, which can create unique challenges for both formal and informal leaders (Ruben, 1976). However, in developing a culturally diverse network, leaders gain access to differing perspectives, attitudes, and values that have the potential to positively influence and enrich group interactions and outcomes.

Much of the literature on intercultural competence highlights three components—knowledge, skill, and motivation. Intercultural *knowledge* provides a useful foundation, but knowledge of a culture alone is not sufficient to ensure successful interactions with others. Rather, *behaviors* are particularly important and should take account of and reflect an understanding of those cultures (Ruben, 1976). The desire or *motivation* to communicate with members of another culture is a third factor which can be influential (Spitzberg & Cupach, 1984).

To become an interculturally competent leader requires you to have knowledge of the specific communicative behaviors that are likely to be effective within a specific context and the skill to enact behaviors that reflect this knowledge. In addition to developing knowledge, leaders must also become aware of their own underlying assumptions and beliefs about their own cultures and the cultures of others. Finally, developing a genuine appreciation for cultural diversity, as well as an interest in and motivation to engage with others from different cultural backgrounds, can strengthen your skills as an intercultural communicator.

As noted throughout this book, the knowledge developed through careful observation can provide a solid basis for effective communication and action. Like anything else, however, having the opportunity to practice these behaviors will only strengthen your competency in this area. Developing expertise and applying the following seven communicative behaviors will help to strengthen your competence as an intercultural communicator (Ruben, 1976):

1. Displaying an interest in and respect for others through verbal and non-verbal behaviors such as eye contact, body posture, pitch, and tone of voice.
2. Responding positively to others in a non-judgmental way by using descriptive instead of evaluative language to strengthen the relationship.
3. Recognizing that others might have differing beliefs concerning what is "true" or "right."

4. Showing empathy for others while attempting to understand their perspective, as well as recognizing that others may show empathy in different ways.
5. Developing the ability to flexibly assume various roles in interactions, such as encouraging others to participate or recognize the value of others' contributions.
6. Taking initiative to manage group interactions in a constructive manner, such as managing turn-taking or moving the agenda forward based on an understanding of the needs and desires of others.
7. Embracing and developing a tolerance for new or ambiguous situations.

Becoming an interculturally competent leader is not easy; that said the beneficial outcomes such as greater cohesion and satisfaction as well as productive processes and achievements within the team, group, organization, or community are worth the effort.

CONCLUSION

There has arguably never been a more important time for understanding and appreciating cultural differences than this current moment. According to a 2015 United Nations report on trends in international migration, there are approximately 244 million people living in a country other than where they were born, an increase of 41% since reported in 2000 (United Nations, 2015). And, the degree of global migration is predicted to grow considerably. In addition to national diversity, society is becoming increasingly diverse in the areas of religion, politics, and lifestyle choices, leading us towards a culture that may be increasingly differentiated, and in some cases, fragmented (Martin, 1992).

Developing intercultural competence will help you to manage the inevitable tensions that arise when people representing differing cultural values and beliefs work together. The position we take here is that cultural diversity, can be highly beneficial for groups, teams, organizations, and communities. Diverse groups composed of individuals who have had different life experiences have the potential to generate new knowledge and develop novel insights for addressing existing problems (Jehn et al., 1999). Also, it is a widely accepted belief that diversity contributes to a group's ability to be more creative and innovative. By applying the insights and skills discussed in this book, and paying attention to the artifacts, espoused beliefs and values, and underlying assumptions of the various cultural groups you encounter in your personal and professional life, you will be better prepared to effectively lead diverse individuals to work together in pursuit of shared goals.

PART TWO:

Your Personal Approach to Leadership

CHAPTER 6

LEADERSHIP IN EVERYDAY ENCOUNTERS: ETHICS, VALUES, AND INTEGRITY

> **⚠ Guiding Questions:**
>
> 1) Why do ethics, values, and integrity matter to the study of leadership?
> 2) What values and guiding principles motivate you to lead?
> 3) How do values play a role in decision making and leadership practice in general?

Think of an individual—family member, friend, coach, teacher, or mentor—whom you admire greatly. What words would you use to describe this person? Perhaps adjectives such as helpful, honest, trustworthy, compassionate, or reliable come to mind. You are likely describing this person by comparing them to a set of values you think are important, your core values. *Core values* are the set of principles that shape your behavior and from which you assess the behaviors of other people. Understanding your core values and guiding principles will help you to understand your motivations to lead, along with the motivations of others around you. Additionally, identifying the values that are most important to you can impact how you go about selecting the individuals that you would most prefer to solicit guidance from in your personal and professional life.

Scholars of leadership, political pundits, journalists, and industry consultants of all kinds often go so far as to declare a "crisis" in contemporary leadership practice—one characterized by an erosion of ethics, values, and integrity. Scandals concerning business leaders, government officials, educational institutions, as well as religious organizations populate the media landscape. In this chapter, we begin to examine the intersection of leadership, ethics, values, and integrity in order to better understand the influence of these factors on both everyday informal encounters as well as formal leadership practices.

ETHICS, VALUES, AND INTEGRITY

© Rawpixel.com/Shutterstock.com

To begin the discussion and bring greater clarity to the topic, we discuss the differences among these three interrelated, but distinct, concepts—ethics, values, and integrity. From an academic perspective, ethics refers to a branch of philosophy concerned with principles of right and wrong conduct and the investigation of ideas associated with morality. Humans have contemplated, debated, and deliberated the meaning of "moral correctness" since the early days of civilization. Religious texts such as the Hindu Vedas, Jewish Torah, Christian Bible, and Muslim Quran all offer ideas regarding what it means to behave in a moral manner. Philosophers such as Socrates, Plato, and Aristotle as well as others throughout the ages have also contended with ideas surrounding ethics and moral action. Stories such as *The Epic of Gilgamesh* and Homer's *Odyssey* offer early accounts of the hero's trials and tribulations and provide testament to the eternal human desire to more fully understand moral action and leadership (Gresseth, 1975). Today, people called "ethicists" contend with ethical dilemmas concerning science, medicine, and law, as well as numerous other pressing and contentious matters. The timeless exploration of these topics is worthy of consideration, and remains important for our purposes in this book. An understanding of ethics, values, and integrity continues to shape the study and practice of leadership.

Ethics. The study of ethics offers a conceptual framework that can help to explain the negotiation of the rules and guidelines for personal and professional conduct. There are three primary branches of scholarship associated with the study of ethics—metaethics, normative ethics, and applied ethics. Metaethics addresses the foundations of moral values, and attends to debates such as the existence of universal moral principles versus the cultural or contextual relevance of moral principles (DeLapp, n.d.). Normative ethics focuses on the principles and standards of behavior that ultimately shape society at large. Applied ethics investigates controversial matters where issues of morality come into play, such as abortion, animal rights, or capital punishment (Fieser, n.d.). Although a more extensive overview of the literature on ethics lies beyond the scope of this book, a number of sources are available if you wish to further explore the connections between each of these three areas and the study and practice of leadership.

At a general level, ethical constructs lead us to consider the following questions: Are there universal moral principles that all formal and informal leaders are expected to follow? What are "right" and "wrong" practices of leadership, and who gets to make this determination? Finally, what are the ethical competencies required for leaders when addressing contentious moral issues? The complexity of these questions reflects the ongoing debates represented in the literature on ethics.

Expectations for ethical behavior are often codified in professional contexts. For example, with an emphasis on "doing no harm," the Hippocratic Oath describes the appropriate conduct and agreed-upon obligations for members of the medical community. The Society of Professional Journalists offers ethical guidelines for their members, which include: seek truth and report it; minimize harm; act independently to serve the public; and be accountable and transparent (Society of Professional Journalists, 2014). The financial and legal professions also have ethical guidelines that inform their members of the expected norms and rules of behavior. Even in one's role as a college student, academic behaviors are subject to ethical guidelines as set forth in an institution's academic integrity policy (Nagel, 2006). Ultimately, leadership in groups, organizations, and society requires an understanding of the broadly agreed-upon standards or norms of behavior. These ethical norms serve to guide our actions and interactions, and "regulate and regularize" behaviors providing rewards, such as recognition or social support, and punishments, such as ostracism or legal penalites (Hackman, 1992, p. 235). From this perspective, leaders must not only consider what they identify as "right" and "wrong" behavior, but as a co-constructed phenomenon, leadership involves an understanding and acknowledgement of what others perceive as acceptable behavior, as well.

Values. Values inform ethics in that they highlight what is important for leaders and followers, and thus, influence actions. Values are enduring and significant beliefs concerning what is good and bad or desirable and undesirable (Cambridge Dictionary Online, 2017). Values can be held by individuals and also may be embraced by groups, societies, organizations, and institutions as well. For example, Johnson & Johnson, the global healthcare company, communicates their core values in their Credo, and individuals are held accountable to these core values. In times of crisis, such as the 1982 tampering of the Tylenol capsules, these core values provide principled guidance for organizational decision-making. By relying on their fundamental principles in responding to the crisis, Johnson & Johnson made organizational decisions that were reflective of their Credo, and weathered the crisis in a way that could model behavior for future organizations.

On an individual level, personal values shape decisions in that they influence "the choices we make, the people we trust, the appeals we respond to, and the way we invest our time and energy" (Posner & Schmidt, 1992, p. 81). When faced with ethical dilemmas, values might be seen as the compass that leaders may use to best navigate through a situation in a way that can help align actions with principles (Schmidt & Posner, 1982).

The interpretation of values can differ from person to person or across social groups as well (Thomassen, 2009). For example, values such as freedom, patriotism, and democracy can be interpreted differently depending on one's allegiance to a particular political party. The language of leadership is often value-laden in that specific principles are embedded in terminology and these ideas are sometimes contested. Consider the word "loyalty," which implies consistent support or allegiance to a person or institution. On the surface, it appears to have a positive connotation. However, if "loyal" followers are required to lie to protect a leader, then loyalty does not reflect ethical behavior.

Values-based leadership focuses on aligning personal values with organizational values to encourage follower identification with and commitment to organizational objectives. Recall from Chapter 5, values are a defining feature of organizational culture in that they can influence how individuals interact with and work together. Leaders who communicate values through behaviors and explicit messages highlight what matters most for a group, a community, or an organization, and encourage similar behaviors in others (Schein, 2010). Consistency between values and actions is a critical component for both formal and informal leadership, for a leader's behavior is an expression of his or her personal set of values and beliefs (DePree, 1993). Group and organizational members are sensitive to what a leader says as well as does. For example, a leader who espouses values such as honesty and transparency, but is found to have lied or concealed facts to protect oneself, has diminished social influence and also a weakened ability to lead.

Former chairman and CEO of Baxter International, Harry Kraemer (2011), contends that values-based leadership is the only true form of leadership. He suggests that leading with values requires self-reflection, balance, self-confidence, and humility. Self-reflection involves developing an awareness of one's core values and principles. Balance requires having an open mind and the consideration of multiple viewpoints. Self-confidence refers to an understanding of your strengths and weaknesses as well as a commitment to personal and professional development and the inclusion of others who complement your abilities. Finally, remaining humble in regards to one's accomplishments and achievements is significant. These value-based practices are consistent with what Ruben (2012) calls personal leadership competencies, which are essential aspects of one's leadership knowledge and skills, as discussed in Chapter 2.

Integrity. Integrity refers to "consistency between words and actions" and is a necessary condition for earning respect and trust as a leader (Palanski & Yammarino, 2009, p. 405). We commonly understand integrity to be an aspect of an individual's character that is informed by personally held virtues. However, we can also view integrity as being two-dimensional in that it involves self and others (Nielsen, Marrone, & Slay, 2010). Values such as honesty, loyalty, humility, and civility are all dimensions of integrity, which Calhoun (1995) defines as a "master virtue" (p. 260). When judging an individual or organization based on issues of integrity, we are evaluating the virtuousness of the action as well as the strength of conviction. Integrity is a fundamental aspect of leadership and some would say that it takes precedence over all other matters concerning leadership (DePree, 1993). Integrity forms the basis for a number of more contemporary leadership theories highlighted in Chapter 2, including transformational, ethical, spiritual, and authentic leadership (Palanski & Yammarino, 2009). Leaders who are viewed as demonstrating integrity are more likely to engender trust among followers, which in turn, leads to increased follower satisfaction with the leader. Additionally, leader integrity is related to positive individual and group norms and the development of an ethical climate (Palanski & Yammarino, 2009). Leaders who are perceived as being fair and who treat followers with respect help to create a climate where followers are more willing to actively contribute to the success of the group or organization (Brown & Mitchell, 2010). These behaviors, in turn, lead to a virtuous cycle in which the supportive and helpful actions of a group member encourage others to act similarly, strengthening the ethical culture, as will be discussed in more detail later.

THE PRACTICE OF ETHICAL LEADERSHIP

Over a 30-year period, Kouzes and Posner (2011) asked more than 75,000 individuals from around the world about the qualities they associate with admired leaders, and honesty was one of the most frequently given responses. Similarly, Treviño, Brown, and Hartman (2003) found that ethical leaders were viewed as being honest, trustworthy, principled decision makers, and demonstrating concern for individuals and society in general. Ethical leaders, therefore, are "altruistically motivated, demonstrating a genuine caring and concern for people" and are considered "to be individuals of integrity who make ethical decisions and who become models for others" (Brown & Treviño, 2006, p. 600). Recognizing the role of followers in the co-construction of leadership, the social learning perspective of ethical leadership contends that the behavior of followers is influenced through observations of leadership behaviors (Brown, Treviño, & Harrison, 2005). However, for distant followers, such as those in virtual environments or in larger organizations who may not engage frequently or directly with the senior leader, it is easy to view the leader as "ethically neutral" when his or her behaviors are often invisible (Treviño, Hartman, & Brown, 2000). The leader, as both a "moral person" and "moral manager" (Treviño et al., 2000), is able to influence ethical behaviors in others by modeling the following attributes:

- Acting with integrity, honesty, and trustworthiness
- Consistently doing "the right thing"
- Showing concern for others
- Being approachable
- Engaging in empathic listening
- Maintaining personal morality

By engaging in these practices on a consistent basis, the "moral manager" or what we might consider the "ethical leader," may also model ethical practices for others. This requires leaders to communicate about the importance of ethics and values, reward ethical behaviors, and discipline unethical behaviors. As is apparent from the characteristics and behaviors highlighted above, communication is critical to ethical leadership (Brown et al., 2005).

So, beyond desiring to do the "right thing," why might a leader want to behave in an ethical fashion? Particularly given the many temptations and opportunities to compromise one's standards and to engage in unethical practices, it is important to consider the many positive outcomes that might result from ethical leadership, including the following:

- Perceived leader effectiveness (Avolio, 1999; Brown & Treviño, 2006; Posner & Schmidt, 1984, 1992; Treviño et al., 2003)
- Increased effort made by followers that go beyond minimal job expectations (Brown et al., 2005)
- Followers' willingness to report problems to superiors (Brown et al., 2005)
- Increased perception as a credible and legitimate role model (Brown et al., 2005)
- Stronger connection and commitment to the organization by workers, especially in the case of temporary workers (Philipp & Lopez, 2013)
- Development of ethical climates and cultures (Brown & Treviño, 2006; Carucci, 2016)

Leadership can be messy and the opportunities to engage in unethical behavior are plentiful, but for all of the reasons offered above and many more, we highly advocate that aspiring and seasoned leaders devote serious attention to the notions of ethics, values, and integrity and the critical role they play in leadership development and leadership practice. When the time comes for you to make a high-stakes decision with ethical consequences, do not underestimate the value of ethical leadership. As described in the next section, by modeling ethical behaviors, the leader can dramatically influence the climate and culture of the teams, groups, organizations, or communities that he or she leads.

CULTIVATING AN ETHICAL CLIMATE AND CULTURE

© GaudiLab/Shutterstock.com

As one would infer from previous discussions of climate and culture, the concepts of ethical climate and ethical culture are closely related. An *ethical climate* refers to the prevailing norms of behavior in a group involving "practices and procedures with ethical consequences" (Victor & Cullen, 1988, p. 103). For example, hiding information from colleagues when making a strategic budgetary decision is a practice with potentially ethical consequences, whether it is done to protect the individuals from learning potentially damaging or disruptive details regarding a given topic, or to limit controversy or disagreement associated with the decision. An *ethical culture*, on the other hand, maintains the highest possible standards when it comes to both visible and invisible manifestations of formal and informal control mechanisms, specific policies, procedures, and decision making processes. Within an ethical culture, there is a commitment to decision-making that is participatory, inclusive, and sensitive to ethical matters, and to the existence of reward systems that reinforce or discourage actions taken by members that uphold or undermine ethical principles and practices, such as discouraging the use of divisive or discriminatory language (Brown & Treviño, 2006; Treviño, Butterfield, & McCabe, 1998). There is a relationship between ethical leadership and beneficial outcomes, including a greater commitment to the group or organization (Cullen, Parboteeah, & Bart, 2003), behavior and decision making that reflects ethical principles (Flannery & May, 2000), greater job satisfaction, higher degrees of work efficiency, increased attention to social responsibility, and improved organizational learning (Mayer, Kuenzi, & Greenbaum, 2009). In other words, an ethical climate and culture provide a sensemaking environment through which group members interpret expectations. When faced with a difficult decision, group and organizational members consciously and unconsciously reflect on behaviors and practices that are expected, encouraged, and rewarded to guide their decisions. If the ethical culture is one in which leaders look the other way when questionable activities occur, then followers will also be more willing to engage in unethical behaviors.

Ethical climates and cultures can be fragile, and leaders and followers alike experience pressures, contradictions, and dilemmas that can contribute to the emergence of an unethical climate. For example, the feeling that it is unsafe to speak out about questionable activities, intense pressures to achieve unrealistic goals, unequal treatment of followers, failure to highlight both positive and negative ethical behaviors, and the absence of ethical role models can promote and encourage unethical behavior (Carucci, 2016).

There are a number of practical steps that leaders and followers can take to create and maintain high ethical standards, as outlined by Thorton (2013). These strategies include the following:

1. Both leaders and followers should understand that creating an ethical culture is a continuous process that requires commitment, learning, and reflection.
2. Leaders need to remind followers that maintaining ethical standards can be challenging, and it is often helpful to openly discuss ethical dilemmas among colleagues to reinforce appropriate behaviors.
3. Leaders should aim to link expectations for ethical behavior to all activities, not just the most visible actions or to major decisions.
4. Leaders should communicate about both small and large ethical actions, and celebrate the accomplishments of individuals who maintain high standards relative to ethics.

As you consider the influence of leadership actions within the culture and climate of an organization, it is worth recalling the widely told story of how an IBM employee refused to let Thomas Watson, the Chairman and CEO, into a restricted area because he did not have appropriate identification with him. Watson's response was to commend the guard for his actions and return to his office to retrieve his ID. Stories like this one vividly illustrate the way principles and values are ideally embraced by those in formal leadership roles; and when repeated across the organization, these behaviors help to reinforce a culture and climate that celebrates, encourages, and demands ethical decision making (Johnson, 2015; Martin, 2002).

Given the importance of communication in creating an ethical climate and culture, leaders must work to build trust and nurture a respectful environment where followers are comfortable discussing ethical issues (Thorton, 2013). One approach that might be utilized by leaders is called "ethical dialogue" (Payne & Calton, 2008). Ethical dialogue is a form of community deliberation designed to manage intractable issues or controversies for which there exists wide disagreement among participants. For example, imagine your campus community has invited a controversial guest to speak to students on campus. Some university members might feel it would be a valuable experience to have this person speak despite his or her controversial beliefs or actions, while other members might feel it would reflect poorly on the institution to have this person recognized in a formal way. This debate—along with subsequent protests from members of the college or university community—has been a frequent occurrence across the United States this year. Instead of debate and protest, ethical dialogue encourages the respectful exploration of differing and potentially conflicting perspectives among individuals. The process focuses on helping individuals develop trusting relationships in the service of addressing complex ethical dilemmas (Payne & Calton, 2008).

There is no shortage today of intractable problems that could benefit from ethical dialogue. Think for a moment about the problems that plague your own community or the community of a friend, family member, or colleague—is there a shortage of affordable housing, is there a lack of jobs that pay decent salaries, or does the cost of a college education place it out of reach for some? Ethical dialogue can provide a foundation for a process through which community members can begin to address these questions. So, how can formal and informal leaders facilitate ethical dialogue in their groups, organizations, and communities? Payne and Calton (2008) outline the following strategies:

- Emphasize a collaborative approach to inquiry
- Engage in honest and authentic conversation
- Acknowledge the potential vulnerabilities and discomfort of others
- Demonstrate mutual care and concern for others
- Minimize power differences
- Recognize that learning occurs through dialogue
- Engage in critical reflection of the process

Take a moment to consider your own teams, groups, or organizations. In what ways might you utilize the strategies offered above to shape the ethical culture and climate of your team, group, or organization? Have you encountered ethical dilemmas in the past, and if so, in what ways did your actions and decisions model behaviors for others? In what ways might these proposed strategies help to resolve intractable problems in the future? These strategies can have a dramatic impact on the culture or climate of the team, group, or organization, for they lead individual leaders to consider the ways in which they make strategic decisions, as discussed in the next section.

THE IMPACT OF ETHICS ON DECISION MAKING

© qoppi/Shutterstock.com

Whether one thinks of a formal or informal group, a club, an organization, or a community, leaders must contend with a range of ethical scenarios, including those related to the management of information, the use of power in shaping the lived experiences of others, and the ability to balance competing loyalties, interests, and obligations (Hackman & Johnson, 2013). Followers expect that leaders will make ethical decisions, strive to be fair, and display concern for matters beyond profit, even in corporate entities (Treviño et al., 2000). It is therefore important for leaders to demonstrate an understanding of one's values and principles and how these translate into specific decisions that one might make.

In order to better understand the ways in which ethics shape decision making, it is helpful to explore three theoretical explanations—virtue theories, duty theories, and consequentialist theories. *Virtue theories* focus on the ethical nature of individuals, not specific ethical principles or guidelines. This perspective stresses the importance of moral character development, asserting that an individual with a strong character will naturally engage in ethical behavior. For example, leadership training for West Point Academy cadets focuses on character development and promotes values such as personal sacrifice in service of the country (Avolio & Locke, 2002). According to the virtue perspective, a cadet who recognizes the value of serving one's country and who embodies this value in one's character will instinctively make decisions in accordance with this ethical framework. *Duty theories* focus on the principles that deal with our rights as individuals and our obligations to others. The 17th century English philosopher John Locke, argued that individuals have inherent rights granted by a creator and these include the protection of life, health, liberty, and possessions. These principles echo the similar concepts of life, liberty, and the pursuit of happiness found in The Declaration of Independence. From this perspective, an ethical decision is one that enriches, enhances, or embraces one's obligation to others. Finally, *consequentialist theories* focus on the outcome or consequences of action. If the outcome is more positive than not, then a decision is considered ethical. The following are examples of consequentialist theories:

- **Ethical Egoism**—The underlying principle of this theory is the achievement of self-interest or the greatest good for the individual. An action is therefore considered ethical if the positive consequences outweigh the negative for the individual who acts. For example, an entrepreneur who starts a business to fulfill her desire to become wealthy is guided by ethical egoism.
- **Utilitarianism**—The underlying principle of this theory is the achievement of maximum utility for the greatest number of individuals, or what is often described as "the greatest good for the greatest number of people." Therefore, an act is considered ethical if the positive consequence of an action benefits most in some way. For example, universal healthcare can be seen as reflecting utilitarianism principles in that the goal is to provide some benefits for all citizens.

■ **Altruism**—The underlying principle of this theory is to serve the best interests of others over the interest of the self. Therefore, an act is considered ethical if the outcomes are more beneficial for others, rather than for the individual who acts. For example, an individual who sacrifices part of his salary so that others can keep their job is demonstrating principles of altruism.

The challenges, tensions, and dilemmas that leaders encounter are inherently messy. For this reason, it is important to take time to better understand the principles that shape your ethical framework, along with the ethical principles emphasized by others, in order to make sense of the debate surrounding contentious matters. As depicted in Table 6.1, a group of scholars from Brown University developed the following framework as a way comparing and constrasting the three normative ethical theories—virtue, duty, and consequentialism—discussed above. Each of the theories illuminates a different approach to decision making. We would encourage you to use this framework as you lead the members of your club, group, organization, or community through any type of decision making process.

In addition to the different ethical normative theories that influence decision making processes, leaders often face dilemmas in situations where there are competing or contradictory values. The recent case of a pharmaceutical company CEO who significantly increased the price of a drug that had been on the market since the 1950's illustrates one such dilemma arising from competing ethical frameworks. The leader's decision resulted in widespread consumer outrage, as well as criticism from government officials and the medical community. Nevertheless, the CEO defended his

Table 6.1. Ethical Decision Making Framework (Brown University, 2013)

	Virtue	Duty	Consequentialism
Individual concern	What kind of person should I be (or try to be), and how will my actions reflect on my character?	What are my obligations, and what are the things I should never do?	What kind of outcomes should I achieve (or try to achieve)?
Underlying principles	What are the character traits (virtues and vices) that are, or could be, motivating those involved?	What are the duties and obligations that exist prior to the situation?	What are the outcomes of an action and all who will be directly or indirectly affected by the decision?
What is ethical conduct?	Ethical conduct is whatever action a virtuous person would take.	Ethical conduct means carrying out one's duty.	Ethical conduct is the action that will achieve the best outcome.
Objective	Aim is to develop one's character.	Aim is to perform the right action.	Aim is to produce the most good.

decision, claiming that the price increase was needed to enable the company to fund research to develop new and more effective treatments. Although the CEO's actions were legal, some asserted that it was nonetheless unethical and unfair to consumers who relied on the drug. In this case, we see the tension between decisions based on a concern for duty—focusing on obligations to the company, versus utilitarianism—providing a benefit to the greatest possible number of individuals at an affordable price. Balancing the interests, expectations, and needs of the many individuals with a stake in your club, group, or organization, is perhaps the ideal strategy for leaders, but we also recognize that there will be situations where this option may not exist, resulting in difficult ethical choices for leaders.

THE ETHICAL USE OF POWER

© Jirsak/Shutterstock.com

As you might expect, the concept of power is very much embedded in issues surrounding ethical leadership. Building upon our discussion of power and authority from Chapter 4, French and Raven (1959) describe social power as the potential to influence or bring about a change using available resources. They identify five bases of social power that exist in leader-follower relationships—legitimate, coercive, reward, expert, and referent power. Informational power was subsequently added (Raven, 2004). Although the framework was developed with formal leadership in mind, these sources of power are relevant in informal leadership contexts as well. Whereas formal leadership can draw from all bases of power, informal leaders often lack legitimate power and authority and thus must rely more on other sources to influence followers. With formal leadership comes authority, defined as "the exercise of legitimate influence by one social actor over another" (Johnson-Cramer, 2008, first para).

Let us take a moment to summarize these five sources of power, for they are helpful constructs for considering our own use of power and they can also inform how we understand the nature of power in ethical decision making. *Legitimate power* is that which comes from having a formal title or position and by extension, the authority to demand compliance. Having legitimate power also supports coercive power (i.e., the threat of punishment to gain follower compliance) in that a formal leader has the authority to punish non-compliant behavior. For example, a formal leader has the authority to threaten an employee with job termination, whereas an informal leader with less coercive power could choose to ignore the suggestions of a group member. *Reward power* is relevant for both formal and informal leadership. It is the exchange of a benefit or compensation for complying with the requests or wishes of a leader. In a formal leadership context, an example would be a leader who provides a follower with a monetary reward for meeting a job performance goal, whereas an informal leader might reward a committee member with special recognition or a token of appreciation in exchange for help with a difficult task. *Expert power* is the use of specialized or superior knowledge or skill to gain compliance. Followers are typically more willing to comply with a request from either a formal or informal leader who has a high degree of expertise in an area closely related to the matter at hand. *Referent power* is at play when followers feel an affinity with a leader and identifies with her or him. A follower who admires the personal qualities of a formal or informal leader would likely comply with his or her requests as a sign of respect and admiration. Finally, *informational power* is derived from having access to or possessing information that others want. Withholding information to maintain control over followers is generally regarded as an unethical use of informational power. Not only is the knowledge of these different types of power useful for understanding one's own influence and the influence of others, but an understanding of these concepts can also help one to consider how best to tap into the other available bases of power in formal and informal leadership situations.

As with many other leadership resources, power can be used in the service of good just as easily as evil. Lord Acton's well-known maxim, "power tends to corrupt, and absolute power corrupts absolutely," presents an unavoidable conundrum that is the result of the concentration of power in formal and informal leadership (Acton & Himmelfarb, 1948). This tension between constructive and unscrupulous uses of power to influence followers is reflected in Bass and Steidlmeier's (1999) discussion of the two faces of transformational leadership. Recall from Chapter 2 how transformational leadership focuses on the ability of leaders to create positive change in the lives of those they lead in pursuit of the collective good (Northouse, 2015). Bass and Steidlmeier distinguish authentic transformational leadership as the use of power in the service of good, from pseudo-transformational leadership, which is characterized as the unethical use of power for self-interest. An example of pseudo-transformational leadership would be the decision by a leader that supports a short-term gain for a group or an organization, making him or her popular for the moment, but leading to an outcome that has long-term negative consequences that will not be realized until the leader is gone. Some political actors are pseudo-transformational leaders in that they take actions that will help them get reelected in the short term, yet the negative consequences of that action may not be realized for many years to come. For a more extensive discussion of transformational leadership, see Chapter 2.

Although leadership is co-constructed between leaders and followers and is not possible without willing followers, we recognize that the power that leaders hold in many situations, particularly in formal positions of authority, can influence follower actions. With this power comes great responsibility, and in many instances, power may be shared or distributed across teams, groups, organizations, or communities. Referring back to one of the themes from the introduction of this chapter, the contemporary "crisis of leadership" often reflects an obsession with and/or abuse of power. For this reason, an understanding of ethics, values, and integrity is essential in keeping power "in check" as one pursues leadership for positive social influence.

CONCLUSION

As suggested throughout this chapter, the practice of formal and informal leadership requires a sturdy and deliberate foundation that is built upon one's core values and ethical principles. We believe that both leaders and followers are more influential when they act with integrity, maintain consistency between words and actions, demonstrate consideration of and respect for others, and deliberately work to create ethical climates and cultures. Finally, leaders have a responsibility to model ethical behaviors for others, to understand and use power wisely, and to guide followers through challenging decisions and circumstances. Having a fundamental understanding of the ethical framework you and others operate from, as well as a clear notion of the personal values that guide your behavior, will help you to further develop the necessary personal competencies to lead with integrity.

CHAPTER 7

THE FOUNDATIONS OF PERSONAL AND PROFESSIONAL LEADERSHIP: PHILOSOPHY, PASSION, AND GOALS

> ⚠️ **Guiding Questions:**
>
> 1) What is your leadership philosophy, and why is it important to consider goals, values, and purpose as one pursues formal and informal opportunities for social influence?
> 2) How does the process of developing an individual leadership plan compare to the process of strategic planning at the organizational level?
> 3) What role do learning and resilience play in developing and sustaining a personal and professional leadership plan?

As discussed thus far, our approach to the topic of leadership in this book emphasizes the importance of communication and social influence, ethics, and personal and professional development and goals. This chapter focuses primarily on this last element—the importance of establishing a personally relevant approach to leadership. This issue is an important one because ultimately, the pursuit of leadership excellence is an individual matter, one that must begin with a personally defined and personally relevant sense of purpose and a passion for making a difference in the lives of others.

However, as suggested throughout this chapter, pursuing your passion and goals is not a straightforward matter—there is always potential for misalignment between an approach to leadership that you find to be personally relevant and what might be considered effective leadership for one's group, team, or organization. Furthermore, leadership effectiveness also involves an understanding and consideration of the expectations of other leaders and colleagues in organizations of which you are a member—and those to whom you may report in formal organizations.

A LEADERSHIP PLAN FOR NAVIGATING COMPLEX TERRAIN

© Sergey Nivens/Shutterstock.com

The challenges facing leaders in all contexts and at all levels are substantial. This is certainly true for today's college students, as it is for formal and informal leaders of professional and community groups, and healthcare, educational, governmental, or business enterprises. Leaders in the workplace, community, and society must negotiate a diverse array of personal and professional responsibilities and commitments. This balancing act can become quite a challenge when the various responsibilities begin to conflict with one another in terms of the desired goals, competing values, or the impact on one's schedule. Students interested in leadership face the additional challenge of pursuing opportunities for social influence while simultaneously investing time and effort in their academic growth and development.

As we consider one's journey as a leader, the terrain is often rough, the conditions are often unpredictable, and the final destination is often uncertain. Despite variables that are beyond the leader's control, the decision to pursue leadership opportunities must be made with intention and purpose. In navigating an often messy and complicated landscape, it is very helpful if leaders have developed a personal and professional guide for navigating the complex terrain. This guide, similar to an organization's mission statement as described below, outlines who you are and who you intend to be as a leader. Additionally, when you encounter roadblocks or crises along the way, the guide can provide direction and may clarify preferred paths and those that you should avoid. This chapter provides a series of concepts and questions that are important to consider in formulating your personal guide to leadership.

CLARIFYING YOUR LEADERSHIP PHILOSOPHY AND PURPOSE

The development of one's leadership philosophy—which is the foundation for your guide—begins with identifying and gaining clarity on one's aspirations.

By thinking about the type of leader you want to be, you engage in a process that allows you to move forward with intentionality and purpose. Clarifying your leadership philosophy and purpose requires you to consider both your mission as a leader—your primary purpose, and your vision as a leader—the leader you aspire to be. As described by Warren Bennis (2003),

> The leader has a clear idea of what he or she wants to do—personally and professionally—and the strength to persist in the face of setbacks, even failures. Unless you know where you're going, and why, you cannot possibly get there. (pp. 31–32)

Identifying role models and reading the leadership literature, including biographies of and professional and practical advice from respected leaders, are helpful actions during this process. Writing for Forbes.com, Hendricks (2014) highlights the personal mission statements of 13 influential CEOs, including Oprah Winfrey, Denise Morrison from Campbell Soup Company, and Richard Branson from The Virgin Group—each of whom identified a mission by which they would live their lives in the pursuit of excellence.

Your guiding philosophy will serve as a reminder of what matters most to you as an individual, and can also serve as an important guide when making difficult decisions. As you consider your personal philosophy for leadership, we encourage you to consider the following four questions:

1. What is your *leadership mission*—your primary purpose as a leader, and *vision of leadership*—the leader you aspire to be?
2. What *leadership identity* would you like to establish among your peers, colleagues, and family and friends—the way you would like to be viewed by others?
3. How would you like to be uniquely known as a leader—your *leadership brand*?
4. What would you like your lasting contribution to be—the *leadership legacy* you would like to leave behind?

Taken together, these four aspects comprise your leadership philosophy (Ruben et al., 2017). This process of developing a leadership philosophy is akin to what Stephen Covey (2013) describes as "beginning with the end in mind"—a rich opportunity to imagine the possibilities of who you are and who you intend to be. As a formal or informal leader, this process of clarifying your leadership philosophy challenges you to think about your own aspirations and the principles that shape your approach to leadership, while simultaneously considering the expectations, perceptions, and attitudes of the many stakeholders with whom you might engage. In his book and corresponding TED Talk, *Start With Why*, Simon Sinek (2009) acknowledges that "People don't buy what you do, they buy why you do it." Self-awareness and self-discovery are intricately connected to this important step. More will be said about this process of clarifying your leadership philosophy and translating it into a personal leadership strategy in the following chapter.

WHAT VALUES AND GUIDING PRINCIPLES MOTIVATE YOU TO LEAD?

© marekuliasz/Shutterstock.com

Returning to the theme of ethics in the previous chapter, we indicated that having a clear understanding of your personal values can help you to align your principles with actions. Ethical leadership is defined as "knowing your core values and having the courage to act on them on behalf of the common good" (The Center for Ethical Leadership, para 1). To highlight the role of values in leadership, The Center for Ethical Leadership has developed a core values exercise, which we have adapted here for your consideration. The exercise is also useful for groups that want to establish common ground around shared values to build a foundation for productive working relationships or to better manage conflicts. The words offered in this exercise are somewhat arbitrary, so you will likely want to add some of your own values to the list below.[1]

- Step 1: Review the list of words below. Add other values that are not listed, but are important to you.
- Step 2: Review the entire list of values and those that are important to you.
- Step 3: Narrow your list to the eight most important values.
- Step 4: Narrow your list to the five most important values.
- Step 5: Finally, narrow your list to the three most important values—these may be considered your core values.

1 The complete exercise can be accessed at: http://www.ethicalleadership.org/uploads/2/6/2/6/26265761/1.4_core_values_exercise.pdf

❏ Authenticity	❏ Kindness
❏ Achievement	❏ Knowledge
❏ Balance	❏ Love
❏ Community	❏ Peace
❏ Curiosity	❏ Power
❏ Family	❏ Recognition
❏ Friendship	❏ Responsibility
❏ Happiness	❏ Status
❏ Influence	❏ Success
❏ Joy	❏ Wealth
❏ Justice	❏ Wisdom

Once you have identified your core values, you can take this a step further to develop a personal leadership credo. Credo is a Latin word meaning "I believe" (Merriam-Webster, 2017). You will recall the discussion in the preceding chapter of Johnson & Johnson's Credo that displays and communicates the core values of the company. A personal credo is a statement of beliefs or core values that guide individual behavior. Kouzes (n.d.) suggests that developing yourself as a credible leader requires you to articulate "who you are, what you believe in, and what you stand for"—essentially your leadership credo. Practitioners and scholars offer various approaches for developing your personal credo. For example, "This I Believe," an international organization based on a 1950s radio program of the same name, has collected more than 125,000 essays focused on the core values that guide individuals daily.[2]

WHAT IS YOUR PASSION?

As you may have noticed in considering the four questions in the previous section, it is very difficult to define your leadership philosophy without first understanding what it is that energizes you both personally and professionally. What motivates you to do what you do as a student, professional, family member, or citizen? What aspects of leadership most excite you? What contributes to your desire to leave a legacy at your college or in the community? Answers to these can help you to identify your sources of passion. Although you may have not yet clarified all dimensions of your passion as you assume leadership roles early in your career, your leadership philosophy is inextricably connected to your personal interests and values. For example, when you wake up in the morning, what parts of your day do you most look forward to? If you are a student, are you most enthusiastic about a specific class in your primary field of study, an experience you are having with an internship, the conversations you tend to have with friends over lunch or dinner, the opportunities to work with technology, engage in a sport, pursue a unique talent, or savor the moments of quiet reflection on your walk between classes, or attend the evening meetings for a club or an

2 You can find instructions for writing a personal credo at: http://thisibelieve.org/guidelines/

© Art Stocker/Shutterstock.com

organization? For full-time working professionals, are you most excited for the time to reflect during your commute to work, the meetings and tasks planned throughout the day, the casual encounters by the water cooler or in the dining hall, or the opportunity to chart a vision for the future of your unit, department, or organization? The type of leader you want to be is ultimately shaped by the parts of your life that most interest and motivate you, and it is our hope that you will pursue leadership roles and careers that directly align with your most fundamental passions.

As you consider these areas of passion, it is worth introducing an important concept in the human motivation literature. Frederick Herzberg (1959), a seminal writer on motivation theory, distinguished hygiene factors from motivating factors. Hygiene factors are external elements of work, that if not present in a personal or professional setting, would cause an individual to be dissatisfied, such as compensation and work conditions. Motivators, on the other hand, include challenging and meaningful work, recognition, and responsibility—which Herzberg identifies as the source of genuine personal and professional satisfaction. Understanding the difference between these two factors is critical, and as Christensen, Allworth, and Dillon (2012) posit, "it is frightfully easy for us to lose our sense of the difference between what brings us money and what causes happiness" (p. 40). These ideas are complemented by Pink (2011) who writes about the deeply motivating and gratifying ability to choose one's activity (autonomy), do things well (mastery), and engage in something that makes a difference (purpose) in the workplace. Although their primary focus is centered on workplace employment, we can extend this way of thinking to any leadership endeavor that you may pursue. Think about what motivates and satisfies you most as you pursue leadership opportunities in your college or university, in the community, and in the workplace, and make every effort to direct your energies in those directions.

Passion for certain projects, for a specific group, team, organization, or company, and for the people involved, is key to successful leadership. Many of the most effective leaders in political and popular culture have shown their ability to share their enthusiasm with those around them. As Morgan (2015) suggests, "people want to follow a passionate leader. Someone who cares about not only the cause for which he or she is working, but also the other people who are involved in the effort" (para 6). Consider the following examples of individuals who have exercised a great deal of social influence by pursuing tasks in alignment with their core passion: Martin Luther King Jr.'s passion for justice, Ellen DeGeneres' passion for comedy, Walt Disney's passion for imagination, Mario Lemieux's passion for hockey, Steve Jobs' passion for innovation, J. K. Rowling's passion for storytelling, and Mother Teresa's passion for public service. By pursuing careers and projects that captured their passion, these individuals had—and for some, continue to have—an exceptional level of influence on their fields and the many individuals involved. Leadership is difficult work, and to do it well requires a clear sense of purpose and a genuine interest in the work at hand.

Recognizing the importance of one's passion, take some time to consider the following questions.

1. What are your core values as an individual—the set of principles or perspectives that guide and influence your behavior?
2. What and/or who motivates you to do what you do as a student, student leader, or working professional?
3. To what do you aspire as an individual?
4. What accomplishments would be particularly meaningful to you?

LEADERSHIP GOALS

© Rawpixel.com/Shutterstock.com

In much the same way as one might identify resolutions prior to the New Year, the process of proactively identifying goals as a leader is critical to one's leadership effectiveness. While we may not often articulate our goals on a daily basis, the goals that we set for ourselves operate in the background of our consciousness and generally guide our choices and behaviors. Your leadership philosophy identifies the guiding principles for *why* you lead; the goals you set for yourself help to operationalize *how* you might fulfill this broader philosophy or purpose. These goals represent tangible expressions of our means for pursuing our aspirations and/or addressing significant gaps that can hinder that progress. Further, our goals provide us with a reference point against which to measure the outcomes resulting from those choices and behaviors.

It is tempting to begin first with the process of setting goals; however, without a clear sense of purpose, goal-setting could easily proceed in less than useful directions. Goals should be broad and far-reaching in scope, and they should describe what one must do to achieve the high-level aspirations articulated in one's leadership philosophy. In establishing both short-term and long-term leadership goals, it is important to resist pressures to create a catalogue of tasks that might be undertaken. While the formulation of an expansive list of suggested projects may seem like a good idea, it is important to first clearly formulate and articulate goals that represent your aspirations and the critical needs of the team, group, or organization that you are leading. Also, generating a list of potential projects without first carefully formulating goals, typically results in the creation of an unfocused, undifferentiated, and unwieldy list of activities, which may not address key priority areas for your personal advancement or for the advancement of the team, group, or organization.

A PERSONAL STRATEGIC PLAN

The process of developing a personal or professional guide for leadership resembles the way a group or organization would design their strategic plan. Each type of planning is important to organizational excellence, and in both cases, the process of planning is arguably more important than the plan itself. Similar to strategic planning at an organizational level, it is not so important to articulate a comprehensive leadership philosophy or to craft the perfect goals for living this philosophy and fulfilling one's purpose. Rather, the focus should be on developing a workable, but, perhaps, less-than-perfect leadership guide, to translate your aspirations into goals that drive those activities. As Tromp and Ruben (2010) describe the process of strategic planning,

> Too often planning begins with a flurry of activities (the "how") and works backward to the goals (the "what") those activities would support. When that occurs, the result is often a drafting of a list of projects that focus on symptoms rather than root causes, and the expenditure of energy, resources, and commitment on smaller issues and problems, rather than on broader benefits to the organization and its beneficiaries. The key here is to be certain that the goals effectively capture your vision and aspirations. Only then can the details of how to accomplish them be addressed. (p. 66)

This might sound familiar to your own experiences inside and outside of the classroom or work setting. We spend so much time focusing on the tasks and responsibilities at hand, and there is a tendency to lose sight of our deeper purpose.

In his op-ed in *The New York Times* entitled "The 'Busy' Trap," Kreider (2012) writes about our obsession with keeping busy—and telling others how busy we are. As he goes on to suggest, "The space and quiet that idleness provides is a necessary condition for standing back from life and seeing it whole, for making unexpected connections and waiting for the wild summer lightning strikes of inspiration—it is, paradoxically, necessary to getting any work done" (para 10). Taking the time to consider your leadership philosophy, your values, principles, and sources of passion, and the necessary goals for fulfilling your purpose as a leader are critical, yet often missing, in leadership practice. By making self-reflection a habit, you can better align your priorities and decisions with your leadership purpose, and you will be better able to adjust behaviors over time to deal with the unpredictable, yet inevitable, roadblocks and challenges that you will encounter in the future. As you will notice, future chapters in the book will build upon this theme of intentionality, for it is critical to effectively leading change initiatives, leading teams in conflict, and leading in a formal and informal manner.

Tromp and Ruben (2010) developed a set of guidelines for goal setting at the organizational level and these are slightly adapted below as an aid in individual goal setting. These guidelines can help you to articulate goals that will help move you closer to achieving the philosophy or purpose identified earlier. It is important to express these goals in terms that allow for tracking progress and measuring outcomes, particularly goals that are clear, achievable, and focused as much on the process as the outcome (Tromp & Ruben, 2010).

Guidelines for Goal Setting

Alignment with mission and vision. Goals should define the top four or five high-level aspirations or achievements that will lead you closer to achieving your vision and/or addressing significant gaps. These goals should be both specific and measurable. Be sure that your goals take account of your stated leadership mission and vision, and the mission, vision, and goals of leaders and other groups and organizations with which you will be interacting.

Importance to stakeholders. When identifying goals at the organizational level, it is important to consider the impact that these goals might have on the stakeholders with an interest in the organization. In much the same way as organizational goals should ultimately benefit stakeholders, individual goals should ultimately benefit you and the individuals that you intend to lead now and into the future.

Collaboration. Who should set goals? Since this is your personal leadership guide, it is most important that you identify, understand, and buy into your own leadership goals. However, given that leadership is a process that is co-constructed between the leader and others with whom you interact, we would encourage you to seek feedback and reaction from individuals that you collaborate and work with as you are developing your goals. You might also consider sharing these goals with trusted family members or friends who know you, your strengths, and your aspirations.

Prioritizing, sequencing, and timing. Each high-level goal represents a primary theme and direction for growth or change. Having too many goals—which implies too many themes—can dilute planning and improvement efforts, resulting in only a mediocre effort. Prioritize key goals and determine how many and which ones can be reached in the first year, second year, third year—all the way through the last year of the plan. While it may be possible to complete some work on all goals simultaneously, this is generally not recommended. Therefore, you may choose to identify different phases for each goal over the next five years. Some may be front-loaded and others may be ongoing, with the work spread out over the years. Or you may choose to prioritize those deemed most critical and focus on all aspects of those goals in a specific year.

Writing goals. Articulate the goals in simple, easily understandable terms. By writing the goals and placing them in a location where you are likely to see on a regular basis, you are often reminded of them and of their importance to your work as a leader.

Measurability. Express the goals in such a way that you can chart your progress and easily determine whether you have met them. You should be able to answer these questions: "Are these the right indicators for success?" and "How do I know I have achieved the desired outcome?"

Resources. What resources will you need in order to accomplish these stated goals (e.g., financial, relational, intellectual)? Understand the current availability of these resources, and be prepared to adjust your goals should you encounter a dramatic change in resources?

Approach. Establish achievable goals—but ones that require a "stretch" in creativity, innovation, and energy to achieve. Since these goals will shape your direction as a leader, it is important to set goals that align with your passion and values. In other words, be sure you are pursuing goals that are worth achieving.

As you consider your personal and professional leadership goals that will help you to operationalize ways of fulfilling your core mission or purpose as a leader, bear in mind the following considerations related to setting goals:

- Given your leadership philosophy, what major areas should be the focus of your individual leadership guide?
- What, specifically, do you want to accomplish this year, and in the next three to five years?
- What are your most pressing issues, and why are they particularly critical? What is the urgency or potential impact associated with these issues?
- How can those pressing priorities or gaps be expressed as goals?
- Do the goals you have articulated align with your purpose, values, and passion? Do these goals align with your current and future priorities?
- What goals, if any, are you currently pursuing, and are those goals of your selection, or were they recommended or mandated by the institution or organization of which you are a part? How can present goals be integrated or aligned with newly established goals?
- Is it within your control and capability to effectively address the selected goals?
- What constraints and/or approval channels exist for establishing goals within your current organization?
- Do the goals fall into a logical sequence? That is, is the reaching of some of them a prerequisite to pursuing others?
- What key factors affect your ability or inability to achieve your goals?

Table 7.1 provides a worksheet that you might complete in order to identify SMART (Specific, Measurable, Attainable, Relevant, and Time-bound) goals that will help you to fulfill your aspirational purpose or mission as a leader.

Table 7.1. SMART Goal Worksheet

Specific: Is the goal focused and written in easily understandable terms?	
Measurable: How will you know when you have achieved the goal? Are these the right indicators for success?	
Attainable: What actions do you need to take to realize this goal? What obstacles will you face in working toward this goal? What resources will you need in order to accomplish this goal (e.g., financial, relational, intellectual)?	
Relevant: Does this goal align with your purpose, values, and passion? Does this goal align with your current and future priorities?	
Time-bound: In what time frame will you realize this goal? Is this a short-term (one year), mid-term (three years), or long-term goal (five years)?	

THE USE OF DASHBOARDS TO MONITOR PROGRESS

Measurement systems—variously termed performance metrics, key performance indicators (KPIs), scorecards, and dashboards—have become increasingly popular in organizations of all kinds. As summarized in Ruben et al. (2017), it was estimated in 2005 that a majority of business organizations had developed, or were developing, a performance measurement system (Eckerson, 2005). Figure 7.1 provides an example of the ways in which assessment data can be displayed using graphics of various kinds. Figure 7.2 illustrates a hypothetical dashboard of the sort that might be used to display financial performance results. The "dashboard" concept draws its name from the analogy to the dashboard of an automobile, which aggregates and displays a few critical measures that the driver can monitor without diverting attention from the fundamental task of driving—or leading, in the case of an organization or a community.

Displaying Assessment Results

Figure 7.1: Assessment Results Graphics

A Sample "Financial Performance" Dashboard

Figure 7.2: Financial Performance Dashboard

As you consider the various elements of your personal and professional leadership plan offered in this chapter, you might also consider ways of presenting these items in a dashboard template so that you can easily highlight key metrics, monitor progress, and display results. In a group, team, or organizational setting, these dashboards are also important for documenting outcomes, setting future targets, and "telling one's story" of accomplishments, progress, and future aspirations to internal and external groups. For example, if you make your progress as a leader of a volunteer group an area for focus, components you would want to track might include: number of meetings held, attendance rates, identification of key projects to be completed, progress on each project, and level of group member engagement. For each of these dashboard components, you would also identify "red," "yellow," and "green" indicators. Red indicators would require immediate attention, yellow indicators may encourage you to pay more attention to this area, and green indicators would call for celebration and continued success.

In much the same way as you would attend to key indicators on the dashboard of a vehicle, so too might your personal and professional dashboard help you monitor progress as it relates to your personal and professional leadership plan. Remember that the path to leadership begins with you, and that the philosophy, goals, values, and motivations that guide your approach to leadership require care and attention. The dashboard imagery is one of many options available to help you sustain your focus on these areas over time.

LEARNING AND RESILIENCE

© piya kunkayan/Shutterstock.com

As noted at the outset of this chapter, one's journey as a leader is often characterized by a rough terrain, unpredictable conditions, and uncertain final destination. Given the many distractions, roadblocks, and obstacles that may emerge on one's journey, it is worth concluding this chapter by emphasizing the importance of learning and resilience as a leader. A commitment to both learning and resilience can help leaders to not only better understand the impediments that may be present, but can also help prepare one in overcoming these obstacles.

In their writing on this topic, Brown and Posner (2001) situate the importance of learning in an environment marked by significant change and disruption: "Today's turbulent economic marketplace requires people who thrive on the challenge of change, who can foster environments of innovation, who encourage trust and collaboration, and who are prepared to chart a course into unchartered territories" (p. 1). A commitment to learning lies at the intersection of these various leadership imperatives. By engaging in transformational learning opportunities (Taylor, 2000) and creating the conditions for others to pursue opportunities for leadership development and learning, leaders and the individuals that they lead will be more nimble, agile, adaptable, and ultimately, effective. We applaud you for taking the time to read a book on leadership, and as you consider additional opportunities for enhancing and enriching your leadership journey, we hope this hunger for learning more about leadership will never tire.

Finally, as you prepare for the inevitable obstacles that lie ahead as you pursue various leadership opportunities—personal and professional setbacks, expected and unexpected challenges, internal and external threats, and the exhausting juggling act that leaders must often perform—we would encourage you to identify opportunities for building resilience.[3] A subject of increased scholarly and professional attention, resilience can be defined as a "personal quality that predisposes individuals to bounce back in the face of loss" (Allison, 2011/2012, p. 79). Biro (2014), writing for *Forbes Magazine*, posits the following four strategies for becoming a more resilient leader:

1. Realize it's not all about you.
2. Control what you can, and don't beat yourself up for what is beyond your control.
3. Build and maintain enduring relationships.
4. Think positively.

In addition to these strategies, it is also important for resilient leaders to carefully consider how their communication with others can contribute to a positive, inspiring, and future-oriented vision of what the future might have in store (Boyatzis & McKee, 2005). As Biro (2014) notes,

> We all have the choice to be trapped in the present bad thing, or to learn from it and rebound. Sometimes it seems too difficult to choose; there's something compelling about being a victim of circumstances. But passivity is a trap. Resilient people, and organizations, take action, own what's theirs, and learn from the rest. Choose to bounce back. Choose to learn. Be resilient. Stay true to you and the people who believe in you.

In order to pursue your proposed leadership plan(s) with intentionality, purpose, conviction, and clarity, you must also be prepared to keep moving forward with resilience and courage in the face of whatever obstacles might lie ahead.

CONCLUSION

We would like to conclude this chapter by referring to another important insight from the book by Christensen, Allworth, and Dillon (2012), *How Will You Measure Your Life?* As the authors suggest, "The type of person you want to become—*what* the purpose of your life is—is too important to leave to chance. It needs to be deliberately conceived, chosen, and managed. The opportunities and challenges in your life that allow you to become that person will, by their very nature, be emergent" (p. 197). The connections between this passage and the concepts raised in this chapter are quite compelling. Decide who you want to become as a leader—and then move forward purposefully as you embark on this noble journey of leadership in order to become that leader, all the while remembering your compass and map to guide you through the process.

3 Angela Duckworth calls resilience "grit"—"a combination of passion and perseverance for a singularly important goal" (Scelfo, 2016). Her research focuses on two traits that correlate with achievement—grit and self-control. Her research finds that on average, individuals who demonstrate grit also demonstrate more self-control (http://angeladuckworth.com/research/). You can assess your level of grit by taking the Grit Scale assessment at http://angeladuckworth.com/grit-scale/.

CHAPTER 8

BECOMING A BETTER LEADER: PERSONAL ASSESSMENT AND LEADERSHIP DEVELOPMENT

> ⚠️ **Guiding Questions:**
>
> 1) What is leadership development?
> 2) What steps can help to guide one's development and growth as a leader?
> 3) In what ways can an individual contribute to his or her own development as a leader?

To begin this chapter, we would like you to consider the following questions: What motivated you to read this book on the topic of leadership and social influence? Are you reading this book to fulfill the requirement of a university course, a professional development program, or for your own personal advancement? Are you hoping to learn more about specific concepts and strategies for leadership that you can use in a position you occupy now or for your more general development as a leader? If leadership is a topic of significant interest to you, perhaps you may also be reading this book to inform the ways in which you think about your own leadership behaviors both now and into the future. It is our hope that regardless of the purposes you bring to the reading of this book, you are regularly considering the connections to the concepts discussed and their personal relevance for your overall development as a leader. By treating your experiences inside and outside of the classroom or workplace as laboratories for leadership development, you can experiment with various leadership styles, reflect on your successes and areas for further development, and learn from personal and professional challenges that can ultimately contribute to your approach to leadership opportunities in the future.

As we are hoping to demonstrate in this book, leadership is an exceedingly complex concept. No single or simple definition will adequately capture all facets of leadership as a concept, and no simple formula will adequately prescribe the behaviors necessary for success or effectiveness as a leader. In many ways, the first step of leadership effectiveness involves an acknowledgement of this inherent complexity. This chapter will provide one approach for thinking about your development as a leader, but it is important to recognize that this formula does not disregard the complexity. Rather, as you think about your development as a leader, you must regularly consider the multi-faceted dimensions of leadership, many of which have already been discussed in this book—the importance of context or situation, the diverse (and often competing) perceptions of stakeholders or followers, and the alignment with your purpose, passion, and core values, and those of others in groups or organizations with whom you interact.

The pursuit of leadership excellence must begin with a personally defined and personally relevant sense of purpose. As you will recall from the preceding chapter, by thinking about the type of leader you want to be, you engage in a process that allows you to move forward with intentionality and purpose. That sense of purpose may be unique to each formal or informal influence position that an individual pursues or in which a person finds himself or herself. And it is also the case, given the multiple challenges and opportunities afforded by any such position, individuals can always improve their understanding and skills over time. Personal leadership development, according to Day, Zaccaro, and Halpin (2004), involves both the desire to learn and the willingness to change. It is always possible to become a better leader, and this developmental process is ongoing throughout the duration of one's life (Kegan, 1982; Luthans & Avolio, 2003). This emphasis on leadership development and continuous improvement is especially helpful to consider, particularly when you encounter personal or professional setbacks or challenging situations.

The writing and research on leadership development points clearly to the following premise: Before you can begin to lead others, it is important that you are able to understand and lead yourself. As described in the previous chapter, there are many variables that influence one's leadership journey, any number of which are beyond the leader's control. The desire to grow as a leader requires a deliberate commitment to learning, discovery, and self-awareness, and by pursuing leadership development with clear intention and purpose, a leader may be better prepared to deal with the obstacles and challenges that lie ahead. One of the great challenges in this pursuit goes beyond identifying a specific plan of action; the more significant challenge is maintaining the commitment to one's plan for personal and professional development. With this in mind, this chapter will lay out a series of concepts and guides for pursuing and sustaining your own leadership development.

PERSONAL LEADERSHIP DEVELOPMENT

© ra2studio/Shutterstock.com

Leadership development, as highlighted by Day (2001) and Fulmer (1997), is a continuous process that is not limited to formal professional development programs or classroom learning. Individual leader development focuses on the cultivation of the "individual-based knowledge, skills, and abilities associated with formal leadership roles" (Day, 2001, p. 585), much like the competency approaches discussed in Chapter 2. Leadership development offers the potential for an individual to enhance one's social capital, which can also benefit the groups, organizations, and communities with which one is involved. In this regard, personal leadership development is meaningful because of its emphasis on the individual in relation to others.

McCauley, van Velsor, and Ruderman (2010), editors of the *Center for Creative Leadership Handbook of Leadership Development*, outline the following items that can be positively influenced by an investment in leadership development:

- Leading oneself
- Self-awareness
- Ability to balance conflicting demands
- Ability to learn
- Leadership values
- Leading others
- Ability to build and maintain relationships
- Ability to build effective work groups
- Communication skills
- Ability to develop others
- Leading the organization

- Management skills
- Ability to think and act strategically
- Ability to think creatively
- Ability to initiate and implement change

Given the many individual and collective benefits of enhanced leadership knowledge and skills, the value of self-assessment and self-improvement for individual leaders must also take account of the context in which you lead and the followers who look to you as a leader. An investment in your own leadership development has the potential to significantly impact your relationships with others and contribute to the ultimate success of the team, group, or organization that you lead.

THE PATH TO BECOMING A BETTER LEADER

©PhotoElite/Shutterstock.com

The lifelong process of leadership development begins with a genuine and deliberate commitment on behalf of the individual leader. What follows is a leadership development model developed by Brent Ruben and used by the Center for Organizational Development and Leadership at Rutgers University that outlines key steps in this process. This model, presented in Figure 8.1 and described also in Ruben et al. (2017), highlights the various key dimensions for individual leadership development that one may pursue over time.

The first step in the learning and change process is to define your leadership philosophy and the standards to which you aspire, as was discussed in the previous chapter. The second stage is determining where you stand relative to these standards. The gaps between your current performance—in general or in particular situations—and the standards you identify represent potential areas for improvement that can only be addressed through a genuine commitment to change. The next step is to translate that commitment to action into specific plans and strategies for improvement. The

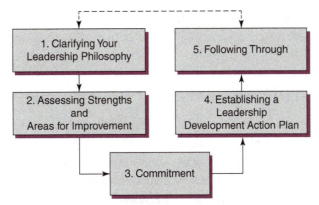

Figure 8.1: The Path to Becoming a Better Leader

final and perhaps most critical step is to ensure follow-through on those plans. As the dotted line in the figure implies, the learning and change process is ongoing and involves a recursive cycling through the steps. This model of learning and change is applicable in a wide range of contexts, including personal, social, and organizational situations, and it is particularly relevant for leadership development. Existing leadership styles and skills should not be regarded as permanent fixtures. On the contrary, you should continue to be aware of and refine your leadership style throughout your education and career. The learning and change model presented in Figure 8.1 outlines the process by which that can occur.

1. Clarifying Your Leadership Philosophy

As detailed in the preceding chapter, a sound approach to leader development begins with gaining clarity in terms of personal and professional aspirations. This initial phase begins with the identification and clarification of your leadership philosophy. By thinking about the type of leader you want to be, you engage in a process that allows you to move forward with intentionality and purpose. Identifying role models and reading the leadership literature—including professional and practical advice and biographies of respected leaders—are helpful actions in this stage. Recall these four questions that were offered in Chapter 7:

1. What is your *vision of leadership*—the leader you aspire to be?
2. What *leadership identity* would you like to establish among colleagues—the way you would like to be viewed?
3. For what will you be uniquely known as a leader—your *leadership brand*?
4. What would you like your lasting contribution to be—the *leadership legacy* you would like to leave behind?

Self-awareness and self-discovery are intricately connected to this initial phase, and the process of assessing strengths and areas for improvement as a leader builds upon this important first step.

2. Assessing Strengths and Areas for Improvement

The next step on the path to becoming a better leader involves the assessment of your strengths as well as areas in need of improvement. This phase allows you to understand where you stand currently relative to the aspirations and philosophy identified in the previous step. As you consider the ways that you approach leadership situations in your current clubs, organizations, and internships, and the ways that you hope to lead as you advance in your education and career, we would encourage you to conduct a candid assessment of your strengths that can be leveraged and also those areas in most need of improvement.

One approach to self-assessment might involve a consideration of the various competencies needed for effective leadership, using a tool such as the Leadership Competencies Scorecard discussed in Chapter 2, that outlines various competencies that contribute to leadership excellence, including positional competencies, analytic competencies, personal competencies, communication competencies, and organizational competencies (Ruben, 2012). This self-assessment phase of the leadership development model involves several steps. First, as you reflect on your past leadership experiences, it is useful to identify several competency areas where you currently excel. Perhaps you are confident of your ability to rally others around a shared goal in your student club or organization, or you might indicate your organizational effectiveness and attention to detail as a member of a group project as an area of personal strength. You might also consider your success in dealing with conflict in a previous internship or your ability to cultivate effective and durable relationships with a diverse group of individuals as a leader in the community. Upon identifying these strengths, the second question challenges you to consider the competency areas that are potential vulnerabilities for you as a leader. For example, individuals who demonstrate particular strengths with broader organizational competencies, such as setting a vision and rallying others around this shared vision, may find personal or positional competencies to be an area for development. Others may feel comfortable communicating with a diverse group of stakeholders, but may find the analytic problem solving competencies to be an ongoing source of difficulty. An additional step of potentially great value is to ask one or more friends, classmates, and mentors to complete a formal assessment of your leadership competencies as they see them. Comparisons between your own assessment results and those of a friend, classmate, or mentor can be useful in achieving a more detached perspective on your strengths and areas of growth. The final phase to this self-assessment process involves the identification of those competencies that must be refined or developed in order to achieve the aspirations put forward in your leadership philosophy. Be sure to identify how you will know whether you are successful in making these changes, which might include keeping a personal journal or asking others for feedback. This approach to personal assessment is one of many that are available in the leadership literature. For a sample of other leadership inventories, descriptions of the tools as offered on their websites, and the various metrics that they seek to assess, see Table 8.1 (Ruben, et al., 2017).

A more extensive summary of these inventories and the insights they are intended to provide, along with other leader and leadership assessments, is beyond the scope of this chapter; however, there are a number of important themes that cut across these various self-assessment tools. First, all of the inventories encourage honest self-awareness in responding to the various inventory questions. The very act of completing these

Table 8.1. Summary of Relevant Behavioral and Leadership Inventories

Inventory Tool	Description	Key Metrics	Website
Campbell Leadership Descriptor	A self-assessment designed to help individuals identify characteristics for successful leadership, recognize their strengths, and identify areas for improvement	• Vision • Diplomacy • Personal styles • Management • Feedback • Personal energy • Empowerment • Entrepreneurialism • Multi-cultural awareness	http://www.ccl.org/leadership/assessments/CLDOverview.aspx
DiSC Personality Test	A self-assessment measure of personality and behavioral style intended to improve work productivity, teamwork, and communication	• Dominance • Influence • Steadiness • Conscientiousness	https://www.discprofile.com/what-is-disc/overview/
Emotionally Intelligent Leadership Inventory for Students	A 57-item evidence-based assessment that measures how often students engage in behaviors that align with emotionally intelligent leadership	19 Emotionally Intelligent Leadership capacities categorized into 3 domains: • Consciousness of Self • Consciousness of Others • Consciousness of Context	http://www.wiley.com/WileyCDA/WileyTitle/productCd-1118821661.html
Leadership Competencies Scorecard 2.0	Provides a competency-based framework that identifies and integrates a diverse array of characteristics described in scholarly and professional writings as being important for effective leadership	• Analytic Competencies • Personal Competencies • Communication Competencies • Organizational Competencies • Positional Competencies	http://odl.rutgers.edu/wp-content/uploads/2015/10/lcs-leadership-inventory.pdf

Inventory Tool	Description	Key Metrics	Website
Leadership Practices Inventory (LPI)	A 30-item self-report measure that assesses leadership behaviors based on the Five Practices of Exemplary Leadership model	• Model the Way • Inspire a Shared Vision • Challenge the Process • Enable Others to Act • Encourage the Heart	http://www.leadershipchallenge.com/professionals-section-lpi.aspx
Leadership Style Inventory (LSI)	Designed to assist in the reflective learning process, to help people explore and better understand their own approach to leadership by distinguishing two leadership style preferences	• Directive style • Consensual style	http://www.nacubo.org/Products/Organizational_Development_Series/Organizational_Development_Series_The_Leadership_Style_Inventory.html
Myers-Briggs Type Indicator (MBTI)	A self-report questionnaire that indicates personality types based on the psychological preferences identified by Carl Jung. These preferences are indicative of how individuals perceive the world and make decisions	• Sensation • Intuition • Feeling • Thinking	http://www.myersbriggs.org/my-mbti-personality-type/mbti-basics/
Strengths Finder	Based on a 40-year study of human strengths, Gallup created a language of the 34 most common talents, and developed the Clifton Strengths Finder assessment to help people discover and describe these talents	34 strengths including but not limited to the following: • Achiever • Belief • Consistency • Empathy • Includer • Strategic • Woo	http://strengths.gallup.com/default.aspx
True Colors Personality Test	A self-report assessment of personality traits identifying individual strengths and challenges across four personality types	• Green = independent thinkers • Gold = pragmatic planners • Orange = action-oriented • Blue = people-oriented	https://truecolorsintl.com/

instruments may enhance one's understanding of self, other, and context. Next, the potential leadership inventory findings are broad enough to be made relevant to the leadership work needed across student clubs and organizations, majors, and careers. Finally, the listed inventories present a series of metrics for what is understood to be important to effective leadership practice. All have the potential to be useful for encouraging reflection, which is arguably more valuable than the score or descriptive profile any inventory provides. Tracking your scores on these various inventories over time, perhaps through the use of a dashboard as discussed in the previous chapter, may help to further clarify your strengths and areas of improvement. It is important to note that inventories and self-ratings are always subject to the limitations of our self-report and self-perception. The way we see ourselves and the way we intend to behave are often inconsistent with how others may see us. For this reason, there is value in gaining the perspectives of others on our leadership performance, needs, and strengths. Mentoring and assessment methods that allow colleagues or friends to constructively share their perspectives—methods like 360-degree feedback—can be most helpful in this regard.

3. Committing to Reflective Practice

As described in Chapter 2, the idea of enhancing one's leadership competencies is particularly compelling because of the relationship between knowledge and behavior. Competencies have *both* knowledge and skill components. Knowledge refers to leaders' understanding of a concept. Skill refers to leaders' effectiveness in operationalizing the knowledge they possess and their strategic ability to act on this information at the right time and in the right way (Ruben, 2012). Both an understanding of the competency and a proficiency associated with the "doing" of the competency are important. Leadership issues often arise because of the gap that often exists between theory and practice—or knowing versus doing (Pfeffer & Sutton, 2000). It is important to acknowledge that an understanding of a leadership theory or concept does not naturally translate into action. It is also often the case that in our self-assessments we blur the distinction between knowing and doing. In fact, without input from others, it is very difficult to separate our knowledge and good intentions from the way these play out in practice from the perspective of others.

Reflective practice is essential to connecting knowledge and practice. Simply put, reflective practice involves a commitment to consciously monitoring and reviewing your actions as a leader, the understandings that guided those actions, and the outcomes that result (Dewey, 1933; Lewin, 1952; Schön, 1984). Schön describes this practice as follows:

> The practitioner allows himself to experience surprise, puzzlement, or confusion in a situation which he finds uncertain or unique. He reflects on the phenomenon before him, and on the prior understandings which have been implicit in his behavior. He carries out an experiment which serves to generate both a new understanding of the phenomenon and a change in the situation. (p. 68)

In essence, the idea is to apply the scientific method to your own performance as a leader—to become, in effect, a leadership researcher—where the focus of study is your own understanding and behavior, and the outcomes that result.

However knowledgeable your understanding and skills are, becoming a better leader is a lifelong process. Continuous improvement requires regular experimentation and reflection. Through reflective practice, you can revisit both the leadership philosophy and self-assessment findings as a way of assessing continuing gaps, tracking progress on these areas of improvement, and identifying new areas in need of attention. Part of this process includes receiving feedback from those who observe your actions and reactions in specific contexts and situations. This provides a check on self-assessments that may be overly self-critical or overly self-congratulatory.

© pixs4u/Shutterstock.com

Committing to reflective practice implies that time will be spent debriefing at the end of interactions, meetings, or events—that is, rethinking the leadership concepts that guided our actions, reexamining the way those understandings were put into practice, and reflecting on those outcomes. You might consider using a dedicated notebook for these reflections so you can periodically review what you have learned and any patterns that emerge. The following are some key questions that can help guide you in the reflective process:

- What was I trying to accomplish?
- What understandings—theories or concepts—guided my actions?
- How effective was I at translating my understanding into practice?
- Was the outcome what I expected or hoped for?
- If not, why not?
- What options should I have considered?
- What refinements to my thinking and actions should I consider in the future?

A commitment to reflective practice will help you as a leader to translate the findings from self-assessment inventories into an applied and realistic plan for practice. Furthermore, by focusing on your own leadership behaviors as a specific unit of analysis, demonstrating a commitment to solicit and use feedback, and treating every leadership situation as a learning opportunity, you can continue to experiment with and learn which approaches to leadership best meet the needs of the group, team, or organization that you might be leading.

4. Establishing a Leadership Development Action Plan

The three previous steps will eventually lead you to a point where you can begin to establish a clear, realistic, thoughtful, and action-oriented leadership development plan. Your plan might contain any number of specific goals, such as the following:

- To become a student of leadership theory and practice
- To identify role models from whom you can learn
- To make every situation a learnable moment and an opportunity to become a better leader
- To seek informal and formal opportunities to lead and learn both within and beyond your college or university
- To establish goals and a plan in every influence situation
- To monitor your behavior
- To debrief leadership situations to assess your effectiveness (compare your goals and plan the outcome)
- To solicit third-party assessments from others, when possible

There are many components that one might include in a leadership development action plan. McCauley, Kanaga, and Lafferty (2010, p. 45) list a number of potential sources of leadership development, organized into five broad categories:

1. **Developmental relationships**
   - Mentors
   - Professional coaches
   - Manager as coach
   - Peer learning partners
   - Social identity networks
   - Communities of practice
2. **Developmental assignments**
   - Job moves
   - Job rotations
   - Expanded work responsibilities
   - Temporary assignments
   - Action learning projects
   - Leadership roles outside work
3. **Feedback processes**
   - Performance appraisal
   - 360-degree feedback
   - Assessment centers

4. **Formal programs**
   - ❐ University programs
   - ❐ Skill training
   - ❐ Feedback-intensive programs
   - ❐ Personal growth programs
5. **Self-development activities**
   - ❐ Reading (books, articles, online resources)
   - ❐ Speakers and colloquia
   - ❐ Professional conferences and trade shows
   - ❐ Fireside chats, town hall meetings, and all-staff meetings

There is great value in creating an action plan for development—one that intentionally bridges theories and concepts with the insight and goals that emerge from self-reflection and self-assessment—and commit yourself to addressing the elements of the plan.

5. Following Through

The fifth step on your developmental journey as a leader is following through on the identified plan. The plan, along with the ongoing process of self-assessment and self-reflection, are only worthwhile if they are put into action to improve your own leadership practice and to strengthen the project or entity that you lead. This emphasis on action is consistent with what Herminia Ibarra (2015b) offers in her text, *Act Like a Leader, Think Like a Leader*. In what she identifies as the outsight principle, "the only way to think like a leader is to first act: to plunge yourself into new projects and activities, interact with very different kinds of people, and experiment with unfamiliar ways of getting things gone" (p. 5). These new ways of acting change not only how we think, according to Ibarra, but also who we become along the way. She continues by acknowledging the following important point about leadership development:

> Who you are as a leader is not the starting point on your development journey, but rather the outcome of learning about yourself. This knowledge can only come about when you do new things and work with new and different people. You don't unearth your true self; it emerges from what you do. (p. 5)

For Ibarra, it is through action—and what we would describe as following through on the plans you establish for yourself as a leader—that you can begin to learn how to lead. As she suggests, "Knowing the kind of leader you'd like to become is not the starting point on your development journey, but rather the result of increasing your outsight" (p. 186). The value of "following through" and acting upon these leadership plans cannot be underestimated.

It is worth acknowledging at the conclusion of this model that a commitment to personal leadership development—like any personal change—is challenging. As will be discussed in the following chapter, change in behavior is extremely difficult, and by creating a plan for one's development, you may be more likely to take the important, and sometimes lonely, unpredictable, and difficult, steps on this journey to becoming a more effective, impactful, and influential leader.

CONCLUSION

Similar to how you might improve your competencies as a musician or athlete, the process of enhancing leadership competencies and behaviors requires time, attention, and practice. Specifically, leadership development that is both constructive and meaningful requires one to commit to further broaden one's knowledge and skills, devote serious attention to reflective practice, seek opportunities and helpful tools to aid in genuine self-reflection, solicit others' evaluations and suggestions for improvement, identify and learn from others who possess the desired knowledge and skills, pursue opportunities to practice and improve, and ultimately, to stay the course. The lifelong leadership development journey may seem arduous, unpredictable, and complex—yet, by maintaining a commitment to continually developing your skills as a leader, there will likely be an opportunity to enrich and enhance your overall leadership experience. Both you and those with whom you interact as a leader will be grateful for this investment.

PART THREE:

Applied Leadership Communication in Personal and Professional Settings

CHAPTER 9

PLANNING AND CHANGE: PRINCIPLES AND PRACTICES

⚠️ **Guiding Questions:**

1) What is organizational change and what makes change complex in a personal, group, and organizational context?
2) What are the predictable sources of resistance to change, and why is this resistance both a problem and an opportunity?
3) What are the common stages associated with the acceptance or rejection of change efforts?
4) Which strategies are most useful for leading change efforts?

In the previous chapters, our focus has been on the nature and importance of leadership and the processes involved in understanding and developing one's personal leadership knowledge and skills. Beginning with this chapter, the focus shifts to an emphasis on the knowledge and skills that are necessary to facilitate change within the context of groups, organizations, and communities.

Bringing about changes and improvements of various kinds is often one of the first priorities on the minds of newly selected, elected, or appointed leaders, and change is often an equally important concern for individuals who serve in continuing leadership positions. Examples of the types of changes a leader may wish to pursue include undertaking a new project or initiative, expanding membership, recruiting new individuals to serve on the leadership team, reexamining the mission or aspirations of the group or organization, beginning a new project or initiative, or enhancing the group or organization's internal or external reputation. However simple and straightforward it may be to imagine and describe a particular change, successfully achieving that change is typically a daunting task, one that requires substantial leadership knowledge and skill, including an understanding of the dynamics of change, developing a plan for change, and having the knowledge and commitment necessary for successful implementation and follow-through. This chapter will address the dynamics of change and will highlight a number of models and strategies that you may wish to use as you engage in planning and change efforts in your current club, group, or organization.

We have described our view of leadership as social influence and explained the dangers of glamorizing a leader's role in the influence process. As noted, without people willing to collaborate—to become what are traditionally referred to as "followers"— leadership is not possible. Even in formal groups or organizations where individuals have designated titles that define their responsibilities, followers are crucial due to their willingness to support and collaborate with their leader, to engage with others as participatory team members, and to contribute to the goals, mission, and vision of the entity. From this perspective, changes and improvements—like other outcomes of social influence—occur through a complex array of communicative interactions that take place among leaders and followers.

THE BIG PICTURE: UNDERSTANDING THE DYNAMICS OF CHANGE

© shutterataken/Shutterstock.com

There is no question that the capacity to change and evolve in various ways is critical to the progress and survival of any group or organization. In this regard, groups and organizations have much in common with individuals, and one way to better understand the challenges presented by change in these social entities is to begin by considering the dynamics through which personal change occurs. How often do we contemplate the need to make personal changes—study more, make more time for friends and relatives, exercise more, develop additional skill in a particular sport or with a musical instrument? And in so many instances, despite one's very best of intentions, successful change proves extremely complex and difficult (Aiken & Keller, 2009; Kotter, 1996; Lewis, 2011; Ruben, 2012).

Our attention to change is underscored each New Year's Eve when millions of people make resolutions about things they need, want, and intend to change in themselves. Few of us have a shortage of topics we might list as worthy candidates for personal change. Unfortunately, despite our resolutions, and best intentions, we often fail in our efforts to achieve these goals. The failure rate for New Year's resolutions is between 75% and 80%, and as suggested by Fury (2016), "'Fail Friday' is the name given to the date, about three weeks into each New Year, when resolutions generally fall by the wayside" (para. 2). Weight control is one area where many of us engage in change efforts, and the statistics on the success of those efforts across the population are quite revealing. For example, Ayyad and Andersen (2000) found that in an analysis of 17 comprehensive studies including a total of more than 3,000 dieters, only an average of 15% were successful in effecting change—defined as losing and maintaining a weight loss of at least 20 pounds for three years or more. So often our hopes and good intentions for weight control and other changes are dashed as we slip back into old habits and traditions that have been, and will continue to be, very powerful forces in our lives.

In so many cases, disappointment is perhaps the most predictable outcome of personal change efforts. While these disappointments often result in frustration, they also teach a powerful and important lesson—hope and good intentions, in and of themselves, are not necessarily effective strategies for change. This lesson draws attention to one of the most fundamental insights to emerge from the study of human behavior: the single best predictor of what we are likely to do in the future is not what we say, intend, hope, or plan, but rather what we have done in the past and what we are doing in the present. Simply said, *behavior is the best predictor of behavior* (Ruben, 2012).

Despite the fact that change is difficult, and our attempts to change sometimes fail, as we will explain in the pages ahead, understanding the change process and consciously mapping out a plan for change can contribute to greater success. Let's begin an exploration of the dynamics of change by considering each of the steps that are involved. The process, as illustrated in Figure 9.1, begins with the first stage of *attention*, and relates to gaining an awareness of and perceiving a need for change. Clearly, if one sees no need for change and is unaware of proposals to address these needs, nothing happens. Once an individual becomes aware of the need, the next step in the change process is *engagement*. To become engaged is to personally consider the potential need and issues involved, to discuss this desired change with others, and generally, to invest time and effort in the process. With engagement, the probability of successful change is advanced. On the other hand, without such engagement, it is unlikely that an individual will be motivated to further consider the need for change or prospects for new and/or innovative ideas, behaviors, or actions. The likelihood of *commitment*—the third stage—increases as a consequence of meaningful engagement.

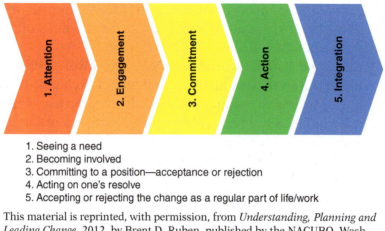

1. Seeing a need
2. Becoming involved
3. Committing to a position—acceptance or rejection
4. Acting on one's resolve
5. Accepting or rejecting the change as a regular part of life/work

This material is reprinted, with permission, from *Understanding, Planning and Leading Change*, 2012, by Brent D. Ruben, published by the NACUBO, Washington, D.C.

Figure 9.1: Stages in the Acceptance or Rejection of Change Efforts

Commitment is a precursor to *action*—stage four. In the final stage, a change must be accepted and fully *integrated* into our daily routine, or it is likely to fade from practice over time. Generally, successful personal change requires a progression through all five stages, but as is typically the case with unsuccessful change efforts, the process can stall at any point.

LEADING CHANGE IN GROUPS AND ORGANIZATIONS

Whereas personal change involves only one individual, exercising some direct control over group, organizational, community, or societal change involves many people— all with their own personal agendas, needs, hopes, fears, and sensemaking styles and habits. Recall from Chapter 3, that it is through the act of sensemaking that human actors "structure the unknown" (Waterman, 1990, p. 41) as a way of constructing that which then becomes sensible to themselves and others (Weick, 1995). The way these interpretations are made, the manner in which expectations are formulated, and the approach to making sense of the aspirations of individuals in a given group or organizational setting are acts that, by their very nature, contribute to reinforcing the status quo and generally make change difficult. As Machiavelli (1532) wrote in *The Prince*: "There is nothing more difficult to take in hand, more perilous to conduct, or more uncertain in its success, than to take the lead in the introduction of a new order of things" (Chapter 6). Offering convincing contemporary support for Machiavelli's caution are studies of the success rate of planned organizational change efforts, which indicate that as few as 30% of these initiatives are considered successful (Aiken & Keller, 2009; Kotter, 1996; Smith, 2007). Although technical and resource considerations are often the first factors to be blamed for a high failure rate, as we shall discuss, failure to understand

and address personal, cultural, and communication issues generally are the more fundamental sources of the problem.

Critical to these failure statistics is what the literature has termed *resistance*. Resistance to personal as well as group and organizational change results from any number of factors. A proposed change may be resisted because it:

- is viewed as implying a criticism of particular individuals, or of present systems, processes, and/or structures
- may not be regarded as necessary, and the added benefits are unclear
- requires too great an investment of time, when there is already too much to do
- calls for new routines, knowledge, or skills
- triggers concerns that the necessary resources will not be available
- threatens present positions, status, stature, or roles
- assumes there is trust and confidence in leaders, when this trust and confidence may not be present

The expression of resistance can take many forms—some quite obvious, some much less so. Depending on the culture and traditions of the group and organization as well as other factors, forms of resistance may include overt or covert avoidance, questioning, challenging, redirecting, delaying, withdrawal, or sabotage. Recall from our discussion in Chapter 5 that organizational cultures have the power to both help and hinder the ability of groups and organizations to effectively work and this is true with regard to change efforts as well.

For leaders advocating change of various kinds, there is a tendency to view resistance as a problem to be solved or an obstacle to be surmounted. For individuals or groups who believe that they will be negatively affected by a proposed change, however, resistance may be seen as a solution rather than a problem. In such instances, resistance becomes a strategy for stopping, delaying, or redirecting the initiative. Thus, the determination as to whether resistance is an asset or liability often depends on one's role, goal, perspective, and experience with change. It is important to note, also, that even for advocates of change, resistance can have important benefits such as creating opportunities to gather valuable feedback—whether through face-to-face interaction, written surveys, or public polling. Resistance can be particularly useful when it highlights unanticipated problems in the plan, suggests potential improvements, or identifies individuals and groups with whom additional time and effort should be spent to enhance the plan or secure support. If carefully analyzed and attended to, resistance offers important information suggesting ways in which a change initiative can be revised, reframed, or more clearly communicated to achieve broader support. Finally, it is important for leaders to understand the reasons for resistance—is the resistance due to a specific change or is it a general resistance to the tendencies of some leaders to introduce every new fad, perhaps leading to a general fatigue with change? By attending to these questions and considerations, leaders may be better able to introduce and implement more effective and sustainable change efforts that are well-received by the individuals most directly impacted by the planned change.

LEMONS TO LEMONADE

© etorres/Shutterstock.com

Fostering change is an area of wide-ranging importance for leaders in any group or organizational setting. Take a moment to consider a specific change that you have attempted to introduce in a formal or an informal leadership role. Perhaps you may have advocated for a new process of collaborating with others on a project, or the change might involve the design of a new program, initiative, or event. Building on the previous discussion, it is helpful to understand that the aim of change leadership is to first design and then implement a plan that will successfully guide others through the stages in the change process described above.

As much as we would like there to be a simple formula for leading change, no such formula exists. However, an understanding of the stages through which successful change efforts must generally pass can serve as a helpful foundation for leaders in designing and executing change initiatives. The more complicated the envisioned change, the more complex the group or organization, the larger the number of people affected, the more it represents a departure from the status quo, the more it deviates from traditions or existing practices, or the more it challenges group or organizational culture, the more it becomes necessary to adopt a systematic approach to leading change. In this section, and summarized in Figure 9.2, we present a five-step model that translates the foregoing insights related to the change process into specific steps and strategies that a leader can follow in guiding change initiatives (Ruben, 2012).

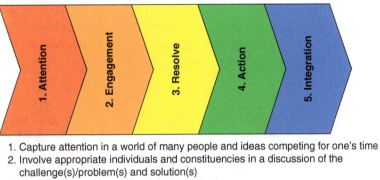

1. Capture attention in a world of many people and ideas competing for one's time
2. Involve appropriate individuals and constituencies in a discussion of the challenge(s)/problem(s) and solution(s)
3. Commit to a position—acceptance or rejection
4. Translate knowledge, attitudes, and beliefs into action – current and best practices
5. Integrate and institutionalize the change (or absence of change) into the culture

Adapted from Understanding, Planning and Leading Change, 2012, by Brent D. Ruben, published by the National Association of College and University Business Officers, Washington, D.C.

Figure 9.2: Strategies for Leading Change

Capturing attention.   The first step, depicted in Figure 9.3, consists of gaining the attention of those who have a need to understand and support the change initiative. While this may seem to be a simple and straightforward undertaking, capturing the attention of others in a world where there are many messages and people competing for time and interest can be a significant challenge—particularly if the topic seems to have little immediate relevance or consequence.

The attention-gaining process should emphasize the need for change and generate a sense of importance or urgency. Ideally, the stage also creates "a burning platform"— which involves imparting the sense that change is necessary because continuing on the present course of action (or inaction)—the status quo—will lead to undesirable outcomes.

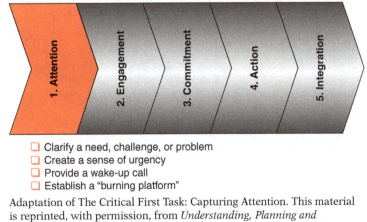

☐ Clarify a need, challenge, or problem
☐ Create a sense of urgency
☐ Provide a wake-up call
☐ Establish a "burning platform"

Adaptation of The Critical First Task: Capturing Attention. This material is reprinted, with permission, from *Understanding, Planning and Leading Change,* 2012, by Brent D. Ruben, published by the NACUBO, Washington, D.C.

Figure 9.3: The Critical First Task: Capturing Attention

Gaining attention for your agenda and issues is essential, but avoiding the *attention paradox* is also a consideration. For instance, the use of highly dramatic, fear-inducing, or shocking message strategies will likely gain attention, but if overdone, these may create a "backlash," and actually contribute to denial or avoidance, or the possible alienation of intended supporters.

Creating engagement.   Strategies that heighten awareness and receptivity should be followed by efforts to engage individuals in discussions of the need(s), challenge(s), or problem(s) and potential solutions, as illustrated in Figure 9.4. A leader's first consideration in this stage is identifying and communicating with key stakeholders—individuals and groups who will have a stake and who should care about the outcome of the proposed change. Consideration should also be given to individuals, groups, and organizations who may be critical sources of support or resistance, have particularly useful insights, control relevant resources, or in other ways can play an important role in building support for, planning, and implementing the change. Depending on the circumstances, the list of relevant stakeholders would likely include individuals from within the group, organization, or community, and perhaps representatives from various external constituencies such as members of advisory boards, leaders and members of other groups, organizations, the media, and perhaps the local community. As noted, the primary goal at this point in the process is facilitating dialogue with internal and external stakeholders in order to generate a shared understanding of the reasons for the proposed change, what the change will involve, and how it will be an improvement over the current situation.

☐ Identify and involve all individuals and constituencies with a stake in the outcome—especially those who will be directly affected
☐ Consider other key stakeholders—particularly those with positional power, credibility, and resources
☐ Facilitate meaningful dialogue and discussion to create a shared sense of the challenge(s), problem(s), and solution(s)

Adaptation of Creating Engagement. This material is reprinted, with permission, from *Understanding, Planning and Leading Change,* 2012, by Brent D. Ruben, published by the NACUBO, Washington, D.C.

Figure 9.4: Creating Engagement

Developing resolve.   Developing resolve—promoting a commitment to the advocated change—is the third aim of the change process. As depicted in Figure 9.5, this stage includes identifying and focusing on areas of agreement, and also addressing and working through obstacles. Typically, these goals include ensuring the availability of needed resources, providing opportunities for input and influence, and ultimately building consensus and working coalitions.

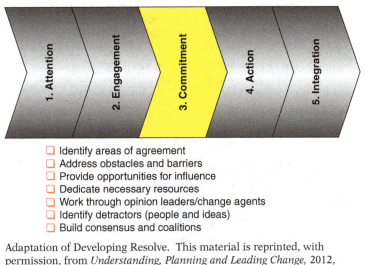

☐ Identify areas of agreement
☐ Address obstacles and barriers
☐ Provide opportunities for influence
☐ Dedicate necessary resources
☐ Work through opinion leaders/change agents
☐ Identify detractors (people and ideas)
☐ Build consensus and coalitions

Adaptation of Developing Resolve. This material is reprinted, with permission, from *Understanding, Planning and Leading Change,* 2012, by Brent D. Ruben, published by the NACUBO, Washington, D.C.

Figure 9.5: Developing Resolve

Motivating action.   Motivating action is the fourth step in the change leadership process, as shown in Figure 9.6. Intuitively, a call for action seems like a logical starting point in efforts to lead change initiatives. However, leaders who begin at this stage often become quickly frustrated with the resistance they encounter—often the result of a lack of effort invested in the foundational stages of attention-gaining, engagement, and commitment-building.

Motivating action builds on successful efforts in each of the prior stages, and this stage involves clarifying intended change outcomes, promoting the desired behavior, identifying the tasks or actions that need to be implemented, providing the necessary resources and training to support the desired behaviors, prompting activities that move the initiative in the desired direction, and continuing these efforts until the intended change outcomes are realized.

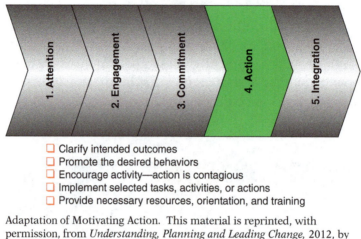

☐ Clarify intended outcomes
☐ Promote the desired behaviors
☐ Encourage activity—action is contagious
☐ Implement selected tasks, activities, or actions
☐ Provide necessary resources, orientation, and training

Adaptation of Motivating Action. This material is reprinted, with permission, from *Understanding, Planning and Leading Change,* 2012, by Brent D. Ruben, published by the NACUBO, Washington, D.C.

Figure 9.6: Motivating Action

Assuring integration.   When the goals of each of the prior stages have been achieved, the final challenge—and by no means an insignificant one—is sustaining the change. All too often, even with changes or improvements that seem to have been successful, the passage of time, waning attention, or a change in leadership leads to a gradual backsliding. To prevent this outcome, leaders should undertake measures to mitigate these tendencies. Such activities could include showcasing and celebrating changes, publicly recognizing and rewarding innovators, developing reinforcing processes and structures, and implementing mechanisms for regular review and improvement, as shown in Figure 9.7.

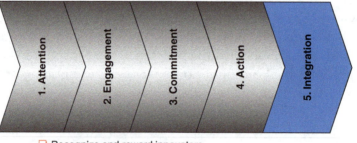

☐ Recognize and reward innovators
☐ Celebrate changes and other outcomes
☐ Develop reinforcing processes, structures, and mechanisms
☐ Implement mechanisms for ongoing review and refinement

Adaptation of Assuring Integration. This material is reprinted, with permission, from *Understanding, Planning and Leading Change, 2012,* by Brent D. Ruben, published by the NACUBO, Washington, D.C.

Figure 9.7: Assuring Integration

Unless these and other reinforcing steps are initiated, whether applied to planned personal or organizational advances, it is likely that advances will gradually regress to the older behaviors, patterns, or traditions. This is all-too-often the unfortunate case with the example of weight loss, as discussed earlier, where evidence suggests that losing weight, while difficult, is far easier than maintaining the lower weight, and it is also often the case with innovations of one kind or another introduced in groups or organizations. Generally, successful change requires a progression through all five stages, but the process can stall at any point.

Recall the example of a change that you have attempted to introduce as a formal or an informal leader. Would you consider the change a major success, a minor success, or a failure? If the change was a success, which of the phases presented above did you intentionally or unintentionally move through in your change efforts, and which of these did you find most influential, helpful, or advantageous? On the other hand, if the change was deemed a failure, might an investment in one or more of these phases have potentially led to a different outcome?

KEY CROSS-CUTTING FACTORS: *FIVE-BY-FIVE MATRIX FOR PLANNED CHANGE*

© Uber Images/Shutterstock.com

Five cross-cutting factors are important for the success of change leadership in each of these stages: planning, leadership, communication, culture, and assessment. We have found that the Five-by-Five Matrix for Planned Change, illustrated in Figure 9.8, provides an exceptionally useful framework for thinking about and helping a leader develop and facilitate a planned change strategy (Ruben, 2012). The matrix displays the five stages of change as columns and the five cross-cutting success factors as rows. Each cell represents a point of intersection between the two sets of considerations, and each is an important area for attention by leaders as they undertake a change initiative. This

STAGES > FACTORS	1. Attention	2. Engagement	3. Commitment	4. Action	5. Integration
Planning					
Leadership					
Communication					
Culture					
Assessment					

Figure 9.8: **Five-by-Five Matrix for Planned Change**

framework can be used by a leader to conceptualize, plan, and implement a desired change on his or her own. In general, however, the benefits are greater—both in terms of the quality of the finished product and the value of the process—if it is developed in a collaborative way by a team with collective responsibility for the change effort.

Planning involves thinking through what is needed to keep the change effort on track in each stage of the process and maximizing the probability of success over- all. The primary aim of planning is to ensure a clear understanding of the purpose and intended outcomes of the project, and to coordinate actions that need to be taken. Except for the most minor changes or improvements, collaborative planning is essential to ensure shared understanding and commitment to the rationale for the envisioned change, specific goals and priorities, and necessary action steps at each stage. When multiple stakeholder groups are involved, planning challenges are sig- nificantly magnified. Critical to the planning process are: (1) developing a succinct and clear statement of the need for and purpose of the change initiative; (2) identi- fying environmental factors that will have an impact on the proposed change; and (3) clarifying project goals, strategies, and action steps necessary for the implemen- tation of the change effort (Tromp & Ruben, 2010).

Leadership considerations are also important in each stage of the change initiative. Leadership in this context has two dimensions: personal leadership and project leadership architecture or structure (Ruben, 2006, 2009). Personal leadership involves identifying the critical personal competencies for coordinating a particular change initiative, and selecting an individual, or individuals, with the appropriate strengths to coordinate each stage of the initiative. Often, successfully guiding an initiative through the five stages requires a number of people to play leadership roles of one kind or another. Decisions as to whether to form a team, how to structure that team, who should be named to partici- pate, who will serve as spokespersons for the team, and what roles individuals will serve during particular stages of the change process are all components of what is referred to as the leadership architecture.

As noted previously, with all but the simplest change initiatives, it makes sense to cultivate a team of leaders. With a team, it is possible to draw on the collective leadership strengths and insights of multiple individuals, which is likely to strengthen the overall impact of the group. That said, as the leadership architecture becomes larger and more complex, more time and effort is required to coordinate that team—in essence, to lead the leaders. The primary point here, is that careful consideration needs to be given to the leaders and a leadership structure that is appropriate for the various stages of a given change initiative, recognizing that no two projects are alike.

Communication refers to designing and implementing a process of engagement—information-sharing, listening, and collaboration—with those involved with, knowledgeable about, and/or affected by the planned change. Communication is vital at every stage of change leadership, and the challenges it presents can be daunting. Differences in experience, perspective, and motivation all come into play within each stage of planned change, and addressing these effectively is essential to successful outcomes. Key questions for leaders to consider for each stage of the change process include the following:

- Who are your internal and external target audiences?
- What are your intended outcomes?
- What are the potential sources of resistance?
- What are the appropriate messages for each audience?
- What are the most effective channels for reaching each audience with your message?
- Who is the most appropriate spokesperson?
- What impact are you expecting from your messages?
- What are the appropriate channels through which to collect feedback from stakeholders?

Possible communication goals for specific stages of the change process might include gaining attention, increasing awareness, providing information, gathering feedback and reactions, overcoming resistance, creating buy-in, motiving actions, promoting sustainability, or any number of other goals. The important point here is that there are many potential communication goals that might be pursued, and it is essential to develop consensus around these goals. Also important is identifying which channels are most appropriate given the specific goals, messages, and audiences, and determining which goals are most appropriate for each stage. When it comes to the selection of communication channels, there are also many available options including face-to-face communication, email, websites, focus groups, surveys, meetings, posters, and many others. Leaders want to carefully consider the various available channels and make selections for communication during each stage in the change leadership process in light of the multiple goals, audiences, messages, and other relevant factors.

Culture, as discussed in Chapter 5, involves taking account of the organization's language, history, norms, rules, and traditions that may influence the dynamics of change. Cultures may be supportive, but more generally, there is likely to be a general resistance to change. Particularly when the cultural traditions of a group or an organization are perceived to be challenged or threatened by a proposed change, resistance is predictable. Additionally, as discussed previously, a group or an organizational culture might be highly differentiated—that is, made up of various subcultures that co-exist in fluctuating states of agreement, conflict, or apathy making the achievement of consensus difficult. While there may well be no way to avoid some degree of resistance, it is important to do the historical and analytic homework necessary in order to avoid being surprised by what are often predictable reactions. Moreover, armed with cultural knowledge it is quite possible to avoid and minimize some sources of resistance during various stages of the change process, and to identify and enlist the support of allies who will see value in change that others may not.

Assessment relates to developing and implementing a systematic approach to monitoring progress as the change process unfolds and to evaluating the overall outcomes of the planned change. While this process might seem at first consideration to be a needless luxury, further analysis suggests that assessment is necessary to evaluate the effectiveness of the change leadership process at various stages. This information is valuable in its own right, but more so if it directs a leader or leadership team in directions that enhance the project and the path toward intended outcomes. Assessment need not be an overly complex task, but should ask and seek answers to the following questions for each stage: (1) What are the aims of this stage? (2) How can progress or outcomes be assessed? (3) How successful are we in achieving the aims? What is working well? What improvements are needed? You might consider developing a dashboard as discussed in Chapter 7 to highlight key metrics, monitor progress, and display results to stakeholders.

CONCLUSION

The stages and critical factors in the change process discussed in the chapter and listed in the *Five-by-Five Matrix for Planned Change* provide a useful framework for leaders to consider in the change leadership process. It is a practical tool that a leader or leadership team can use in conceptualizing, designing, and facilitating change. Successfully leading change—whether in a small or large group, a project team, a club, an organization, or a broader community—is perhaps one of the greatest leadership challenges and tests of one's ability to exercise social influence. Factors such as the size of the group, the magnitude of the change, and the extent of resistance and polarization all play a critical role in defining the challenges and opportunities confronting the leader as he or she endeavors to guide a change initiative. Notwithstanding these factors, the importance of understanding the dynamics of change, core leadership concepts, careful planning, strategic communication, an understanding of the culture, and an ongoing assessment of the effectiveness of one's efforts are always essential to the pursuit of the desired aims.

CHAPTER 10

DEFINING AND PURSUING A VISION OF EXCELLENCE: A FRAMEWORK FOR GROUPS, CLUBS, AND ORGANIZATIONS

> ⚠️ **Guiding Questions:**
>
> 1) What factors contribute to excellence in groups, clubs, and organizations?
> 2) What are the characteristics of outstanding formal groups and organizations?
> 3) Which "best practice" models or frameworks can a leader adopt to define and pursue a vision of excellence?
> 4) How might a leader adopt this way of thinking to inform the planning, assessment, and improvement processes in clubs, groups, and organizations?

Developing and vigorously pursuing a vision of excellence for your group or organization is one of the most fundamental contributions you can make in your role as leader. And while every leader wants his or her group or organization to be excellent, determining what excellence means in this context is not an easy task. In this chapter, our focus will be on the tools and best practices available for leaders as they define and systematically pursue a vision of excellence for their group, team, club, or organization. Unquestionably, having a reference point for understanding excellence can be of great value for leaders across settings and sectors. An understanding of what constitutes excellence may help to shape day-to-day sensemaking and decision making, and can also serve as a guide for planning and priority-setting.

© Rawpixel.com/Shutterstock.com

Of the various approaches that may be helpful in these ways, none has been more successful or more influential than the Malcolm Baldrige model[1] (Baldrige National Quality Program, 2017). The Baldrige model was named after the U.S. Secretary of Commerce, Malcolm Baldrige, who served from 1981 until his death in 1987. The Baldrige model provides a framework for assessment and improvement based on a blend of academic concepts, principles from the professional literature, and successful leadership practices. The framework draws on many sources, and can serve as a helpful guide for leaders as they envision and pursue excellence in a variety of contexts and settings. While the primary application of the model has been within formal organizations, many of the concepts are equally applicable for envisioning and creating outstanding groups—work groups, clubs, community or service organizations, or business enterprises, for instance.

A FRAMEWORK FOR GROUP AND ORGANIZATIONAL EXCELLENCE

The Baldrige framework is built around a series of core values and principles that are relevant across various sectors, applications, and adaptations (e.g., Ruben, 2016a, 2016b, 2016c). Specifically, the model highlights seven categories or components of excellence that are illustrated below in Figure 10.1. These categories are described here using terminology that is general enough to be broadly applicable to any formalized club, group, or organization.

Organizational excellence, based on this framework, is the result of careful attention to the following components:

1. **Leadership**—An effective leader and/or leadership team that provides guidance and ensures a clear and shared sense of direction and a vision for the future, a commitment to continuous review and improvement of leadership practices, and an exemplar of both social and environmental consciousness.

1 For further information on the Baldrige National Quality Program, visit http://www.nist.gov/baldrige/.

A Baldrige-inspired framework adapted to higher education language and cultures

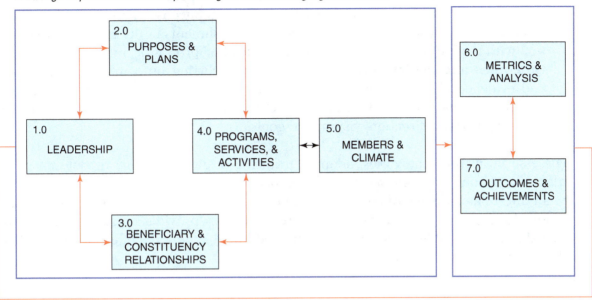

Figure 10.1: A Framework for Group and Organizational Excellence

"A Framework for Group and Organizational Excellence", adapted from *The Excellence in Higher Education Guide: A Framework for the Design, Assessment, and Continuous Improvement of Institutions, Departments and Programs - 8th edition* by B. D. Ruben. Sterling, VA: Stylus Publishing, LLC, 2016.

2. **Plans and purposes**—A systematic planning process and coherent plans that translate the group or organization's purposes, directions, and vision for its future into clear and measurable goals that are widely understood and effectively implemented. As we discussed in Chapter 9, the goal of planning is to ensure a clear understanding of the purpose and intended outcomes, and to coordinate actions that need to be taken.

3. **Beneficiary and constituency relationships**—Knowledge and understanding of the needs, expectations, and satisfaction or dissatisfaction levels of those served by the group or organization, as well as practices in place that are responsive to these needs and expectations. Additionally, the implementation of evaluation processes to stay current with, and anticipate the evolving needs and expectations of those who benefit from the activities of the group or organization.

4. **Programs and services**—Quality programs, services, and activities to ensure effectiveness, efficiency, consistency, and compatibility with the needs and expectations of those served by the group or organization.

5. **Members and climate**—A culture and climate that attracts, encourages, recognizes, and rewards member commitment and contributions toward group or organizational excellence while advancing the overall purposes of the group or organization.

6. **Measurement and information use**—The development and use of indicators of group or organizational performance that reflect its purpose, directions, vision, and goals, and provide a way to compare the accomplishments of the group or organization with those of peers, competitors, and/or leading groups or organizations.

7. **Outcomes and achievements**—Methods for reporting outcomes, achievements, and evidence of accomplishments in all of the preceding categories in order to demonstrate and document the effectiveness of the group or organization in relation to their purposes, direction, vision, and goals.

These seven distinct categories, adapted from the original Baldrige model and other adaptations, such as *Excellence in Higher Education* (Ruben, 2016a), are understood to be an interrelated system of components of excellence relevant to any group or organization. As discussed in the next section, the framework provides a useful roadmap for formal and informal leaders who are interested in enhancing the effectiveness of their club, group, or organization.

THE SELF-ASSESSMENT PROCESS

© airdone/Shutterstock.com

As you consider ways to utilize this framework in your current or future club, group, or organization, consider undertaking a detailed assessment process to determine how the unit currently measures up in each of the key categories—either by doing this yourself as a leader, or even better, engaging most or all members of the group or organization. This kind of reflective exercise helps everyone involved to develop an understanding of the components of a vision for group and organizational excellence. This process also helps participants identify the core strengths and areas of improvement for the club, group, or organization.

For each of the seven categories, there are a series of questions that relate to key issues and considerations that correspond with each component of excellence. Thinking through and answering these questions provides a helpful foundation for leaders and others involved in the assessment process. The "yes" answers identify current areas of strength; and obviously enough, the more "yes" answers there are, the greater the level of excellence. The items which yield "no" responses are equally important, because they point to areas where improvements should be seriously considered and they form the basis for an agenda for change and improvement. As you read through the questions offered below, you might take some time to actively consider a group or an organization that you are currently involved in—or one that you might hope to join in the future.

Excellence Categories and Key Issues

Category 1—Leadership

Focuses on leadership approaches, how leaders and leadership practices encourage excellence and innovation, and how leadership practices are reviewed and improved.

- Is the leadership structure clearly defined and understood by all?
- Do leadership practices effectively advance the group or organization's mission, directions, and aspirations, and promote follow-through on plans and goals?
- Are clearly defined leadership goals in place?
- Do leaders and leadership practices promote active engagement by all group and organization members?
- Are formal and informal leadership review and feedback methods in place, and used effectively?
- Is leadership development a core value?

Category 2—Purposes and Plans

Focuses on the planning process, and how purposes, directions, aspirations, and values are developed and communicated, how they are translated into goals and action steps, and how members are engaged in these processes.

- Is there a formalized planning process?
- Are members engaged in developing and implementing plans?
- Does an up-to-date, written plan currently exist?
- Does that plan effectively translate the purposes, directions, vision, and values into priorities, measurable goals, and action steps with specified roles and responsibilities?

- Does the plan take account of current strengths and areas in need of improvement, innovation, or elimination?
- Does the plan consider resource needs, along with potential constraints associated with obtaining resources?
- Are the plans and goals synchronized with those of other relevant groups or organizations?

Category 3—Beneficiary and Constituency Relationships

Focuses on the individuals and groups inside and outside of the group or organization that benefit from your programs or services, other groups or organizations with which you collaborate, and the needs and satisfaction or dissatisfaction of these individuals and groups.

- Is there a shared view of the relative priority of the groups for which the program, department, or organization provides its programs, services, and/or activities?
- Is there a systematic approach to monitoring needs, expectations, satisfaction levels, and your reputation with each group?
- Is information about needs, expectations, satisfaction, and perceptions systematically gathered, well-organized, analyzed, disseminated, and used for improvement or change? How is this done?
- Are mechanisms in place to ensure effective communication with members of each of these external groups?
- Is there a broad commitment to enhancing communication and improving relationships with those who are critical to fulfilling your mission, aspirations, and goals?

Category 4—Programs, Services, and Activities

Focuses on methods for assuring high standards in programs, services, and activities that are critical to the group or organization's mission.

- Is there clarity and consensus as to the group or organization's critical functions—why the group or organization exists, what it does, and how these functions fit with your mission and aspirations for the future?
- Are procedures in place for regular review of programs, services, or activities to assure their quality, continuing relevance, consistency, and alignment with the group or organization's mission and aspirations for the future?
- What procedures are in place to assure high standards in the design and implementation of new programs, services, or activities?
- What actions will be taken if there is a potential need to refine, revise, or discontinue particular offerings, or to create new programs and services if the need arises?

Category 5—Members and Climate

Focuses on attracting and retaining committed members; encouraging and recognizing their contributions; promoting personal and professional development; and creating and maintaining effective group or organizational structures and maintaining a positive culture and climate.

- Are effective procedures in place for identifying, attracting, welcoming, and orienting new members?
- Are effective approaches in place for encouraging, documenting, and recognizing member contributions and accomplishments, particularly emphasizing those that are consistent with the mission, aspirations, and values of the group or organization?
- Is personal and/or professional development promoted and facilitated?
- Are procedures in place for the regular review and assessment of the effectiveness and efficiency of the group or organization's structure?
- Is there a formalized approach for regularly assessing workplace climate and culture as well as member satisfaction?

Category 6—Measurement and Information Use

Considers the methods used for review and evaluation of the effectiveness of the group or organization. Focuses on how assessment methods are developed and used to identify and document accomplishments and needs for improvement, innovation, or the discontinuation of programs, services, or activities.

- Is there a well-defined, shared view as to what standards to use in assessing the effectiveness of the group or organization in achieving its mission and living its values?
- Are standards in place for assessing effectiveness in each category—leadership practices, planning, beneficiary and constituency relationships, member satisfaction and climate, and assessment systems?
- Are there effective approaches for sharing assessment results?
- Is this information effectively used to guide group or organizational improvement—refinement, innovation, redesign, and/or the discontinuation of particular programs, services, or activities when appropriate?
- Is trend and comparative information from peers and exemplary groups or organizations gathered, analyzed, and used to evaluate, improve, and innovate?
- Is outcome information used in internal and external communication, priority setting, planning, resource allocation, reward, and recognition?

Category 7—Outcomes and Achievements

Focuses on documenting outcomes and achievements, your progress over time relative to plans and goals, and your effectiveness compared to peer and exemplary groups and organizations.

- Does objective outcome information indicate your group or organization's success in achieving its mission, vision, plans, goals, and priorities?
- Does objective outcome information indicate the effectiveness of each of the programs, services, and activities that are critical to your mission?
- Does the available information indicate the effectiveness of leadership, planning, beneficiary and constituency relations, member satisfaction, assessment and knowledge sharing, and the documentation and reporting of outcomes?
- Does evidence and information compare trends with those of peers and exemplary groups and organizations?
- Is outcomes information used for continuing improvement and innovation, and for communicating with internal and external constituencies?

Ways of Utilizing the Framework

© QiuJu Song/Shutterstock.com

Collectively, these seven categories provide the basis for defining a vision of excellence, and the questions posed in each category offer a tool for clarifying specific strengths or potential needs for improvement in each area as you pursue this vision. Leaders or members of a group or organization can use this framework in any number of ways. For example, a leader—alone or with members of the leadership team—may decide to use it as the basis for an informal evaluation of the strengths and shortcomings of the organization, as a stimulant for informal discussion regarding the current state of the group or organization, and/or as a way of identifying areas where future planning and improvement are warranted. A more formal option is to complete a questionnaire which asks for a list of strengths or needed areas of improvement across the seven categories, as a part of a planned retreat or workshop that includes some or all members of the group or organization. Regardless of the approach that is used, the great value of the framework lies in having a comprehensive and proven model for assessing the current state of the group or the organization, and for identifying strengths and possible improvement topics as the group or organization moves forward.

To illustrate how the framework might be used in a retreat or workshop, consider the following description. As discussed, the *Purposes and Plans* category focuses on the development and implementation of group or organizational directions, aspirations, and plans. During a meeting, workshop, or retreat, a leader or member of the group or organization—or an outside facilitator—might structure the session by talking with members of the unit about how they establish, review, and refine their mission, aspirations, values, and broader goals. The leader or facilitator may then guide the discussion into a more detailed exploration of how these directions are translated into priorities and action steps and the ways they may be implemented in a coordinated manner to foster continuing innovation and improvement.

In exploring the themes of each category and assessing how thoroughly the group or organization addresses each of these elements within the category, the discussion within the group may focus on the strengths and areas for improvement. Lists can be made of strengths and improvement needs—which might include minor refinement or major changes. The discussion would continue until all participants felt they had fully discussed the topic and shared thoughts and suggestions related to the category.

Once the discussion has been completed for all seven categories, the list of areas of strength and those in need of improvement would be reviewed and discussed further. Next, multi-voting could be used to rank-order the priority areas for improvement across all categories based on their importance, potential impact, and feasibility.

The four to five most highly ranked priorities for improvement become the focus of attention for the unit and its leadership. Depending on the approach being utilized, the next step may be the formation of committees or teams to draft action plans for projects that would address each of the priority areas. The action plan typically would include a list of what needs to be done—the project mission, a list of key steps, identification of the individuals or roles that should be involved in the project, a proposed team leader, a project timeline, an estimate of resources, and the identification of important outcomes.

The leaders and others within the group or organization would also decide how to move forward with the various improvement projects. Those leading the efforts could be charged with reporting on the progress of each project on a regular basis. As the selected priority projects are completed, the group could return to the list of remaining areas for improvement to determine the next series of projects. Ideally, this process would be undertaken on an annual or semi-annual basis as a way of regularly engaging leaders and members of the group or organization in a process of continuing assessment and improvement as the ideals of excellence are pursued.

© BeeBright/Shutterstock.com

Another less complex approach that can be used for reviewing and reflecting on the current state and needs of a group or an organization would be to use the checklist provided in Appendix B of this book. The checklist includes brief statements that also highlight the major themes in each category. Ratings for each theme may be completed by individuals or through group discussion. As with the option discussed above, a next step would be to determine where the priority improvement needs are, and to develop plans to address these needs.

CONCLUSION

As noted in the opening of this chapter, having a vision of excellence is a significant challenge facing any leader. What are the components of excellence for the group or organization? What needs to be done to move the group or organization forward? What standards exist that can provide guidance, so that the framework a leader adopts has established validity and utility, and is not simply one that emerges by default based on the way things have always been done, or from one's own experience or imagination? The Baldrige framework, adapted in the preceding pages for use with formal groups and organizations, provides one useful model for addressing these challenges. It offers an analytic framework for leaders, a rubric for defining excellence and for assessing the current strengths and limitations of a group or an organization, a method that engages group and organization members in the review and improvement process, and perhaps most importantly, a strategy for cultivating and embedding an attitude and process of continual improvement within the existing culture of any club, group, or organization.

CHAPTER 11

TEAMWORK AND CONFLICT IN ORGANIZATIONS: LEADERSHIP TRENDS AND IMPLICATIONS

RICHARD DOOL

⚠️ **Guiding Questions:**

1) How are teams used in organizations and what are their key characteristics?
2) How does a leader create and lead a high performing team?
3) Is conflict in teams inevitable? If so, how can a leader mitigate conflict?
4) What are the best practices for leading teams and managing conflicts?

In pursuing the aspirations of an organization, as well as in the pursuit of ongoing improvements of various kinds, teams can be an extremely helpful tool. The use of teams is growing in both popularity and importance in organizations of all sizes and purposes as globalization continues to expand the scope, structures, and strategies of organizations, and as technology broadens the array of possibilities for networking and teamwork opportunities. This chapter will discuss both the benefits and challenges associated with teamwork, and will also highlight several strategies that leaders may consider when leading teams and managing conflict in group settings.

TRENDS AND THEIR IMPLICATIONS

The growing relevance of teamwork is supported by research, which indicates that nearly three in four employers rate teamwork and collaboration as "very important" (Queensland University, n.d.). A recent Deloitte (2016) study, entitled Human Capital Trends, also identified a key shift from the traditional functional hierarchy to one characterized as a "network of teams" by General Stanley McChrystal, in his book, *Team of Teams*: "This new mode of organization—a 'network of teams' with a high degree of empowerment, strong communication, and rapid information flow—is now sweeping businesses and governments around the world" (para 2). In the Deloitte survey of more than 7,000 companies, 92% of respondents indicated that the top challenge was "redesigning the way we work," and perhaps not surprisingly, the "rise of teams" was critical in this redesign. As the study noted, "Two major factors are driving change . . . [T]he pressure to make products and services more readily and rapidly available, combined with a desire for greater empowerment among the workforce, is making teams a more natural and productive way to work. Small teams can deliver results faster, engage people better, and stay closer to their mission" (Deloitte, 2016, p. 19).

The growing emphasis on teams and the importance of teamwork is not limited to the workplace, as you have likely engaged in numerous group tasks in classes and co-curricular experiences, as well as in club, group, and community contexts. Given these broader trends in the environment, teamwork is now regarded as an "essential" career skill (National Association of Colleges and Employers, 2016), and according to a Department of Labor report (2015), teamwork was ranked as one of the most important competencies in the workplace.

Despite this trend, many organizations and leaders struggle to develop effective teams. According to a report by the Blanchard Companies (2011), the development of "team building skills" was listed as a key challenge by an average of 50% of the more than 9,000 leaders who participated in the study. The evidence seems clear that the trend of forming, leading, and participating in teams will continue, and the ability to participate in and lead a team will become increasingly important in professional and well as personal settings.

The opportunities for teamwork are expansive, and so too are the challenges associated with leading a team. The Center for Creative Leadership (2016) included "leading a team" in their list of the top six leadership challenges, particularly as it relates to how to instill pride in a team, support the team, lead a large team, and take over a new team. According to Mackin (2012), "Teaming is not easy, nor is it our natural state of being" (para 6). The United States is an individualistic culture, as discussed previously, and teamwork requires a collective orientation. The primary role of a team is to combine resources, competencies, skills, and bandwidth to achieve organizational objectives, and the role of the leader in helping teams accomplish their goals cannot be underestimated. The underlying assumption of a well-functioning team is one of synergy, which is to say that the output of a team will be greater than the sum of each individual's contribution (Boundless, 2017). Or as Lencioni (2007) puts it, "As difficult as teamwork is to measure and achieve, its power cannot be denied. When people come together and set aside their individual needs for the good of the whole, they can accomplish what might have looked impossible on paper" (p. 3).

KEY CHARACTERISTICS OF TEAMS

The Purpose and Formation of Teams

A simple Google search of the "definition of teams" results in over 45 million "hits." There are obviously many different points of view, and they can be somewhat contextual and situational. For the purpose of this chapter, we suggest the following definition of teams, based on Katzenbach and Smith (2005): "A team is a small number of people with complementary skills who are committed to a common purpose, performance goals, and approach for which they hold themselves mutually accountable" (p. 45). Critical to this definition are the concepts of a grouping of people, shared goals, and mutual accountability. One of the main purposes for working in a team is to achieve shared goals that are recognized as important by the larger unit, organization, or community. There are many other reasons for why teams might be formed. Teams can be a powerful tool for influence, whether to address an area needing improvement, clarify an emerging opportunity or threat, deliver a key project or event, implement a new process, or investigate an operational problem and brainstorm a solution. Katzenbach and Smith (1993) summarized three fundamental purposes of teams: teams may run things, teams may make or do things, or teams may recommend things. Such teams are variously referred to as work teams, project teams, cross-functional teams, quality circles, taskforces, problem solving teams, committees, or task teams.

The popularity of teams can be explained by many factors, including the following:

- A lack of focused expertise in a particular area within an organization.
- Growth in the use of flatter, leaner, more networked organizational structures. Teams may better support flatter and leaner structures, with less hierarchy.
- Efforts to promote cross-functional cooperation and mitigate some of the challenges related to "silos" in organizations.
- Encouraging the sharing and integration of diverse perspectives in an efficient manner.
- Building camaraderie and cohesion.
- Creating positive peer pressure to encourage shared ownership of problem solutions.
- To achieve results and complete projects at a rate that is much quicker than would be possible for individuals working alone. When teams of people with complementary skills work together to accomplish shared goals, the team may complete work faster than otherwise would be possible.

The Stages in the Evolution of Teams

Similar to individuals, groups, and organizations, teams typically move through a series of lifecycle stages. Psychologist Bruce Tuckman (1965) characterized the stages of teams as *forming*, *storming*, *norming*, and *performing*, each of which are described in some detail below. In 1977, Tuckman, jointly with Mary Ann Jensen, added a fifth stage: *adjourning*. There will be some contextual and situational differences, but in general, a familiarity with these stages will be useful for leaders in helping them understand and guide the dynamics of a team experience.

Forming.   The first stage of team development is known as the forming stage. The forming stage represents a time often characterized by anxiety and uncertainty as the team begins to come together. In the forming stage, personal relations are characterized by dependence and caution. Team members have a desire for acceptance by peers and a need to know that the team environment is safe. Conflict, controversy, and personal opinions are avoided even though members begin to form impressions of each other and gain an understanding of the teaming process. During this stage, teams tend to gain an understanding of their goals and purpose, their organizational structure, roles and responsibilities, major deliverables, and the resources available for the team to use.

Storming.   A second phase of group development is known as storming. The storming stage is where conflict and competition are most likely to occur, as team members work to reconcile their individual views of the team's goals, purposes, and major tasks with those of the group. During this phase, there is an increased confidence as members begin to address some of the more important issues surrounding the team and its process. Individual members of the team may have to adapt their feelings, ideas, attitudes, and beliefs to suit the team at this stage. Because of concerns or even fears, there will be an increased need for leadership that establishes clear expectations and rules for communication. Although conflicts may or may not surface as team issues, it should be assumed that they do exist. More dominant team members also tend to emerge during the storming stage, while other, less confrontational members may suppress their feelings just as they did in the forming stage. There may be wide swings in members' behavior based on emerging issues of competition or conflicting opinions. Questions surrounding leadership, authority, rules, responsibilities, structure, evaluation criteria and reward systems also may arise during the storming stage.

Norming.   Once a team gains the clarity the members seek, the team can move on to the third stage of development, known as norming. During this phase, the team evolves into a more cohesive unit. In this stage, team members tend to engage in the active acknowledgment of all members' contributions in pursuit of solving team challenges. Members are willing to modify their preconceived ideas or opinions on the basis of the facts and opinions presented by their peers, and they actively solicit and share feedback and opinions among the members of team. Morale might increase as team members actively acknowledge the talents, skills, and experiences that each member brings to the group. Furthermore, as the team becomes highly focused on a common goal, community may be established during this phase and team members may become more flexible, interdependent, and trusting of one another. Leadership tends to be shared during this phase, and cliques often dissolve. Finally, information may flow seamlessly as a result of the sense of security that members experience in this stage.

Performing.   In this stage, people can work independently, in subgroups, or as a total unit. Their roles and authorities dynamically adjust to the changing needs of the team and individuals. This stage is marked by interdependence in personal relations, and problem solving becomes an actively shared process. At this point, the team should be most productive. Team identity is strong, team morale is high, and group loyalty is intense, all driven by the cohesion created around the shared goal. Unfortunately, all teams do not reach this particular stage.

Adjourning.   Tuckman's final stage involves the planned and coordinated conclusion of the team's lifecycle. It usually includes recognition of participation and achievement and an opportunity for members to share insights and perspectives regarding the team experience and process. Adjourning a team can create some apprehension and feelings of separation. The termination of the team involves giving up membership in the team, along with the termination of any social energy that came from the teaming process.

There are practical challenges associated with each stage. The most challenging tend to occur during the "bookend" phases of formation and adjournment. As the leader of a team, it is critical to form and disband a team in an efficient and productive manner that takes into account the needs, goals, and emotions of the members of the group. Too often, teams are formed based on expediency, convenience, or availability. There are certainly time pressures that must be managed, but shortcuts in team formation often lead to downstream team dysfunction. On the other end, it is critical that teams reflect on the process and outcomes before disbanding in order to discuss, collect, and archive for future use any positive and negative lessons learned.

As Bonebright (2010) suggests, Tuckman's team stages model has become the most widely recognized in organizational literature. It has proved useful for practitioners by describing the ways that people work together and has helped team members understand what was happening throughout the teaming process. Recent theories tend to be more broad and nuanced than Tuckman's model, particularly in explaining the complexity of team dynamics in contemporary society, which are not easily represented in a simple model. More recent models provide a more detailed discussion of the many aspects of team dynamics from forming through adjourning. Teams may, in fact, cycle through the various stages in an unpredictable manner depending on contextual factors. These models also examine external factors affecting team development, such as organizational roles, resource allocation, and pressure from external stakeholders. They do not, however, provide the same breadth of application that is offered by the Tuckman model, which is very useful for understanding the lifecycle of teams across a variety of settings.

ATTRIBUTES OF HIGH-PERFORMING TEAMS

© kentoh/Shutterstock.com

As you consider the various teams of which you are a part, you will be able to identify a number of positive behaviors that contribute to the effectiveness of the group, many of which are often cultivated by formal and informal leaders. A number of practitioners (Lencioni, 2007; Ricci & Wiese, 2012) have identified the key attributes of high-performing teams. As you will notice in the summary below in Table 11.1, these are very much interrelated; for example, trust develops through communication and interaction, but open communication also depends on the existence of trust.

Table 11.1. Summary of Attributes of High-Performing Teams

Attitude	The phrase, "There is no 'I' in team" is more than a teaming cliché. It emphasizes the expectation that the team members should have a "team first" attitude and a "we" mentality.
	• Team cohesion arises from the development of a collective mindset and the creation of a team identity.
	• Team cohesion requires members who value the power and synergy of collaboration.
	• Collaboration is what happens when team members look beyond individual needs to the common good that can be served by the group; individuals are able to determine when to put aside personal differences for the common good.
Trust and Respect	Trust is one of the foundational components of successful teams, in much the same way as it is critical to successful leadership. Some suggest that it is, in fact, the most important attribute for team success (Lencioni, 2007), for without trust, it becomes very difficult to build a productive or cohesive team.
	• Members of great teams trust one another on a fundamental, emotional level, and they are comfortable being vulnerable with each other about their weaknesses, mistakes, fears, and behaviors.
	• Respect includes acknowledging other points of view and a willingness to listen and learn from others.
	• Feelings and ideas are more likely to be expressed when there is a high degree of trust in each other and in the team's purpose (Ricci & Wiese, 2012).
	• Building trust requires open communication that allows members to know and understand the values, skills, and behaviors of all team members so that activities can be structured to take advantage of each member's unique expertise and talents.
	• Trust grows and is strengthened as team members demonstrate personal accountability for the tasks they have been assigned, when individuals are honest, willing to self-disclose, and respectful of others.
	• Teams that have built trust are more willing to engage in honest and passionate dialogue concerning key issues and decisions, without filtering their discussions. In the spirit of finding the best answers, discovering the truth, and making great decisions, team members do not hesitate to disagree with, challenge, and question one another (Lencioni, 2007).

Dialogue and Open Communication	Just as in a relationship, open communication is critical—misunderstandings as well as misalignment in expectations, attitudes, and goals have contributed to the failures of many teams. • Unspoken assumptions and issues can be destructive to productive team functioning. Therefore, commitment to open and constructive communication, in which team members share their thoughts, ideas, and feelings with respect to one another, is critical for a healthy communication climate and successful teamwork. • Open communication requires individuals to be inclusive, giving everyone the opportunity to contribute, including introverts (Ricci & Wiese, 2012). • Team members should express thoughts and ideas clearly, directly, honestly, and show appreciation for others as well as the team.
Commitment and Engagement	An effective team has members who are intensely focused on and actively engaged in the work of the team. This includes a commitment to active participation in team processes, such as proactively working on individual activities that contribute to the achievement of shared goals. • Engaged team members enthusiastically add value to other team members' work, and seek to improve themselves and their contributions to team objectives. • Team members do not pursue individual interests at team expense.
Flexibility	Team cohesion is more likely when members are flexible—open to new ideas and diverse viewpoints, and are willing to get to know one another, particularly those with different interests and backgrounds. • This requires understanding the need to balance team cohesion with the need for individual expression without becoming locked into a particular position. • Members must remain flexible enough to adapt as the team's needs change over time.
Constructive Conflict	Teams that engage in unfiltered conflict are able to achieve genuine buy-in around important decisions, even when various members of the team initially disagree—they ensure that all opinions and ideas are put on the table and considered, giving confidence to team members that issues have been fully examined (Lencioni, 2007). • Team members proactively diffuse tension and friction in a relaxed and informal atmosphere (Ricci & Wiese, 2012). • Disagreement is viewed as a good thing when conflicts are managed. Criticism is constructive and is oriented toward problem solving and the removal of obstacles (Ricci & Wiese, 2012).

Accountability and Reliability	Team goals can suffer when individual commitments are not fulfilled. Hence, team members must take their individual assignments seriously, complete individual commitments as scheduled, and be accountable for completing scheduled tasks and meeting commitments in pursuit of team goals. • Team members should be clear on how to work together and how to accomplish tasks; each member must carry his or her own weight and respect the team processes and other members (Ricci & Wiese, 2012). • Teams that commit to decisions and standards of performance do not hesitate to hold one another accountable for adhering to those decisions and standards. • Team members should not rely solely on the team leader as the primary source of accountability—they go directly to their peers (Lencioni, 2007). • The leadership of the team shifts from time to time, as appropriate, to drive results. No individual members are more important than the team—each is equally accountable (Ricci & Wiese, 2012).
Focus on Team Objectives	Teams that commit to team objectives and hold members accountable are very likely to set aside their individual needs and agendas and focus almost exclusively on what is best for the team. • Team members must not give in to the temptation to place their departments, career aspirations, or personal status ahead of the collective results that define team success (Lencioni, 2007). • Everyone should be clear on both team and individual performance goals and know what is expected (Ricci & Wiese, 2012). • All team members must be working toward the same goals.

In summary, effective team members share three common features: they "buy into" and develop a commitment to the team goal(s); they possess the essential skills, experience, and competencies to accomplish their primary tasks; and they have a strong desire to contribute to the team in a collaborative manner. These positive teaming behaviors can contribute to team cohesion—a dynamic process that is reflected in the tendency of a team to stick together and remain united in pursuit of its goals and objectives despite difficulties and setbacks (Oxford, 2016). Even though group cohesion is extremely important, one of the major risks for teams is falling victim to what is typically termed "groupthink," where people withhold their opinions and criticisms if they are different from those of the majority for fear of offending others or alienating themselves (Janis, 1972).

DYSFUNCTIONAL TEAM BEHAVIORS

It is important for students of leadership to understand and recognize not only the attributes of a high-performing team, but also those characteristics and behaviors of dysfunctional teams. As often suggested, it can be as instructive to be familiar with "worst practices" to be avoided, as it is "best practices" to be followed. As you read through the following list of behaviors that may dilute team performance, detract from team effectiveness, and undermine team cohesiveness, consider your previous and current experiences with ineffective teams, whether it be in a professional or personal setting such as the classroom, extracurricular activity, or in a work or community setting. Ironically, it is often easier to recall negative team experiences than it is to recall more positive experiences. Many of these situations are likely to embody one or more of the dysfunctional behaviors described in the following section.

Subversive behavior. There are times when team members may engage in subversive behavior that actively undermines the team. These individuals may deliberately destroy the goodwill among team members or between the team leader and the team for personal gain, ego enhancement, misguided intentions, or distorted motives. Subversive team members may use gossip, whispers, subtle resistance, or even social media to undermine the team or leader and/or to derail the direction of a group.

Negativity. There is a difference between occasional disagreement and consistent negativity. Some people may undermine the team with their negative attitude or display of passive-aggressive behaviors, such as stubbornness, procrastination, sullenness, or resentment when they do not get their way. They are rather consistently gloomy and pessimistic and have a tendency to share this outlook with others. For such individuals, any idea is met with a cynical response that the particular task or project will not work. On the other hand, a member who is critical, but who offers constructive alternatives, can be a major asset to the team.

Blame and excuses. The use of excuses, defensive responses, and blame are common behaviors in dysfunctional teams. In such cases, an individual tends to assume, and often assert, that the fault lies with others, the leader, the process—anyone or anything other than himself or herself. Such individuals may also take credit for the work others completed, claiming achievements that are not rightfully theirs.

Domineering behavior. Sometimes one individual may attempt to dominate the directions of a team. This could be the result of having a a forceful personality, a strong belief in the direction of the organization, or the perception of having greater abilities than others in the group. The team member may bully other members by spreading rumors, making unfounded accusations, yelling, interrupting, undercutting, undervaluing, humiliating, or sabotaging other members of the team. Such actions create an ineffective and unsatisfying work environment. The "I-Know-Everything" attitude has the clear potential to disturb the work flow and relations of the team.

The "five dysfunctions of a team" posited by Lencioni (2007) are listed in Table 11.2. These detrimental behaviors, along with the others noted above, are destructive, can be

Table 11.2. Summary of the "Five Dysfunctions of a Team" (Lencioni, 2007)

Dysfunction #1: Absence of Trust: *Members of teams with an absence of trust...*
- Conceal their weaknesses and mistakes
- Hesitate to ask for help or provide constructive feedback
- Hesitate to offer help outside of their own areas of responsibility
- Jump to conclusions about the intentions and aptitudes of others
- Fail to recognize and tap into one another's skills and experiences
- Hold grudges
- Dread meetings and find reasons to avoid spending time together

Dysfunction #2: Fear of Conflict: *Teams that fear conflict...*
- Have boring meetings
- Create environments where back-channel politics and personal attacks thrive
- Ignore controversial topics that are critical to team success
- Fail to tap into all the opinions and perspectives of team members
- Waste time and energy with posturing and interpersonal risk management

Dysfunction #3: Lack of Commitment: *A team that fails to commit...*
- Creates ambiguity among the team about direction and priorities
- Watches windows of opportunity close due to excessive analysis and unnecessary delay
- Breeds a lack of confidence and fear of failure
- Revisits discussions and decisions again and again
- Encourages second-guessing among team members

Dysfunction #4: Avoidance of Accountability: *A team that avoids accountability...*
- Creates resentment among team members who have different standards of performance
- Encourages mediocrity
- Misses deadlines and key deliverables
- Places an undue burden on the team leader as the sole source of discipline

Dysfunction #5: Inattention to Results: *A team that is not focused on results...*
- Stagnates/fails to grow
- Rarely defeats competitors
- Loses achievement-oriented employees
- Encourages team members to focus on individual goals and careers
- Is easily distracted

contagious, and must therefore be addressed early by the formal or informal leader or fellow team members. Left unaddressed, these behaviors have the potential to erode the very fabric of the organization.

LEADING TEAMS: CHALLENGES AND OPPORTUNITIES

As emphasized throughout this book, leadership is co-constructed between leaders and followers; without followers, leadership is not possible. The same holds true when considering the leadership of teams. Team performance is a consequence of symbiotic relationships between the team leader and other team members. It is quite a challenge to have an effective team without an effective leader. Also, how effective would a team leader be without engaged and effective team members? Team leadership can take on many forms from appointed, elected, or assumed leaders, to sponsors outside of the direct team, or even self-managed teams. In all cases, the influential role of a leader in fostering the support of followers cannot be understated.

Morgeson, DeRue, and Karam (2010) noted that leaders of teams have two essential tasks: (1) aligning the composition of the team with the task environment and ensuring this alignment is preserved over time as the task environment shifts and (2) ensuring the team not only has the requisite knowledge and skills for task performance, but also that the team is composed in such a way that team members form trusting and cooperative relationships. They go on to note that leaders must assure the occurrence of these key actions:

- Define the mission
- Establish expectations and goals
- Structure and plan the team's work
- Train and develop team members
- Provide feedback
- Guide sensemaking, which involves identifying essential environmental events, interpreting these events, and communicating this interpretation to the team

Folkman (2016) noted five dimensions commonly shared by leaders of high-performing teams:

1. *Team leaders inspire more than they drive.*
   The ability of the leader to gain collective buy-in for the team vision helps to determine the success of the team. Leaders in high-performing teams know how to create energy and enthusiasm so that team members feel confident that they are on a worthwhile mission.

2. *Team leaders resolve conflicts and increase cooperation.*
   Conflicts can tear teams apart and leaders need to work to help resolve differences quickly and promote cooperation. This requires a level of maturity in team members. When there is a high degree of trust and accountability among members, disputes can be resolved more easily. Team leaders that emphasize competition over cooperation rarely achieve outstanding results.

3. *Team leaders set stretch goals.*
   Leaders who know how to set stretch goals create an internal drive in the team to accomplish the impossible. Individuals in high-performing teams want to do something extraordinary and accomplish goals no other team can. Extraordinary accomplishments contribute to a feeling of being personally capable and competent, all the while increasing pride and engagement across the group.

4. *Team leaders communicate the vision and direction.*
   Leaders need to "be a broken record" when it comes to reminding team members to stay focused on their vision. High-performing team leaders stay on message, continuously communicate, and keep people focused on the vision, mission, and strategies for accomplishing goals. They keep people informed, up-to-date, and on track.

5. *Team leaders are trusted.*
   Trust is critical to inspiring team members, resolving conflicts, and encouraging a shared vision for the future. A lack of trust has the potential to derail these efforts. Folkman (2016) identifies three basic pillars for building trust—relationships, knowledge and expertise, and consistency. First, we trust people who we like, therefore building positive relationships increases trust. Second, we trust people who have the necessary knowledge and expertise to provide insight, give a right answer, or solve a problem. Third, we trust people who demonstrate consistency and who follow through on their commitments.

The use of teams, in a variety of forms, continues to multiply, but the complexity and speed of change in today's dynamic environment present multiple challenges leaders must confront. As Flint and Hearn (2015) suggest, the challenges associated with forming, deploying, leading, and disbanding teams, particularly as they seek to build trust, overcome conflict, create transparency, entice and sustain engagement, and manage change presents a complex reality for team leaders and also for team members. Additionally, leaders can expect to face difficulties in securing buy-in from team members as well as the larger organization or community in which they are embedded. The lack of patience with or resistance to change among various stakeholder groups may create further barriers. Because the approach a leader takes to develop, manage, and lead a team so significantly impacts morale, productivity, cohesion, and performance, formal and informal leaders must be thoughtful and skilled in guiding the team through each phase of its work.

High-functioning teams are not the result of coincidence. They achieve greater levels of participation and collaboration because their members trust one another, share a strong sense of team identity, and have confidence in their abilities and effectiveness (Ross, 2006). As suggested previously, a leader should aspire to create team cohesion, which is characterized by high morale and is the result of frequent communication, a friendly team environment, loyalty, and team member contributions throughout the decision making process (Daft & Marcic, 2009). Cohesive teams also demonstrate higher levels of motivation, satisfaction, emotional adjustment, and task performance (Carron & Brawley, 2000; Boundless, 2016). Team building depends on the ability to blend the styles and temperaments of different people so that the skills of each can be used to benefit the entire group. The process of team building has the potential to improve communication, reduce conflict, foster greater enthusiasm among team members, and create a sense of shared purpose. Although team building often involves individual members subordinating their personal needs for the good of the team, effective leaders also provide opportunities for individual needs to be satisfied (Oxford Dictionary, 2016).

MANAGING CONFLICT IN TEAMS, GROUPS, AND ORGANIZATIONS

Conflict is a widely defined concept in the scholarly literature. Common definitions view conflict as "a process of social interaction involving struggle over claims to resources, power and status, beliefs, and other preferences and desires" or "disagreements and frictions among the team members generated by perceived incompatibilities or divergence in perceptions, expectations, and opinions" (Geels, 2012, para 2).

Not surprisingly, conflict is common within teams, as it is in groups and organizations more generally, especially during the storming phase of team development. However, conflict is not limited to this stage and can be present or may surface at any point in the team's lifecycle. It can be argued that conflict in teams is inevitable since creative collaboration, which requires risk taking and divergent thinking, is often the team's reason for existence (Kling, 2009). Differences are inevitable when passionate people work together and conflict is arguably a necessary part of teamwork. It is important to note that conflict is neither inherently good nor bad. When conflict is managed well, creativity can be enhanced because ideas are more rigorously debated, however, poorly managed conflict can damage morale, weaken cohesion, and negatively impact team performance.

Weiss and Hughes (2005) found that organizational efforts to improve collaboration often fail because leaders overlook the fact that the root cause of the problem is conflict. Learning to manage conflict effectively makes it possible to benefit from the team's diversity while still working together to achieve common organizational and personal goals.

The Sources of Conflict

© wavebreakmedia/Shutterstock.com

Before you can appropriately deal with conflict as a leader, it is necessary to first determine which type of conflict the members of your team face. The process of resolution and the steps necessary will depend upon this diagnosis. Thompson (2011) examined three conflict types that are most relevant to team settings: task, relationship, and process.

The first type of conflict is *task conflict* or cognitive conflict. This type of conflict is not about interpersonal issues, but rather involves plans, ideas, or projects—the work the group has been formed to undertake.

The second type of conflict examined is *relationship conflict*. Relationship conflict is also referred to as affective, emotional, or type A conflict (Thompson, 2011). Relationship conflict is interpersonal in nature, and often involves issues related to ego, gender, culture, or title. Relationship conflict is the area that most managers and leaders struggle with and often times try to avoid. This type of conflict has the greatest long-term negative effects on teams. Because of this, it is imperative that leaders work to effectively address relationship conflicts, recognize them early, and have the necessary tools to help members reach resolution (Geels, 2012). If ignored, relationship conflict interferes with the ability of team members to give full effort on the completion of a task because of time spent worrying about threats, struggling to leverage power, and reconciling relationship issues (Geels, 2012).

The third type of conflict that is mentioned by Thompson (2011) is *process conflict*. Like task conflict, process conflict does not have the interpersonal aspects that are found in relationship conflict. The difference between process conflict and task conflict is that this form of conflict does not relate to the task itself, but rather in the approach to handling the task. Process conflict is the result of disagreement regarding individual responsibilities and the process by which goals are achieved across the group. (Geels, 2012).

In addition to the three sources of conflict noted above, you might also consider the following reasons for team conflict presented by Witt (2015): conflict over positions, strategies or opinions, goal misalignment, mistrust, uneven communication, personality clashes, power issues, and personal agendas. Other common sources of conflict in teams include: lack of role clarity, inconsistent leadership behaviors, differences in priorities conflicting time pressures, different opinions or approaches, or gaps in skills.

APPROACHES TO MANAGING CONFLICT

The Thomas-Kilmann model (1974) was designed by psychologists, Kenneth Thomas and Ralph Kilmann, to illustrate the options leaders or team members have when handling conflict. This widely used model explores two dimensions of conflict (1) assertiveness, the extent to which the person attempts to satisfy his own concerns, and (2) cooperativeness, the extent to which the person attempts to satisfy the other person's concerns. From these two dimensions, five approaches were developed for leaders and teams to manage or mitigate conflict: *Competing, Accommodating, Avoiding, Collaborating,* and *Compromising*. Leaders may be capable of effectively deploying all five conflict-handling modes. It should not be assumed that one approach is necessarily correct. The best choice is both situationally and contextually dependent. You might consult Table 11.3 when determining the best strategy for responding to conflict in a team or group of which you are a part.

If not handled properly, conflict alienates people and inhibits creativity and productivity, and can cause members of the team to become insecure about their value to the team or organization. As Myatt (2012) explains:

> Leadership and conflict go hand-in-hand. Leadership is a full-contact sport, and if you cannot or will not address conflict in a healthy, productive fashion, you should not be in a leadership role. From my perspective, the issues surrounding conflict resolution can be best summed-up by adhering to the following ethos; ***"Don't fear conflict; embrace it—it's your job."*** While you can try and avoid conflict (bad idea), you cannot escape conflict. The fact of the matter is conflict in groups and organizations is unavoidable. The ability to recognize conflict, understand the nature of

conflict, and to be able to bring swift and just resolution to conflict will serve you well as a leader—the inability to do so may well be your downfall. (para 1)

When faced with conflict, it is worth heeding this advice, as well as Berman's (n.d.) recommendations: stay calm, listen to understand, accentuate the positive, use tact, address the issue not the person, avoid the blame game, focus on progress and the future versus the past, and brainstorm and leverage areas of agreement.

Table 11.3. Leadership Approaches to Managing Conflict

Approach	Characteristics	Common Uses
Competing	Competing is assertive and uncooperative, a power-oriented mode. When competing, an individual pursues his or her own concerns at the other person's expense, using whatever power seems appropriate to win his or her position. Competing might mean standing up for your rights, defending a position you believe is correct, or simply trying to win.	• When quick, decisive action is vital—for example, in an emergency • On important issues when unpopular courses of action need to be implemented—for example, cost cutting, enforcing unpopular rules, discipline • On issues vital to group or organization welfare when you know you are right • When you need to protect yourself from people who take advantage of non-competitive behavior
Collaborating	Collaborating is both assertive and cooperative. When collaborating, an individual attempts to work with the other person to find a solution that fully satisfies the concerns of both. It involves digging into an issue to identify the underlying concerns of the two individuals to find an alternative that meets both sets of concerns. Collaborating might take the form of exploring a disagreement to learn from each other's insights, resolving some condition that would otherwise have individuals competing for resources, or confronting and trying to find a creative solution to an interpersonal problem.	• When you need to find an integrative solution and the concerns of both parties are too important to be compromised • When your objective is to learn and you wish to test your assumptions and understand others' views • When you want to merge insights from people with different perspectives on a problem • When you want to gain commitment by incorporating others' concerns into a consensual decision • When you need to work through hard feelings that have been interfering with a relationship

Approach	Characteristics	Common Uses
Compromising	Compromising involves both assertiveness and cooperativeness. When compromising, the objective is to find an expedient, mutually-acceptable solution that partially satisfies both parties. This approach addresses an issue more directly than avoiding, but does not explore it in as much depth as collaborating. Compromising might mean splitting the difference, exchanging concessions, or seeking a quick middle-ground position.	• When goals are moderately important but not worth the effort or the potential disruption involved in using more assertive modes • When two opponents with equal power are strongly committed to mutually exclusive goals—as in labor-management bargaining • When you want to achieve a temporary settlement for a complex issue • When you need to arrive at an expedient solution under time pressure • As a backup mode when collaboration or competition fails
Avoiding	Avoiding is unassertive and uncooperative. When avoiding, an individual does not immediately pursue his or her own concerns or those of the other person. He or she does not address the conflict. Avoiding might take the form of diplomatically sidestepping an issue, postponing an issue until a better time, or simply withdrawing from a threatening situation.	• When an issue is unimportant or when other, more important issues are pressing • When you perceive no chance of satisfying your concerns—for example, when you have low power or you are frustrated by something that would be very difficult to change • When the potential costs of confronting a conflict outweigh the benefits of its resolution • When you need to let people cool down—to reduce tensions to a productive level and to regain perspective and composure • When gathering more information outweighs the advantages of an immediate decision • When others can resolve the issue more effectively • When the issue seems tangential or symptomatic of another, more basic issue

Approach	Characteristics	Common Uses
Accommodating	Accommodating is unassertive and cooperative—the opposite of competing. When accommodating, an individual neglects his or her own concerns to satisfy the concerns of the other person; there is an element of self-sacrifice in this mode. Accommodating might take the form of selfless generosity or charity, obeying another person's order when you would prefer not to, or yielding to another's point of view.	• When you realize that you are wrong—to allow a better solution to be considered, to learn from others, and to show that you are reasonable • When the issue is much more important to the other person than it is to you—to satisfy the needs of others and as a goodwill gesture to help maintain a cooperative relationship • When you want to build up social credits for later issues that are important to you • When you are outmatched and losing and more competition would only damage your cause • When preserving harmony and avoiding disruption are especially important • When you want to help your employees develop by allowing them to experiment and learn from their mistakes

CONCLUSION

© Roman Samborskyi/Shutterstock.com

The use of teams across organizations of all kinds has much momentum and will not likely decline in the foreseeable future. Participation in and the leadership of teams is both complex and multi-faceted; and as discussed in this chapter, as teams grow in importance and occurrence, so too will the inevitable conflicts and need for competent leaders to lead conflict in productive, rather than destructive, directions. The reaction to conflict by team members, along with the leader's ability to manage or mitigate conflict, will have a significant impact on team morale, productivity, cohesion, and performance, as you have likely experienced in your own personal and professional lives. As a current or future leader of a team, it is important that you recognize the dynamics of team behaviors, and cultivate in the team the many positive and effective characteristics noted throughout this chapter. The more that conflict can be framed as a constructive process, the more likely it will become a natural part of the team's DNA and a source of positive energy. Across groups, organizations, and communities, effective leadership can help teams to pursue aspirations, develop high quality solutions to problems, address improvement needs, and foster cohesiveness and a shared sense of identity.

CHAPTER 12

THE DIGITAL WORLD: LEADERSHIP IN AN INTERCONNECTED SOCIETY

> **⚠ Guiding Questions:**
>
> 1) What is the digital world?
> 2) What factors associated with the digital environment have contributed to changes in the study and practice of leadership?
> 3) How do leaders best connect with others in a digital world?
> 4) How can one manage his or her identity as a leader in this digital environment?

In 1962, J.C.R. Licklider, the first head of the computer research program at the Defense Advanced Research Projects Agency (DARPA), dreamed of a "Galactic Network," a globally interconnected set of computers that would enable anyone from anywhere to share data and programs. Today, his dream is a reality with more than three and a half billion computers connected worldwide.[1] In 1962, one could hardly imagine the transformations in communication and interaction that would emerge as a consequence of his dream.[2] The pervasiveness of new electronic communication technologies has ushered in a multitude of changes in our personal and professional lives. Digital platforms such as Facebook, Twitter, LinkedIn, YouTube, Slack, and a myriad of others offer new ways for leaders and followers to engage. Digital communication in the form of electronic signals has changed the delivery and exchange of information, documents, and images, replacing the need for individuals engaged in coordinated activities to be located in the same physical setting.

1 The number of Internet users worldwide as of June 30, 2016 is 3,675,824,813 as reported by Internet World Stats: Usage and Population Statics (http://www.internetworldstats.com/stats.htm)
2 For further information on the history of the Internet visit, http://internetsociety.org.

Historically, a majority of personally and professionally oriented group and organizational activities took place among individuals who were located within a shared physical setting. Most routine financial transactions, for example, took place in a bank; a board of directors meeting took place in a room with all parties attending in-person; the sale of products and services typically required sales workers and customers to be present in the same physical facility—a store of one kind or another—at a common point in time. Access to books and other information sources generally required a trip to the library or bookstore; the purchase of entertainment media required an in-store purchase of tapes or records; the development of photographic images required film to be physically transported to a vendor who could develop and print the film, and then be picked up by the customer. Analogous changes have occurred in healthcare, journalism, education, and many other areas of our personal and professional lives, so much so that physical barriers no longer inhibit how we work, play, and communicate. In fact, one of the authors recently received a message from an auto dealer indicating that his car had emailed the dealer to say it (the car) needed service.

© bestfoto77/Shutterstock.com

Over the past 25 years, changes in digital media as well as the widespread diffusion of information and communication technologies (ICTs) have transformed nearly all aspects of our lives—how we do business, how we make purchases, and how we communicate, organize, and interact in dyadic, group, and organizational settings. At the same time, these technologies have transformed the nature of work, the definition of "workplace," and of particular relevance for our purposes in this book, the way individuals interact within groups and organizations. These changes have many implications for the conduct of personal and professional activities in general, and for leadership practices in particular.

LEADERSHIP AND FOLLOWERSHIP IN A DIGITAL WORLD

© Vasin Lee/Shutterstock.com

Throughout this book, we have presented a number of leadership principles and theories and highlighted the ways in which leader-follower relationships are shaped by social influence. Many of the perspectives and examples envisioned leaders and followers interacting through face-to-face or written communication within traditional group or organizational structures. Changes in these structures, in the way work is organized, and where it is transacted—co-located versus virtual—present new challenges, but also new opportunities for leaders. This is especially the case for current college students and young professionals who are familiar and comfortable with these new ways of interacting, and who are well-positioned to embrace the role of technology in current and future leadership situations.

As you may recall from Chapter 3, initial conceptualizations of leadership communication portrayed communication as a linear approach whereby the leader delivered a message to followers with some desired result. Within formal groups and organizations, this often comes in the form of "top-down" communication based on the hierarchy of an organization. Newer technologies add greater flexibility to the ways in which leaders communicate. Because of the many affordances of digital technologies, communication is not limited to top-down interactions from those in higher to lower authority roles; rather, these technologies permit, facilitate, and encourage multi-directional communication across the unit, group, or organization. Moreover, new communication technologies and tools make it easier for leaders to reach a broad array of external stakeholders, and vice versa. Referring back to our earlier descriptions of the leader-follower relationship, the differences and distinctions between leaders and followers are often unclear and messy as a result of new technologies.

FACTORS CONTRIBUTING TO THE EVOLUTION OF THE LEADERSHIP ROLE

Three factors have had a notable impact on leadership in our digital age: (1) globalization; (2) the rise of the knowledge worker, and (3) the relentless pursuit and pace of innovation. We provide a brief overview of each of these factors below, along with specific ways of thinking about these factors in relation to your own personal and professional leadership pursuits.

Globalization.   As discussed in the previous chapter, the term "globalization," introduced into popular business discourse in 1983 by Harvard Business School professor Theodore Levitt,[3] refers to the increasing connections across people, technologies, governments, and economic markets worldwide.[4] Although technologies have always played a role in the development of global markets (e.g., consider how the telegraph, telephones, televisions, and airplanes were instrumental in moving information, ideas, and people around the world), ICTs have contributed exponentially to the pace and degree to which globalization has spread. *The New York Times* journalist, Thomas Friedman (2007) describes how globalization was driven primarily by countries and governments seeking to increase power and territory from the years 1492 to 1800, how it was driven by multinational organizations seeking to increase market share from the years 1800 to 2000, and how it is driven today by technologies that enable individuals to collaborate and compete globally. Friedman refers to this new trend as "Globalization 3.0," which is made possible through an array of technologies that enable a vast, integrated web of people, groups, organizations, and governments to connect.

Globalization impacts leadership in a number of important ways. First, organizations increasingly draw from a highly diverse workforce distributed across the globe to access specific skills and expertise. You might consider internships or careers across the world, or perhaps you may have experienced opportunities to study abroad or conduct service internationally. Given the opportunities for global collaborations and the challenges posed by cross-cultural interactions—challenges made all the more complex as leader-follower interactions become mediated by a wide range of constantly evolving ICTs—leadership requires the development, cultivation, and facilitation of trusting and productive relationships with workers from a wide range of cultural, educational, and technical backgrounds. For a more in-depth discussion of leadership and culture, see Chapter 5.

An additional leadership challenge posed by globalization is that the norms for communication and interaction may vary considerably across globally distributed organizations. As suggested by existing research, leaders can find that what works in one location might not necessarily work in others. For example, Dewhurst, Harris, and

3 See Feder (2006) for more information on Theodore Levitt.
4 See Friedman (1999) for a discussion on globalization.

Heywood (2011) found that leaders in global organizations, as compared to those in locally situated organizations, encounter greater difficulty establishing and engaging followers around a shared vision, coordinating and controlling work processes, and encouraging innovation and learning—for what works in one location does not necessarily translate to another.

Finally, organizations are increasingly relying on virtual teams—teams composed of individuals who interact via technology rather than through face-to-face interaction. Virtual teams are dynamic in that they allow for fluid participation from individuals who often represent multiple countries and cultures and who bring a range of expertise and experiences. These teams are often geographically dispersed and rely on a variety of synchronous and asynchronous ICTs to accomplish shared goals (Gibson & Gibbs, 2006). Synchronous and asynchronous technologies enable different modes of communication. For example, synchronous technologies such as the telephone or video conferencing enable the simultaneous sending and receiving of messages, allowing users to respond instantaneously and clarify misunderstandings quickly. In contrast, messages shared through asynchronous technologies such as email or online discussion forums are separated by longer response times. This can be beneficial because it allows users to spend time carefully reading messages and crafting responses, which can be especially useful for global teams composed of members who speak multiple different languages and require more time for translating thoughts and ideas, but it also leads to delays in interaction.

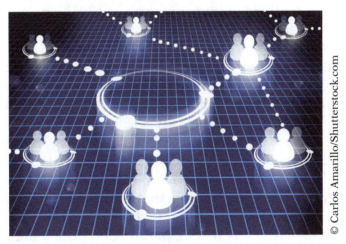

© Carlos Amarillo/Shutterstock.com

The practice of leading virtual teams differs from leading co-located teams in a number of ways. According to Malhotra, Majchrzak, and Rosen (2007), leaders of virtual teams must rely primarily on ICTs to:

1. establish and maintain trust among members by developing and promoting communication norms around technologies
2. understand, appreciate, and leverage diversity, such as pairing diverse team members for different tasks to reduce out-group bias

3. manage virtual work processes and maintain engagement through the use of electronic discussion threads, instant messaging, and announcements
4. monitor team progress by observing patterns of interaction occurring through asynchronous and synchronous technologies
5. promote virtual team contributions, which are often less visible, to others in the organization
6. ensure that team members benefit from their participation on the team by promoting professional development opportunities.

Take a moment to consider the ways in which you and members of a group may have used technology in a professional context or for a group course assignment. What specific aspects of this project did you find most rewarding and most challenging? These challenges are made all the more complex for members of virtual teams who might never meet in person and who use digital technology to complete all aspects of their work assignments.

The knowledge economy.   In 1969, management scholar Peter Drucker described the "knowledge economy" as a future state where the need for knowledge would intensify and where the demand for ideas and information would overtake the demand for goods and services.[5] Consistent with his prediction, in the 1980s, the need for knowledge workers began to outpace demand for routine production jobs such as assembly line or warehouse workers, and non-routine administrative jobs such as filing clerks and bookkeepers. Over the past 30 years, the number of jobs requiring knowledge work has doubled, rising from approximately 28.5 million in 1983 to 60.1 million in 2016 (Zumbrun, 2016). Knowledge work differs from production or administrative work, because workers often deal with complex issues that require creative, non-linear thinking and the development of innovative solutions (Reinhardt, Schmidt, Sloep, & Drachsler, 2011). As management scholar Thomas Davenport (2005) notes, "Knowledge workers think for a living. They live by their wits—any heavy lifting on the job is intellectual, not physical. They solve problems, they understand and meet the needs of customers, they make decisions, and they collaborate and communicate with other people in the course of doing their own work" (pp. 10–11). In a knowledge economy, the development and maintenance of relationships is increasingly important to facilitate the sharing of reliable and useful information. Individuals are more likely to seek information from and provide information to those they have had a reliable exchange with in the past (Powell, 1990). These factors, as well as others, reflect a need to rethink top-down organizing, management, and leadership practices developed in the 20th century, for as Drucker (1999) notes, the productivity of knowledge workers is an imperative for the 21st century.

Whereas the primary objective of leadership and management beginning with the industrial age was to drive efficiency and productivity, in a knowledge economy,

---

5 See Drucker (1999) for a discussion on the knowledge economy and knowledge workers.

leadership takes precedence over management (Drucker, 2001). Leading knowledge workers often requires giving individuals greater autonomy, promoting continuous learning, and providing workers with an inspiring and motivating vision (Wartzman, 2014). As referenced earlier in this text, leaders need to intentionally provide followers with opportunities for mastery, autonomy, and purpose, all of which are critical for motivating the knowledge worker in this contemporary environment (Pink, 2009).

© Ahmet Misirligul/Shutterstock.com

Innovation.   The global marketplace of knowledge workers supported by the widespread network of highly flexible ICTs has contributed to an increasing pace of innovation. Innovation is viewed as a competitive advantage for business and a potential asset for groups and organizations attempting to address community-based and other complex problems, such as climate change, poverty, and disease. Innovations can range from policy reforms, novel organizational structures, redesigned methods or processes, creative products or services, or new market opportunities (Nohria & Gulati, 1996). Examples of innovations include products such as the Apple Watch, services such as Amazon Prime Delivery, or business models such as Uber and Airbnb, which are part of a growing "sharing economy."

Despite the timeworn myth that innovations are derived from the activities of a lone genius, organizations today recognize that breakthroughs often result from networks and teams of individuals with specialized knowledge and expertise. Increasingly, businesses are connecting with individuals beyond organizational boundaries to access new ideas and knowledge in order to innovate. Open innovation, a term popularized by scholar Henry Chesbrough (2011), describes this process as a "more distributed, more participatory, more decentralized approach to innovation, based on the observed fact that useful knowledge today is widely distributed, and no company, no matter how capable or how big, could innovate effectively on its own" (para 2). Successful open innovation therefore requires collaboration with a diverse network of suppliers, customers, partners, and communities. Collaborative tools such as social enterprise networks have the potential to facilitate and accelerate open innovation processes, but our understanding of how to best lead such initiatives has not kept pace with these changes. For all of these reasons, as a student of leadership, we would encourage you to embrace innovative thinking and to consider the ways in which you might help your current and future organizations to think more creatively about solutions for addressing the problems, challenges, and limitations that plague institutions, communities, and societies.

LEADERSHIP PERSPECTIVES FOR A NEW AGE

© GaudiLab/Shutterstock.com

Many of the leadership concepts, definitions, and models presented in this book emerged before the rise of the knowledge worker and before the age of open innovation. Early models of leadership can be traced as far back as the mid-1800s with the "great man theory" of leadership, followed by leadership trait and style models in the 1940s and 50s, and others reviewed in Chapter 2. However, while these theories have been foundational in their significance, some scholars have suggested that we lack an understanding of the ways in which advanced ICTs have impacted leadership in the contemporary age—noting that our theories and research have not changed much with the times (Avolio, Sosik, Kahai, & Baker, 2014).

On the other hand, some experts argue that the fundamentals of leadership remain the same. According to James Champy (2010), "Real leadership requires relationships and personal engagement. Nothing I see in technology has yet to replace these qualities. I believe that technology will enable new business models, but not 'new leadership'" (para 8). This idea, however, is challenged by Avolio and Kahai (2003), who suggest that technology has brought about "a fundamental change in the way leaders and followers relate to each other within organizations and between organizations" (p. 15). The perspective we advance here is that because organizations are complex interconnected systems, the introduction of new technologies can create a cascading set of changes. There is a recursive relationship between leadership and technologies whereby technologies transform leadership, and leadership transforms how technologies are implemented and adopted (Avolio & Kahai, 2003; Katz & Kahn, 1978). While it is true that social influence as well as the development and maintenance of relationships remain fundamental to our understanding of leadership, there is no question that interaction and influence are increasingly happening from a distance and are mediated through a wide array of evolving ICTs. We encourage you to think about your perspective in this debate. In what ways does technology change the nature of leadership—and followership—if at all?

LEADERSHIP FROM A DISTANCE

© Den Rise/Shutterstock.com

Leadership from a distance is not a new phenomenon. Consider, for example, the vast Roman Empire extending from the western shores of the Atlantic to North Africa under the rule of Emperor Augustus. Throughout history, the governance of widely dispersed people depended on the availability of communication technologies, for example papyrus and parchment, to mediate communication between leaders and followers (Innis, 2007). As noted throughout this text, communication is fundamental for leadership effectiveness, and this is certainly the case in our consideration of leadership and followership from a distance.

Computer mediated communication.   Early writing on computer-mediated communication (CMC) focused less on social influence processes and more on technological features, advancing the idea that communication mediated solely through ICTs was seen as inferior to the ideal standard of face-to-face communication. Scholars proposed that because ICTs lacked the same visual, auditory, and social cues that accompany most face-to-face interactions, "social presence" was diminished and it thus impacted how "real" communication partners appeared to each other (Culnan & Markus, 1987). Various forms of mediated communication—such as those utilizing text only, audio only, or video with audio—were categorized along a continuum from low social presence to high social presence according to their capacity to transmit multiple cues (Short, Williams, & Christie, 1976). This idea was extended to information processing in organizations in the writing on media richness theory (Daft, Lengel, & Treviño, 1987; Daft & Weick, 1984), which suggests the richness of media—the number of visual and auditory cues available—influences an individual's ability to understand and reduce uncertainty.

Today, these early theories are considered *technologically deterministic* in that they advance a view of ICTs as having greater power than the individual to shape social interaction. Research in the 1990s positioned other factors as influential in the development of personable relationships and social influence through ICTs, such as the length of time individuals communicate as well as the potential for engaging in future interactions (Walther, 1992, 1994; Walther & Burgoon, 1992).

More recent scholarship advances an "affordance" approach, which abandons technological determinism in suggesting that technologies create possibilities for communicative activities, but that these possibilities are ultimately shaped by the individual's preferences and goals (Aakhus & Jackson, 2005; Gibson, 1979; Hutchby, 2001; Norman, 1999). This perspective, while acknowledging the potential influence of technology, reminds us that both leaders and followers can influence the quality and effectiveness of their interactions. For example, although email and text messaging afford the opportunity to connect with others from any place and at any time, a leader who respects an employee's personal time on the weekend can wait to send a message on Monday. We encourage you to reflect on how you use ICTs to interact with others both as a leader as well as a follower, or as a member of a team, and consider how your actions shape others' perceptions of your leadership style.

Leadership online.   As discussed throughout the book, both formal and informal leadership are sources of social influence that play out in both personal and professional settings. A number of behaviors have been linked to informal leadership online. For example in technical communities and general online discussion groups, such as Google Groups, individuals who interact with many other members, participate by posting, responding, and answering questions, share knowledge, express concern for others, and use a broad vocabulary, are perceived by others to be leaders (Faraj, Kudaravalli, & Wasko, 2015; Huffaker, 2010).

Blogs and podcasts also provide opportunities for individuals to demonstrate leadership. Individuals without formal positional power use these platforms to become opinion leaders—informal leaders, demonstrating their expertise by sharing their knowledge on particular topics. These opinion leaders share information, stimulate conversation, frame issues, and even influence how a particular topic is understood and discussed through their online activities (Huffaker, 2010). Recalling these topics from Chapter 3, in essence, opinion leaders play a critical role in setting an agenda and framing discussion topics for others to explore.

Opinion leadership is an option open to both formal and informal leaders based on their ability to influence the issues that others think about and how they think about these issues. For example, educator Christopher Nesi is an opinion leader and subject expert on technology's role in education. Nesi is passionate about the topic and demonstrates his expertise through his weekly podcast and blog, *House of #EdTech*, which focuses on how technology is changing classrooms and schools. He shares his own experiences as well as the experiences of teachers, education leaders, and content creators to drive change in teaching practices across his profession. Through his ability to combine his personal and professional interests and to use ICTs to reach others with similar interests, he has become a widely respected opinion leader.

LEADERSHIP AND SOCIAL MEDIA

© Rawpixel.com/Shutterstock.com

Organizations and groups today increasingly rely on social media to connect members internally across enterprise social networks such as SharePoint, Slack, and Microsoft OneDrive, as well as through external commercial platforms such as Facebook, Twitter, and LinkedIn to connect with various stakeholder groups such as community members, customers, employees, investors, and suppliers. What make social media distinct from other ICTs such as websites and blogs is the ability of users to construct a public or semi-public profile and make connections with others visible (boyd & Ellison, 2007). This enables like-minded individuals to connect and more easily engage in collective action. Social media have particular affordances that shape leader-follower interactions differently than other ICTs such as email, blogs, or text messages. For example, social media make user activities visible to a broader audience, content is persistent in that it remains available in its original form, its asynchronous properties enable careful editing and crafting of messages, and the connections between and among users and content is visible to others (Treem & Leonardi, 2012).

Social media provide additional opportunities for leaders to engage followers at both the personal level and the strategic or organizational level. However, as will be discussed later it can also present significant challenges. Deiser and Newton (2013) identify six aspects of social-media-literate leadership. At the personal level, this includes producing creative and authentic content, building and sustaining networks of followers, and strategically engaging with content by sharing, linking, and liking content to create context for followers. At the organizational level, leaders can play an active role in supporting and shaping social media usage for followers, integrating vertical and horizontal communication to engage multiple stakeholders, as well as staying up-to-date on the emerging technology trends and innovations. Today, leaders, employees, members of work groups or teams, customers, suppliers, regulators, and institutions are increasingly linked through networks of technologies supported by a variety of platforms, allowing individuals and collectives to interact around social, cultural, and civic matters deemed meaningful (boyd, 2010).

Leaders also use social media to generate new ideas and encourage innovation. For example, crowd sourcing is an online strategy that consists of soliciting new ideas from users, getting input from customers, and accessing social media to take the pulse of stakeholders. Leaders also use social media to create context for followers and build common ground, both of which are made more difficult when there are few opportunities to connect directly. The development of "mutual knowledge" leads to shared interpretations of a situation, which enable groups to act together more productively (Cramton, 2001). But when people have limited opportunities to share a physical context, the development of mutual knowledge or common ground becomes more difficult, presenting a challenge for leadership and followership at a distance. Social media, when used effectively, provide opportunities for leaders to communicate a compelling vision, motivate followers, and create shared context that supports their vision. People like Richard Branson with nearly 10 million followers, and Bill Gates with over 33 million followers, use Twitter to share information and stories that shape their professional identity and inspire followers.

The Challenges of Social Media

Important to note here is how the lines between personal and professional are blurred in the online world, what scholars Marwick and boyd (2010) call *context collapse*. Social media combine elements of interpersonal communication with broadcast media, merging multiple social contexts into a singular amorphous audience, creating potential challenges for the way you present yourself online. Context collapse is the merging of multiple audiences—family, friends, business associates, customers, employees, and employers—into one "imagined audience." In face-to-face interactions, social influence occurs in part through the presentation of a carefully tailored image based on the person or persons you are physically with at the moment. The image you present to a friend is likely different from how you would present yourself to your boss (Goffman, 1959). Social media complicate strategic self-presentation, in part because multiple audiences can view your identity and messages, and at times, not in the original context for which it was intended. This creates new challenges for leaders who in the past could strategically tailor their identity and messages for particular audiences. A message to shareholders could be vastly different from, or even contradict, messages to employees because the audiences were separated. The context collapse created by social media has increased the need for leaders to be consistent across multiple audiences.

Social media enable the unrestricted sharing of information, ideas, and opinions in a single message that can reach millions in a short period of time. While social media can serve as useful tools for leaders to engage followers, they are also ripe for various leadership challenges. The ways in which information is disseminated and shared can have both positive and negative implications due in part to the various affordances—visibility, editability, persistence, and association—previously described. Gone are the days when leaders could carefully control all aspects of a message, their public persona, or the organization's image in the marketplace. Today, social media enhance the ability of distributed stakeholders to quickly organize and express their support or dislike of a leader, group, or organization's actions.

Take for example the case of a university in the United States where an internal crisis played out across multiple social media platforms including Twitter, Facebook, and YouTube. The crisis began when the university board asked the president for her resignation, stating that her approach to leadership was not in line with the university's long-term strategy. Two days later, the president accepted the board's decision and submitted her letter of resignation. However, the president's inclusive and participative leadership style that she cultivated in her first two years in office enabled her to build strong relationships with stakeholders, a fact overlooked by board members who wrongfully assumed their final decision would be respected (Gruber, Smerek, Thomas-Hunt, & James, 2015). Instead, various stakeholder groups including the faculty senate, students, alumni, major donors, as well as other interested parties swiftly expressed disapproval of the board's decision, demonstrating their support for the president. Many took to social media to vent their frustrations and share their opinions. Days later, a graduate student started a Facebook group in support of the president and an alumnus launched an online petition that gathered more than 5,000 signatures in support of the president. Supporters also created and posted videos to YouTube and tweeted, creating a global trending topic on Twitter[6] (Gruber et al., 2015). When a local news outlet obtained emails related to the story, editors shared information about the case on Twitter as well. Some tweets were subsequently picked up and further amplified

6 You can read more about the case involving the University of Virginia here: http://uvamagazine.org/articles/how_social_media_helped_change_university_history

by the national media outlets. The overwhelming support for the president fueled by social media and amplified in traditional mass media resulted in the reinstatement of the president weeks later. While the board embraced a traditional hierarchical approach to leadership, assuming they alone held leadership decision making power and control over communication with stakeholders, the stakeholders in this situation believed that their input should be considered and they took to social media to make sure their voices were heard and their influence was realized.

This particular case illustrates how social media contributed to strengthening the relationship between a leader and her followers. Her formal influence as a leader was shaped throughout her tenure as president, and her informal influence was manifested through support from influential followers via social media. As discussed previously, social media afford *visibility* of user activities and this contributed to the emergence of a community of supporters as well as the dissemination of the story to larger media outlets. The use of hashtags increased the visibility of content shared across social media and triggered attention to content for additional social media users. As we discussed previously, social networks also afford *association*, and in this case revealed the visible connections among users and content.

Research has shown that ICTs can facilitate the development of social capital, defined as the potential to access resources—either tangible such as a financial support or intangible such as the backing for a new idea—that is realized through relationships with others (Coleman, 1988). Social media enable individuals to connect, sustain existing relationships, and aid in the building of community (Quan-Haase, Wellman, Witte, & Hampton, 2002; Treem & Leonardi, 2012; Wellman et al., 2003). The university president's social capital, and thus influence, grew as the members of online communities increased in numbers.

Social media can be a "double-edged sword" with regard to both personal and professional life; while they can help a leader build social capital and influence, social media can lead to its destruction as well. Consider the case of the New York politician whose leadership was undermined through his actions that played out across social media. This former congressman and once mayoral candidate had been considered a savvy user of social media, stating that Twitter was part of his morning routine. He gave great attention to his followers' posts and sometimes incorporated their suggestions (Parker, 2011, May 30). However, his situation changed dramatically when he posted a link to a private and embarrassing photo of himself to his public Twitter account. Although he quickly removed the post, a Twitter user had captured screen shots of the original post, which were subsequently shared on an oppositional website. The story quickly spread from Twitter to broadcast media. As the story unfolded, the congressman was compelled to admit in a press conference that he intended to send the photo as a private message to a young woman who was not his spouse. Although the congressman had a once promising political career, the Twitter scandal cost him public support and the support of congressional leaders, who called for his resignation (Fouhy, 2011). He publically apologized and resigned his position—an act that can be viewed as acknowledging what amounts to bankruptcy of much of the social capital and personal and professional influence he had developed as a leader (Hernandez, 2011).

In thinking about the affordances of social media we previously discussed, this case illustrates aspects of *editability,* the degree to which users can shape content and *persistence*, the degree to which content remains available and in its original form. Although the content was editable in that it could be deleted, the persistence afforded by the digital content resulted in the capture and dissemination of the embarrassing message. Clearly, it was the congressman's unethical behavior that led to his demise, but the affordances of social media contributed to the amplification of his actions.

MANAGING YOUR ONLINE IDENTITY AS A LEADER

© Dragon Images/Shutterstock.com

The case of the congressman highlights a challenge faced by all participants on social media today. The ubiquity of social media require us to be thoughtful in both online and offline contexts, as well as consistent across our thoughts, beliefs, and actions.

As you pursue your leadership aspirations, we suggest that you take seriously how you use social media to present yourself to others. Author and keynote speaker, Erik Qualman, highlights the many challenges we face in managing our digital identities today. Both *What Happens on Campus Stays on YouTube* and *What Happens in Vegas Stays on YouTube* offer students and professionals useful guidelines. We recommend consulting these guides for tips on creating and managing your online identity. Additionally, Table 12.1 outlines a simple framework you can use as you develop both a personal and professional social media persona.

Table 12.1. Developing a Personal and Professional Social Media Persona (Dutta, 2010)

	Personal and Private	Professional and Private	Personal and Public	Professional and Public
Audience	Family and Friends	Work Colleagues	Society	Professional Peers
Message	I want to keep in touch with you	I am a team player, and I want to collaborate with you	I am passionate about ideas and I want to share them with you	I am competent and growing professionally
Goals	• Show commitment to your relationships • Strengthen ties • Stay up-to-date on changes in your network	• Enhance your image at work • Collaborate to boost productivity and effectiveness • Leverage colleagues input	• Become known for your ideas • Find new outlets for your passions • Leverage other's ideas and viewpoints	• Build your recognition • Find new opportunities and show commitment • Boost industry knowledge and develop yourself
Sample Tools	Facebook, Instagram	Slack, Yammer	Blogs, YouTube, Twitter	LinkedIn, Twitter, sector-specific communities

CONCLUSION

This chapter offered an overview of the research and writing on various topics associated with the digital world, highlighted the need for a re-examination of popular leadership theories and practices in light of the changes in technology, described the challenges and opportunities posed by these changes in technology and changes in our virtual environment, and addressed various strategies for creating and managing your identity in a digital world.

It is worth concluding this chapter by revisiting some of the leadership competencies presented in Chapter 2 and the ways in which digital leadership intersects with these competency areas. First, with regard to analytic competencies, understanding stakeholder groups as well as having the knowledge of and skill to use technologies to support your leadership efforts is critical for effectively communicating with followers in groups, organizations, and communities. Second, developing your personal competencies in general and clearly articulating the character, personal values, and ethics you want to present to online audiences will serve you well and will help you develop a thoughtful and consistent identity both online and offline. Third, knowing the technological capabilities of your organization as well as understanding the particulars of information or knowledge management and the practices of boundary spanning can help your group or organization expand its sphere of influence. Finally, knowing how to communicate credibly in order to build trust with others, to understand the processes of influence and persuasion in online environments, and to use technology in order to listen to and learn from stakeholders are all critical skills that will be important to cultivate to be effective within the domain of digital leadership.

EPILOGUE

Attempting to fully address a topic as complex and nuanced as leadership in one book is a daunting task. Our aim for this book was to provide you with a coherent and accessible point of entry into the study of leadership; and it is our hope that you feel inclined to explore the topic further through reading, reflection, and experimentation. The communication approach offered in this book is one of many possible lenses through which to understand the dynamics of social influence in personal and professional settings. We believe that an exploration of leadership without consideration of communication is incomplete, and we remain confident that the communication-centered perspective can complement, enhance, and enrich the many other perspectives offered by other textbooks and resources on the subject of leadership.

It is difficult to ignore the fact that the topic of leadership is one of the most contemplated themes in contemporary life, one that continues to attract a great deal of attention from scholars, practitioners, and pundits. This is due, in part, to a perceived deficit in leadership across groups, organizations, and societies—and the tendency to attribute these deficits to problems in leadership. This perception is heightened by the well-publicized incidents of our time—ethical lapses in corporate entities, the collapse of non-profits and educational institutions during an era of great change and transformation, the growth of global terroristic activity, and the growing mistrust of leadership across sectors, including government (Pew Research Center, 2015). We, too, feel compelled to write about, teach, and develop tools and concepts associated with leadership because of this growing need for effective and ethical leaders who maintain a commitment to the highest standards of leadership, and are also responsive to their followers. We have seen far too many leaders in the private and public sectors model behaviors that are inconsistent with "best practices" and incongruent with the needs, expectations, and desires of their followers. We have also observed too many college students pursue leadership positions for the wrong reasons, and we have learned of many individuals who failed to meet their full potential as leaders due to an inadequate understanding of communication, culture, and planning. This book is one response to these many challenges and difficulties. At the same time, from our perspective, many of the contemporary problems attributed to leaders, can also be thought about as problems in followership.

We remain hopeful about the promise of leadership, particularly its potential in contributing in positive ways to the many group, organizational, community, national, and international challenges we face. Consider the ways in which formal and informal opportunities for social influence may be used for good. In response to the 2013 bombings near the finish line of the Boston Marathon, we witnessed individuals running *toward* the site of the explosions to be of assistance to the victims. In response to bullying and social injustices, we have seen individuals stand up and help to give voice to those most marginalized in our society. In teams and organizations of all kinds, we have observed many formal and informal leaders helping others to reach their full potential. These examples speak to the importance of leadership—leadership that is guided by a clear sense of purpose, and responsive to the needs of followers and the challenges of the situation at hand. As leaders speak, behave, and engage with others, any number of messages—intended or unintended—can have great significance to others who are prepared, able, and ready to receive them. Recalling one of the axioms of communication discussed in Chapter 3, we cannot *not* communicate—and this is of particular importance to individuals who pursue leadership.

Leadership is not simple—and simple answers for how best to lead may be misleading. We attempted to address the complexity and nuances of leadership in this book, while also distilling some of the clear concepts, insights, and themes found in the voluminous literature and research on this topic. Referring back to an opening theme of this text, our goal in this book was to provide a GPS to help readers navigate through the complexity associated with the topic in order to develop an integrated and useful understanding of leadership dynamics. As you pursue opportunities for social influence, it is our hope that the concepts and models highlighted in this book are useful as you attempt to enhance, enrich, and inspire the lives of those who seek your leadership.

REFERENCES

Aakhus, M. & Jackson, S. (2005). Technology, interaction, and design. In K. Fitch & B. Sanders (Eds.), *Handbook of language and social interaction* (pp. 411–433). Mahwah, NJ: Lawrence Erlbaum.

Acton, J. E. E. D. A. & Himmelfarb, G. (1948). *Essays on freedom and power*. Boston: Beacon Press.

Aiken, C. & Keller, S. (2009, April). The irrational side of change management. *The McKinsey Quarterly, 2*. Retrieved August 6, 2017 from http://www.mckinsey.com/insights/organization/the_irrational_side_of_change_management

Allison, E. (2011/2012). The resilient leader. *Educational Leadership, 69*(4), 79–82.

Alvesson, M. & Sveningsson, S. (2003). The great disappearing act: Difficulties in doing "leadership." *Leadership Quarterly, 14*(3), 359–381.

Ashforth, B. E. & Mael, F. (1989). Social identity theory and the organization. *The Academy of Management Review, 14*(1), 20–39.

Association for Talent Development. (2015). *2015 State of the industry*. Retrieved December 8, 2015, from https://www.td.org/Publications/Research-Reports/2015/2015-State-of-the-Industry

Avolio, B. J. & Gardner, W. L. (2005). Authentic leadership development: Getting to the root of positive forms of leadership. *Leadership Quarterly, 16*(3), 315–338.

Avolio, B. J. (1999). *Full leadership development: Building the vital forces in organizations*. Thousand Oaks, CA: Sage.

Avolio, B. J. & Kahai, S. S. (2003). Adding the "E" to E-leadership: How it may impact your leadership. *Organizational Dynamics, 31*(4), 325–338.

Avolio, B. J. & Locke, E. (2002). Contrasting different philosophies of leader motivation—Altruism versus egoism. *Leadership Quarterly, 13*(2), 169–191.

Avolio, B. J., Sosik, J. J., Kahai, S. S., & Baker, B. (2014). E-leadership: Re-examining transformations in leadership source and transmission. *The Leadership Quarterly, 25*(1), 105–131.

Axley, S. (1984). Managerial and organizational communication in terms of the conduit metaphor. *Academy of Management Review, 9*(3), 428–437.

Ayyad, C. & Andersen, T. (2000). Long-term efficacy of dietary treatment of obesity: A systematic review of studies published between 1931 and 1999. *Obesity Reviews, 1*(2), 113–119.

Baird, J. E. & Weinberg, S. B. (1981). *Group communication: The essence of synergy* (2nd ed.). Dubuque, IO: Wm. C. Brown Company Publishers.

Baldelomar, R. (2016, July 21). Where is the line between ethical and legal? *Forbes* (online). Retrieved August 6, 2017 from http://www.forbes.com/sites/raquelbaldelomar/2016/07/21/where-is-the-line-between-what-is-ethical-and-legal/print/

Baldrige National Quality Program. (2017). www.nist.gov/baldrige/

Barge, J. K. (2007). The practice of systemic leadership. *OD Practitioner, 39*(1), 10–14.

Barge, J. K. (2014). Pivotal leadership and the art of conversation. *Leadership, 10*(1), 56–78

Barge, J. K. & Fairhurst, G. (2008). Living leadership: A systemic constructionist approach. *Leadership Quarterly, 4*(3), 227–251.

Barker, R. A. (1997). How can we train leaders if we do not know what leadership is? *Human Relations, 50*(4), 343–362.

Bass, B. (1990). *Bass & Stogdill's handbook of leadership: A survey of theory and research*. New York: Free Press.

Bass, B. & Avolio, B. J. (1994). *Improving organizational effectiveness through transformational leadership*. Thousand Oaks, CA: Sage.

Bass, B. M. & Steidlmeier, P. (1999). Ethics, character, and authentic transformational leadership behavior. *The Leadership Quarterly, 10*(2), 181–217.

Bateson, G. (1972). *Steps to an ecology of the mind*. New York: Ballentine.

Beebe, S. A., Beebe, S. J., & Ivy, D. K. (2013). *Communication: Principles for a lifetime* (5th ed.). New York: Pearson.

Bennis, W. (2003). *On becoming a leader*. New York: Perseus.

Bennis, W. (2007). The challenges of leadership in the modern world. *American Psychologist, 62*(1), 2–5.

Bennis, W. & Nanus, B. (1985). *Leaders: The strategies for taking charge*. New York: Harper & Row.

Berger, P. L. & Luckmann, T. (1966). *The social construction of reality*. New York: Doubleday Anchor.

Berman, L. (n.d.). 13 Tools for resolving conflict in the workplace, with customers and in life. *Mediate.com*. Retrieved February 26, 2017, from http://www.mediate.com/articles/bermanlj3.cfm

Biro, M. M. (2014, May 4). 4 ways to be a more resilient leader. *Forbes*. Retrieved June 5, 2017, from https://www.forbes.com/sites/meghanbiro/2014/05/04/4-ways-to-be-a-more-resilient-leader/#523ec62f3853

Blake, R. R. & McCanse, A. A. (1991). *Leadership dilemmas: Grid solutions*. Houston, TX: Gulf Publishing.

Blanchard, K. (2011). *Corporate issues survey: A nine-year look at the key issues organizations and leaders face*. Retrieved February 8, 2017, from http://www.kenblanchard.com/getattachment/Leading-Research/Research/2011-Corporate-Issues-Survey/Blanchard_2011_Corporate_Issues_Survey.pdf

Blanchard, K. (2016). The role of teams in organizations. *Boundless Management*. Retrieved February 21, 2017, from https://www.boundless.com/management/textbooks/boundless-management-textbook/groups-teams-and-teamwork-6/defining-teams-and-teamwork-51/the-role-of-teams-in-organizations-257-6411/

Bonebright, D. (2010). 40 years of storming: A historical review of Tuckman's model of small group development. *Human Resource Development International. 13*(1), 111–120.

Boyatzis, R. E. & McKee, A. (2005). *Resonant leadership: Renewing yourself and connecting with others through mindfulness, hope, and compassion*. Boston, MA: Harvard Business School Press.

boyd, d. m. (2010). Social network sites as networked publics: Affordances, dynamics, and implications. In Z. Papacharissi (Ed.), *A networked self: Identity, community, and culture on social network sites* (pp. 39–58): New York, NY: Routledge.

boyd, d. m. & Ellison, N. B. (2007). Social network sites: Definition, history, and scholarship. *Journal of Computer-Mediated Communication 13*(1), 210–230.

Bratton, W. J. (1998). *Turnaround: How America's top cop reversed the crime epidemic*. New York, NY: Random House.

Bratton, W. J. (1999). Great expectations: How higher expectations for police departments can lead to a decrease in crime. In R. H. Langworthy (Ed.), *Measuring what matters: Proceedings from the Policing Research Institute meetings* (pp. 11–26). Washington, DC: National Institute of Justice.

Brown, L. & Posner, B. (2001). Exploring the relationship between learning and leadership. *Leadership & Organizational Development Journal, 22*(6), 274–280.

Brown, M. E. & Mitchell, M. L. (2010). Ethical and unethical leadership: Exploring new avenues for future research. *Business Ethics Quarterly, 20*(4), 583–616.

Brown, M. E. & Treviño, L. K. (2006). Ethical leadership: A review and future directions. *The Leadership Quarterly, 17*(6), 595–616.

Brown, M. E., Treviño, L. K., & Harrison, D. A. (2005). Ethical leadership: A social learning perspective for construct development and testing. *Organizational Behavior and Human Decision Processes, 97*(2), 117–134.

Brown University (2013). *A framework for making ethical decisions*. Retrieved August 6, 2017 from https://www.brown.edu/academics/science-and-technology-studies/framework-making-ethical-decisions

Burns, J. M. (1978). *Leadership.* New York: Harper & Row.

Burton, T. I. (2014, January 22). Why are American colleges obsessed with 'leadership'? *The Atlantic*. Retrieved June 5, 2017, from https://www.theatlantic.com/education/archive/2014/01/why-are-american-colleges-obsessed-with-leadership/283253/

Cain, S. (2013). *Quiet: The power of introverts in a world that can't stop talking*. New York: Broadway Books.

Calhoun, C. (1995). Standing for something. *The Journal of Philosophy, XCII*(5), 235–260.

Cambridge Dictionary Online. (2017). Definition of "values". Retrieved from http://dictionary.cambridge.org/us/dictionary/english/values

Carron, A. V. & Brawley, L. R. (2000). Cohesion: Conceptual and measurement issues. *Small Group Research, 31*(1), 89–106.

Carton, A. M. & Cummings, J. N. (2012). A theory of subgroups in work teams. *Academy of Management Review, 37*(3), 441–470.

Carucci, R. (2016). Why ethical people make unethical choices. *Harvard Business Review* (online). Retrieved August 6, 2017 from https://hbr.org/2016/12/why-ethical-people-make-unethical-choices

Center for Creative Leadership (2016). *The top 6 leadership challenges*. Retrieved February 8, 2017, from https://www.ccl.org/articles/leading-effectively-articles/top-6-leadership-challenges/

Center for Ethical Leadership. (n.d.). *Self-guided core values assessment*. Retrieved June 6, 2017, from http://www.ethicalleadership.org/uploads/2/6/2/6/26265761/1.4_core_values_exercise.pdf

Champy, J. A. (2010, May 4). Does leadership change in a web 2.0 world? *Harvard Business Review* (online). Retrieved June 6, 2017 from https://hbr.org/2010/05/does-leadership-change-in-a-we.html

Cherniss, C. (2010). Emotional intelligence: Toward clarification of a concept. *Industrial and Organizational Psychology, 3*(3), 110–126.

Chesbrough, H. W. (2011). Everything you need to know about open innovation. Retrieved June 6, 2017 from https://www.forbes.com/sites/henrychesbrough/2011/03/21/everything-you-need-to-know-about-open-innovation/#6e35637075f4

Christensen, C. M., Allworth, J., & Dillon, K. (2012). *How will you measure your life?* New York: Harper Business.

Cohn, D. (2016, June 23). It's official: Minority babies are the majority among the nation's infants, but only just. Retrieved August 6, 2017 from http://www.pewresearch.org/fact-tank/2016/06/23/its-official-minority-babies-are-the-majority-among-the-nations-infants-but-only-just/

Coleman, J. S. (1988). Social capital in the creation of human capital. Supplement: *Organizations and Institutions: Sociological and Economic Approaches to the Analysis of Social Structure, 94*, S95–S120.

Covey, S. (2013). *The 7 habits of highly effective people: Powerful lessons in personal change*. New York: Simon & Schuster.

Cramton, C. D. (2001). The mutual knowledge problem and its consequences for dispersed collaboration. *Organization Science, 12*(3), 346–371.

Cullen, J. B., Parboteeah, K. P., & Bart, V. (2003). The effects of ethical climates on organizational commitment: A two-study analysis. *Journal of Business Ethics, 46*(2), 127–141.

Culnan, M. J. & Markus, M. L. (1987). Information technologies. In F. M. Jablin, L. L. Putnam, K. H. Roberts, & L. W. Porter (Eds.), Handbook of organizational communication: An interdisciplinary perspective (pp. 420–433). Newbury Park, CA: Sage Publications.

Daft, R. L. & Weick, K. E. (1984). Toward a model of organizations as interpretation systems. *Academy of Management Review, 9*(2), 284–295.

Daft, R. L., Lengel, R. H., & Treviño, L. K. (1987). Message equivocality, media selection, and manager performance: Implications for information systems. *MIS Quarterly, 11*(3), 355–366.

Daft, R. & Marcic, D. (2009). *Understanding management (6th ed.)*. Mason, Ohio: South-Western Cengage Learning.

Davenport, T. H. (2005). *Thinking for a living: How to get better performance and results from knowledge workers*. Boston, MA: Harvard Business School Press.

Day, D. V. (2001). Leadership development: A review in context. *Leadership Quarterly, 11*(4), 581–613.

Day, D. V., Zaccaro, S. J., & Halpin, S. M. (Eds.). (2004). *Leader development for transforming organizations: Growing leaders for tomorrow*. Mahwah, NJ: Erlbaum.

De Lisi, R. & Lawrence, S. (2017). Formal and informal leadership in higher education: Roles and responsibilities. In B. D. Ruben, R. De Lisi, & R. A. Gigliotti. (2017). *A guide for leaders in higher education: Core concepts, competencies, and tools*. Sterling, VA: Stylus.

Deiser, R., & Newton, S. (2013, February). Six social-media skills every leader needs. *McKinsey Quarterly*. Retrieved February 9, 2017 from http://www.mckinsey.com/industries/high-tech/our-insights/six-social-media-skills-every-leader-needs

DeLapp, K. M. (n.d.). Metaethics. In J. Fieser & B. Dowden (Eds.), *The Internet encyclopedia of philosophy*. Retrieved August 6, 2017 from http://www.iep.utm.edu/metaethi/

Deloitte (2016). *Human capital trends*. Retrieved February 9, 2017, from https://dupress.deloitte.com/dup-us-en/focus/human-capital-trends/2016/organizational-models-network-of-teams.html

Department of Labor (2015). Competency models—Communicating industry's education and training needs. *Employment and Training Administration (ETA)*. Retrieved February 10, 2017, from https://www.careeronestop.org/competencymodel/pyramid_definition.aspx#tier9

DePree, M. (1993). *Leadership jazz*. New York: Dell.

DePree, M. (1999). My mentors' leadership lessons. In F. Hasselbein & P. M. Cohen (Eds.), *Leader to leader* (pp. 15–24). San Francisco: Jossey-Bass.

Dervin, B. (1992). From the mind's eye of the user: the sense-making qualitative-quantitative methodology. In J. D. Glazier & R. R. Powerll (Eds.), *Qualitative research in information management* (pp. 61–84). Englewood, CO: Libraries Unlimited.

Dervin, B. (1998). Sense-making theory and practice: An overview of user interests in knowledge seeking and use. *Journal of Knowledge Management, 2*(2), 36–46.

Dewey, J. (1933). *How we think*. Boston, MA: D. C. Heath & Co.

Dewhurst, M., Harris, J., & Heywood, S. (2011). Understanding your 'globalization penalty'. *McKinsey Quarterly*, 1–4.

Diaz-Saenz, H. R. (2011). Transformational leadership. In A. Bryman, D. Collinson, K. Grint, B. Jackson & M. Uhl-Bien (Eds.), *The SAGE handbook of leadership* (pp. 299–310). Thousand Oaks, CA: Sage.

Dichotomies. (2017). In *Merriam Webster Online*, Retrieved July 6, 2017, from https://www.merriam-webster.com/dictionary/dichotomy

Dool, R. (2007). Managing conflict in student team assignments, *eLearn Magazine of the Association for Computing Machinery (ACM)*.

Drucker, P. F. (1999). Knowledge-worker productivity: The biggest challenge. *California Management Review, 41*(2), 79–94.

Drucker, P. F. (2001). *Management challenges for the 21st century*. New York: Harper Business.

DuBrin, A. W. (2004). *Leadership*. New York: Houghton Mifflin.

Dutta, S. (2010). Managing yourself: What's your personal social media strategy? *Harvard Business Review, 88*(11), 127–130.

Eckerson, W. W. (2005). *Performance dashboards: Measuring, monitoring, and managing your business*. New York, NY: Wiley.

Entman, R. M. (1993). Framing: Toward clarification of a paradigm. *Journal of Communication, 43*(4), 51–58.

Fairhurst, G. T. (2007). *Discursive leadership: In conversation with leadership psychology*. Thousand Oaks, CA: Sage.

Fairhurst, G. T. (2009). Considering context in discursive leadership research. *Human Relations, 62*(11), 1607–1633.

Fairhurst, G. T. & Connaughton, S. L. (2014a). Leadership: A communicative perspective. *Leadership, 10*(7), 7–35.

Fairhurst, G. T. & Connaughton, S. L. (2014b). Leadership communication. In L. L. Putnam & D. K. Mumby (Eds.), *The SAGE handbook of organizational communication: Advances in theory, research, and method* (pp. 401–423). Thousand Oaks, CA: Sage.

Fairhurst, G. T. & Sarr, R. (1996). *The art of framing: Managing the language of leadership*. San Francisco: Jossey-Bass.

Falbe, C. M. & Yukl, G. (1992). Consequences to managers of using single influence tactics and combinations of tactics. *Academy of Management, 35*(3), 638–653.

Faraj, S., Kudaravalli, S., & Wasko, M. (2015). Leading collaboration in online communities. *MIS Quarterly, 39*(2), 393–412.

Feder, B. J. (2006). Theodore Levitt, 81, who coined the term 'globalization', is dead. *The New York Times*. Retrieved July 6, 2017, from http://www.nytimes.com/2006/07/06/business/06levitt.html

Fiedler, F. E. (1967). *A theory of leadership effectiveness*. New York: McGraw-Hill.

Fieser, J. (n.d.). Ethics. In J. Fieser & B. Dowden (Eds.), *The Internet encyclopedia of philosophy*. Retrieved August 6, 2017 from http://www.iep.utm.edu/ethics/

Flannery, B. L., & May, D. R. (2000). Environmental ethical decision making in the U. S. metal-finishing industry. *Academy of Management, 43*(4), 642–662.

Flint, M. & Hearn, E. (2015), *Leading teams: 10 challenges and 10 solutions*. London: FT Publishing. Pearson.

Folkman, J. (2016). 5 ways to build a high performance team. *Forbes* (online). Retrieved August 6, 2017 from https://www.forbes.com/sites/joefolkman/2016/04/13/are-you-on-the-team-from-hell-5-ways-to-create-a-high-performance-team/#344598d87ee2.

Fouhy, B. (2011). US congressman admits lying about lewd photo. *AP English Worldstream—English*.

French, J. R., Jr., & Raven, B. H. (1959). The bases of social power. In C. Dorwin (Ed.), *Studies in social power* (pp. 150–167). Oxford, England: University of Michigan Press.

Friedman, T. L. (1999). *The Lexus and the olive tree*. London: Harper Collins.

Friedman, T. L. (2007). *The world is flat: A brief history of the twenty-first century*. New York: Picador/Farrar, Straus and Giroux.

Fulmer, R. (1997). The evolving paradigm of leadership development. *Organizational Dynamics, 25*(4), 59–72.

Fury, A. (2016). Fickle fashion New Year's resolutions—easier than the gym. *Independent*. Retrieved June 6, 2017, from http://www.independent.co.uk/life-style/fashion/features/fickle-fashion-new-years-resolutions-easier-than-the-gym-a6796601.html

Galsworth, G. (2016, December 7). The biggest obstacle: Leadership versus managing. *Visual Thinking*. Retrieved June 2, 2017, from http://visualworkplace.com/2016/12/the-biggest-obstacle-leading-versus-managing/

Gao, G. (2016, July 7). *Biggest share of whites in U.S. are Boomers, but for minority groups it's Millennials or younger*. Retrieved August 6, 2017, from http://www.pewresearch.org/fact-tank/2016/07/07/biggest-share-of-whites-in-u-s-are-boomers-but-for-minority-groups-its-millennials-or-younger/

Geels, T. (2012). *Conflict in teams—Promoting leadership understanding*. Retrieved February 25, 2017 from http://www.mandtsystem.com/blog/conflict-in-teams-promoting-leadership-understanding/

Geertz, C. (1973). *The interpretation of cultures: Selected essays*. New York: Basic Books.

George, B. (2003). *Authentic leadership: Rediscovering the secrets to creating lasting value*. San Francisco: Jossey-Bass.

Gibson, C. B., & Gibbs, J. (2006). Unpacking the concept of virtuality: The effects of geographic dispersion, electronic dependence, dynamic structure, and national diversity on team innovation. *Administrative Science Quarterly, 51*(3), 451–495.

Gibson, J. J. (1979). The theory of affordances. In J. J. Gieseking & W. Mangold (Eds.), (pp. 56–60). New York: Routledge.

Gignac, G. (2010). On a nomenclature for emotional intelligence research. *Industrial and Organizational Psychology, 3*(2), 131–135.

Gill, R. (2012). *Theory and practice of leadership* (2nd ed.). Thousand Oaks, CA: Sage.

Gioia, D. A., & Chittipeddi, K. (1991). Sensemaking and sensegiving in strategic change initiation. *Strategic Management Journal, 12*(6), 433–448.

Goffman, E. (1959). *The presentation of self in everyday life*. New York: Anchor Books.

Goleman, D. P. (1998). *Working with emotional intelligence*. New York: Bantam Books.

Goleman, D. P. (2004). What makes a leader? *Harvard Business Review, 82*(1), 82–91.

Goleman, D. P. (1995). *Emotional intelligence: Why it can matter more than IQ for character, health and lifelong Achievement*. New York: Bantam Books.

Government Dashboards. (2017). Retrieved July 6, 2017, from https://www.idashboards.com/solutions/government-dashboards/

Graen, G. B. & Canedo, J. (2016). The new workplace leadership development. *Oxford Bibliography on Management*. New York: Oxford University Press.

Graen, G. B., & Uhl-Bien, M. (1995). The relationship-based approach to leadership: Development of LMX theory of leadership over 25 years: Applying a multi-level, multi-domain perspective. *Leadership Quarterly, 6*(2), 219–247.

Greenleaf, R. (1977). *Servant leadership*. Mahwah, NJ: Paulist Press.

Gresseth, G. K. (1975). The Gilgamesh Epic and Homer. *The Classical Journal, 70*(4), 1–18.

Grint, K. (2001). *The arts of leadership*. Oxford: Oxford University Press.

Grint, K. (2010). *Leadership: A very short introduction*. Oxford: Oxford University Press.

Gronn, P. (1983). Talk as the work: The accomplishment of school administration. *Administrative Science Quarterly, 28*(1), 1–21.

Gruber, D. A., Smerek, R. E., Thomas-Hunt, M. C., & James, E. H. (2015). The real-time power of Twitter: Crisis management and leadership in an age of social media. *Business Horizons*, *58*(2), 163–172.

Hackman, J. R. (1992). Group influences on individuals in organizations. In M. D. Dunnette & L. M. Hough (Eds.), *Handbook of industrial and organizational psychology* (Vol. 3, pp. 199–268). Palo Alto, CA: Consulting Psychologists Press.

Hackman, M. Z. & Johnson, C. E. (2013). *Leadership: A communication perspective* (6th ed.). Long Grove, IL: Waveland Press.

Hartley (Ed.), *Readings in social psychology* (pp. 459–473). New York, NY: Henry Heath & Co.

Healthcare Dashboards. (2017). Retrieved July 6, 2017 from https://www.idashboards.com/solutions/healthcare-dashboards/

Hendricks, D. (2014). Personal mission statements of 13 CEOs and lessons you need to learn. *Forbes*. Retrieved June 5, 2017, from https://www.forbes.com/sites/drewhendricks/2014/11/10/personal-mission-statement-of-14-ceos-and-lessons-you-need-to-learn/#e2d72861e5ea

Hernandez, R. (2011, June 16). Weiner resigns in chaotic final scene. *The New York Times*. Retrieved August 6, 2017, from http://www.nytimes.com/2011/06/17/nyregion/anthony-d-weiner-tells-friends-he-will-resign.html?_r=1

Hersey, P. (1984). *The situational leader*. Escondido, CA: Center for Leadership Studies.

Hersey, P. & Blanchard, K. H. (1969). Life-cycle theory of leadership. *Training and Development Journal, 23*(5), 26–34.

Herzberg, F. (1959). *The motivation to work*. New York: Wiley.

Hobman, E. & Bordia, P. (2006). The role of team identification in the dissimilarity–conflict relationship. *Group Processes & Intergroup Relations*, *9*(4), 483–507.

Hofstede, G. H. (2001). *Culture's consequences: Comparing values, behaviors, institutions, and organizations across nations* (2nd ed.). Thousand Oaks, CA: Sage.

Hofstede, G. H., Hofstede, G. J., & Minkov, M. (2010). *Cultures and organizations: Software of the mind* (Vol. 3). New York: McGraw-Hill.

Hofstede, G. J. & Minkov, M. (2010). *Cultures and organizations: Software of the mind* (3rd ed.). New York: McGraw-Hill.

Hogg, M. A. & Terry, D. J. (2000). Social identity and self categorization processes in organizational contexts. *Academy of Management*, *25*(1), 121–140.

House, R. J. & Mitchell, T. R. (1974). Path-goal theory of leadership. *Journal of Contemporary Business, 3*(4), 81–98.

House, R. J. (1971). A path-goal theory of leader effectiveness. *Administrative Science Quarterly, 16*(3), 321–339.

House, R. J. (1996). Path-goal theory of leadership: Lessons, legacy, and a reformulated theory. *The Leadership Quarterly, 7*(3), 323–352.

Huffaker, D. (2010). Dimensions of leadership and social influence in online communities. *Human Communication Research*, *36*(4), 593–617.

Hutchby, I. (2001). Technologies, texts and affordances. *Sociology*, *35*(2), 441–456.

Ibarra, H. (2015a). The authenticity paradox. *Harvard Business Review*, January–February, 52–59.

Ibarra, H. (2015b). *Act like a leader, think like a leader.* Boston, MA: Harvard Business Review Press.

Innis, H. A. (2007). *Empire and communications.* Toronto, CA: Dundurn Press.

Jackson, P. (n.d.). *Goodreads quotes.* Retrieved February 21, 2017, from http://www.goodreads.com/quotes/527132-the-strength-of-the-team-is-each-individual-member-the

Jago, A. G. (1982). Leadership: Perspectives in theory and research. *Management Science, 28*(3), 315–336.

Janis, I. L. (1972). *Victims of Groupthink.* New York: Houghton Mifflin.

Jehn, K. A., Northcraft, G. B., & Neale, M. A. (1999). Why differences make a difference: A field study of diversity, conflict, and performance in workgroups. *Administrative Science Quarterly, 44*(4), 741–763.

Johnson, C. E. (2015). *Organizational ethics: A practical approach.* Thousand Oaks, CA: Sage.

Johnson-Cramer, M. E. (2008). Authority. In R. W. Kolb (Ed.), *Encyclopedia of business ethics and society.* Thousand Oaks: Sage.

Kanter, R. M. (1983). *The change masters: Innovation & entrepreneurship in the American corporation.* New York: Simon & Schuster.

Katz, D., & Kahn, R. L. (1978). *The social psychology of organizations.* New York: John WIley & Sons.

Katz, R. L. (1955). Skills of an effective administrator. *Harvard Business Review, 33*(1), 33–42.

Katzenbach, J. & Smith, D. (1993). The discipline of teams. Cambridge, MA: Harvard Business Press.

Katzenbach, J. & Smith, D. (2005). *The wisdom of teams. Creating the high-performance organization.* Boston: Harvard Business Press.

Kegan, R. (1982). *The evolving self: Problem and process in human development.* Cambridge, MA: Harvard University Press.

Kennedy, F.A. & Nilson, L.B. (2008). *Successful strategies for teams: Team member handbook.* South Carolina: Office of Teaching Effectiveness and Innovation, Clemson University.

Kingdon, J. W. (1984). *Agendas, alternatives, and public policies.* Boston: Little, Brown.

Kling, J. (2009). Tension in teams. *Harvard Management Update, 14*(1), 3–4. Retrieved February 3, 2009, from https://hbr.org/2009/01/tension-in-teams.html

Kotter, J. P. (1996). *Leading change.* Boston, MA: Harvard Business Press.

Kotter, J. P. (2012). Accelerate! *Harvard Business Review, 90*(11), 45–58.

Kouzes, J. M. (n.d.). *Composing your personal credo.* Retrieved June 6, 2017, from http://www.leadershipchallenge.com/resource/composing-your-personal-credo.aspx

Kouzes, J. M. & Posner, B. Z. (2011). *Credibility: How leaders gain and lose it, why people demand it.* San Francisco, CA: Jossey-Bass.

Kraemer, H. M. J. (2011). The only true leadership is values-based leadership. *Forbes* (online). Retrieved from http://www.forbes.com/2011/04/26/values-based-leadership.html

Kreider, T. (2012, June 30). The 'busy' trap. *The New York Times.* Retrieved June 1, 2017, from https://opinionator.blogs.nytimes.com/2012/06/30/the-busy-trap/?_r=0

Lawrence, S. E. & De Lisi, R. (2017). Formal and informal leadership in higher education: Roles and responsibilities. In B. D. Ruben, R. De Lisi, & R. A. Gigliotti, *A guide for leaders in higher education: Core concepts, competencies, and tools* (pp. 146-163). Sterling, VA: Stylus Publishing.

Lencioni, P. (2005). *The five dysfunctions of a team*. San Francisco: Jossey-Bass.

Lencioni, P. (2007). *Overcoming the five dysfunctions of a team: A field guide for leaders, managers, and facilitators*. New Jersey: Wiley.

Lewin, K. (1952). *Group decision and social change*. In G. W. Swanson, T. M. Newcomb, & E. L (Eds.). *Readings in social psychology* (pp. 459–473). New York, NY: Henry Heath & Co.

Lewin, K., Lippitt, R., & White, R. K. (1939). Patterns of aggressive behavior in experimentally created "social climates". *Journal of Social Psychology, 10*(2), 271–299.

Lewis, L. K. (2011). *Organizational change: Creating change through strategic communication*. Malden, MA: Wiley-Blackwell.

Liden, R. C., Wayne, S. J., Zhao, H., & Henderson, D. (2008). Servant leadership: Development of a multidimensional measure and multi-level assessment. *Leadership Quarterly, 19*(2), 161–177.

Lovelace, K., Shapiro, D., & Weingart, L. (2001). Maximizing cross-functional new product teams' innovativeness and constraint adherence: A conflict communications perspective. *Academy of Management Journal, 44*(4), 779–793.

Luke, J. S. (1998). *Catalytic leadership*. San Francisco: Jossey-Bass.

Luthans, F. & Avolio, B. J. (2003). Authentic leadership: A positive developmental approach. In K. S. Cameron, J. E. Dutton, & R. E. Quinn (Eds.), *Positive organizational scholarship* (pp. 241–261). San Francisco, CA: Barrett-Koehler.

Machiavelli, N. (1532). Concerning new principalities which are acquired by one's own arms and ability. In *The prince*. (Chapter VI). Retrieved from www.constitution.org/mac/prince06.htm

Mackin, D. (2012). *Teaming in the workplace: Building a team that is "great by choice"*. Retrieved February 11, 2017, from http://www.newdirectionsconsulting.com/leadership-engagement/teaming-in-the-workplace-building-a-team-that-is-great-by-choice/

Malhotra, A., Majchrzak, A., & Rosen, B. (2007). Leading virtual teams. *Academy of Management Perspectives*, February, 60–70.

Martin, J. (1992). *Cultures in organizations: Three perspectives*. Oxford, UK: Oxford University Press.

Martin, J. (2002). *Organizational culture: Mapping the terrain*. Thousand Oaks, CA: Sage.

Marwick, A. E. & boyd, d. m. (2010). I tweet honestly, I tweet passionately: Twitter users, context collapse, and the imagined audience. *New Media & Society, 13*(1), 114–133.

Maxwell, J. C. (1993). *Developing the leader within you*. Nashville, TN: Thomas Nelson.

Maxwell, J. C. (1999). *The 21 indispensible qualities of a leader*. Nashville, TN: Thomas Nelson.

Mayer, D. M., Kuenzi, M., & Greenbaum, R. L. (2009). Making ethical climate a mainstream management topic: A review, critique and prescription for the empirical research on ethical climate. In D. De Cremer (Ed.), *Psychological perspectives on ethical behavior and decision making* (pp. 181–213). Greenwich, CT: Information Age Publishing.

Mayer, J. D., Salovey, P., & Caruso, D. R. (2000b). Models of emotional intelligence. In R. J. Sternberg (Ed.), *Handbook of intelligence* (pp. 396–420). Cambridge: Cambridge University Press

McCauley, C. D., Kanaga, K., & Lafferty, K. (2010). Leader development systems. In E. Van Velsor, C. D. McCauley, & M. N. Ruderman (Eds.), *Center for Creative Leadership handbook of leadership development* (pp. 29–61). San Francisco, CA: Jossey-Bass.

McCauley, C. D., Van Velsor, E., & Ruderman, M. N. (2010). Introduction: Our view of leadership development. In E. Van Velsor, C. D. McCauley, & M. N. Ruderman (Eds.), *Center for Creative Leadership handbook of leadership development* (pp. 1–26). San Francisco, CA: Jossey-Bass.

McChrystal, S., Collins, T., Silverman, D. & Fussel, C. (2015). *Team of teams: New rules of engagement for a complex world*. New York: Penguin Random House.

McCombs, M. E. & Shaw, D. L. (1972). The agenda-setting function of mass media. *The Public Opinion Quarterly, 36*(2), 176–187.

McCombs, M. E. & Shaw, D. L. (1993). The evolution of agenda-setting research: Twenty-five years in the marketplace of ideas. *Journal of Communication, 43*(2), 58–67.

McGrath, J. E. (1962). Leadership behavior: Some requirements for leadership training. Washington, DC: U.S. Civil Service Commission, Office of Career Development.

Meenan, C. (n.d.). *Differences between destructive and constructive conflict. Chron Small Business*. Retrieved February 24, 2017, from http://smallbusiness.chron.com/differences-between-destructive-constructive-conflict-1202.html

Meindl, J. R. & Ehrlich, S. B. (1987). The romance of leadership and the evaluation of organizational performance. *The Academy of Management Journal, 30*(1), 91–109.

Meister, J., & Willyerd, K. (2009). Are you ready to manage five generations of workers? *Harvard Business Review* (online).

Mischel, L. J., & Northcraft, G. B. (1997). I think we can, I think we can ...: The role of self-efficacy beliefs in group and team effectiveness. In B. Markovsky & M. J. Lovaglia (Eds.), *Advances in group processes. Greenwich*, CT: JAI Press.

Mockler, S. (2016). Not all conflicts are created equal: The 3 types of conflicts. Retrieved February 24, 2017, from http://www.vantageleadership.com/our-blog/not-all-conflicts-are-equal-3-types-of-conflict/

Morgan, N. (2015, July 8). The art of passionate leadership. *Forbes* (online). Retrieved June 6, 2017, from https://www.forbes.com/sites/ellevate/2015/07/08/the-art-of-passionate-leadership/#45817e104484

Morgeson, F., DeRue, D., & Karam, E. (2010). Leadership in teams: A functional approach to understanding leadership structures and processes. *Journal of Management, 36*(1), 5–39.

Myatt, M. (2012). *5 keys of dealing with workplace conflict. Forbes* (online). Retrieved February 26, 2017, from https://www.forbes.com/sites/mikemyatt/2012/02/22/5-keys-to-dealing-with-workplace-conflict/#c898c371e95c

Nagel, T. (2006). Ethics. In D. M. Borchert (Ed.), *Encyclopedia of philosophy* (2nd ed., Vol. 3, pp. 379–394). Detroit: Macmillan Reference USA.

National Association of Colleges and Employers (2015). *Job outlook 2016 survey*. Retrieved June 1, 2017, from http://www.naceweb.org/career-development/trends-and-predictions/job-outlook-2016-attributes-employers-want-to-see-on-new-college-graduates-resumes/

Nielsen, R., Marrone, J., & Slay, H. (2010). A new look at humility: Exploring the humility concept and its role in socialized charismatic leadership. *Journal of Leadership and Organizational Studies*, *17*(1), 33–43.

Nohria, N. & Gulati, R. (1996). Is slack good or bad for innovation. *Academy of Management*, *39*(5), 1245–1264.

Norman, D. A. (1999). Affordance, conventions and design. *Interactions*, 38–43.

Northouse, P. G. (2015). *Leadership: Theory and practice* (7th ed.). Thousand Oaks, CA: Sage.

Nowicki, M. & Summers, J. (2008). When participative management leads to garbled communication. *Healthcare Financial Management, 62*(2), 118–120.

Oxford Dictionary (2016). *Oxford dictionary of business and management* (6th ed.). Oxford University Press. Retrieved February 20, 2017, from: http://www.oxfordreference.com/search?q=Team&searchBtn=Search&isQuickSearch=true

Palanski, M. E. & Yammarino, F. J. (2009). Integrity and leadership: A multi-level conceptual framework. *The Leadership Quarterly, 20*(3), 405–420.

Parker, A. (2011, May 30). Congressman, sharp voice on Twitter, finds it can cut 2 ways. *The New York Times*. Retrieved from http://www.nytimes.com/2011/05/31/nyregion/for-rep-anthony-weiner-twitter-has-double-edge.html

Parker, P. S. (2005). *Race, gender, and leadership*. Mahwah, NJ: Lawrence Erlbaum.

Parks, S. D. (2005). *Leadership can be taught: A bold approach for a complex world*. Boston, MA: Harvard Business Review Press.

Payne, S. L. & Calton, J. M. (2008). Ethics of dialogue. *Encyclopedia of business ethics and society*. Thousand Oaks, CA: Sage.

Pew Research Center (2015, November 22). Beyond distrust: How Americans view their government. Retrieved July 06, 2017, from http://www.people-press.org/2015/11/23/beyond-distrust-how-americans-view-their-government

Pfeffer, J. (2015). *Leadership BS: Fixing workplaces and careers one truth at a time*. New York: HarperCollins.

Pfeffer, J. & Sutton, R. I. (2000). *The knowing doing gap: How smart companies turn knowledge into action*. Boston, MA: Harvard University Business School Press.

Philipp, B. & Lopez, P. (2013). The moderating role of ethical leadership: Investigating relationships among employee psychological contracts, commitment, and citizenship behavior. *Journal of Leadership & Organizational Studies, 20*(3), 304–315.

Phillips, K. W., Mannix, E. A., Neale, M. A., & Gruenfeld, D. H. (2004). Diverse groups and information sharing: The effects of congruent ties. *Journal of Experimental Social Psychology, 40*(4), 497–510.

Pink, D. H. (2011). *Drive: The surprising truth about what motivates us*. New York: Riverhead Books.

Pondy, L. R. (1978). Leadership is a language game. In M. W. McCall & M. M. Lombardo (Eds.), *Leadership: Where else can we go?* Durham, NC: Duke University Press.

Popper, K. (2002). *The logic of scientific discovery*. New York, NY: Routledge

Posner, B. Z. & Schmidt, W. H. (1984). Values and the American manager: An update. *California Management Review, 26*(3), 202–216.

Posner, B. Z. & Schmidt, W. H. (1992). Values and the American manager: An update updated. *California Management Review*, *34*(3), 80–94.

Powell, W. W. (1990). Neither market nor hierarchy: Network forms of organization. In B. Staw & L. L. Cummings (Eds.), *Research in organizational behavior* (Vol. 12, pp. 295–336). San Francisco: JAI Press.

Project Management Hacks (2016). 13 Statistics on the state of work in 2016: Meetings, productivity & conflict. Retrieved February 26, 2017, from http://projectmanagementhacks. com/13-statistics-on-the-state-of-work-in-2016-meetings-productivity-conflict/

Qualman, E. (2014). *What happens in Vegas stays on YouTube*. Cambridge, MA: Equalman Studios.

Qualman, E., & Brown, P. G. (2015). *What happens on campus stays on YouTube*. Cambridge, MA: Equalman Studios.

Quan-Haase, A., Wellman, B., Witte, J. C., & Hampton, K. N. (2002). Capitalizing on the net: Social contact, civic engagement, and sense of community. In B. Wellman & C. Haythornthwaite (Eds.), *The Internet in everyday life* (pp. 291–324). Malden, MA: Wiley-Blackwell.

Queensland University (n.d.). *Infographic—Communicating in the modern workplace*. Retrieved February 9, 2017, from: http://online.queens.edu/resource/business-leadership/infographic/ communicating-in-the-workplace.

Raven, B. H. (2004). Power, six bases of. In G. R. Goethals, G. J. Sorenson, & J. M. Burns (Eds.), *Encyclopedia of leadership*. Thousand Oaks: Sage.

Reinhardt, W., Schmidt, B., Sloep, P., & Drachsler, H. (2011). Knowledge worker roles and actions—results of two empirical studies. *Knowledge and Process Management*, *18*(3), 150–174.

Ricci, R. & Wiese, C. (2012). *The collaboration imperative: Executive strategies for unlocking your organization's true potential*. San Jose, CA: Cisco Systems.

Ross, J. A. (2008). Make your good team great. *Harvard Business Review* (online). Retrieved August 6, 2017 from https://hbr.org/2008/02/make-your-good-team-great-1.

Rost, J. C. (1993). *Leadership for the twenty-first century*. Westport, CT: Praeger.

Rothman, J. (2016, February 29). Shut up and sit down. Why the leadership industry rules. *The New Yorker*. Retrieved June 1, 2017, from http://www.newyorker.com/magazine/2016/02/29/ our-dangerous-leadership-obsession

Ruben, B. D. (1976). Assessing communication competency for intercultural adaptation. *Group & Organization Studies*, *1*(3), 334–354.

Ruben, B. D. (2003). General system theory: An approach to human communication. In R. W. Budd & B. D. Ruben, *Approaches to human communication* (2nd ed., pp. 95–118). New Brunswick, NJ: Transaction Publishers.

Ruben, B. D. (2006). *What leaders need to know and do: A leadership competencies scorecard*. Washington, DC: National Association of College and University Business Officers.

Ruben, B. D. (2012). *Understanding, planning and leading organizational change*. Washington, DC: National Association of College and University Business Officers.

Ruben, B. D. (2012). *What leaders need to know and do: A leadership competencies scorecard* (2nd ed.). Washington, DC: National Association of College and University Business Officers.

Ruben, B. D. (2015). Communication theory and health communication practice: The more things change, the more they stay the same. *Health Communication*, *31*(1), 1–11.

Ruben, B. D. (2016a). *Excellence in higher education workbook and scoring instructions* (8th ed.). Sterling, VA: Stylus.

Ruben, B. D. (2016b). *Excellence in higher education facilitator's guide* (8th ed.). Sterling, VA: Stylus.

Ruben, B. D. (2016c). *Excellence in higher education: A framework for the design, assessment, and continuous improvement of institutions, departments, and programs* (8th ed.). Sterling, VA: Stylus.

Ruben, B. D., De Lisi, R., & Gigliotti, R. A. (2017). *A guide for leaders in higher education: Core concepts, competencies, and tools*. Sterling, VA: Stylus.

Ruben, B. D. & Gigliotti, R. A. (2016). Leadership as social influence: An expanded view of leadership communication theory and practice. *Journal of Leadership and Organizational Studies*, *23*(4), 467–479.

Ruben, B. D. & Gigliotti, R. A. (2017). Communication: Sine qua non of organizational leadership theory and practice. *International Journal of Business Communication, 54*(1), 12–30.

Ruben, B. D. & Stewart, L. P. (2016). *Communication and human behavior* (6th ed.). Dubuque, IA: Kendall Hunt.

Ruud, G. (2000). The symphony: Organizational discourse and the symbolic tensions between artistic and business ideologies. *Journal of Applied Communication Research*, *28*(2), 117–143.

Salovey, P. & Mayer, J. D. (1990). Emotional intelligence. *Imagination, Cognition, and Personality, 9*, 185–211.

Scelfo, J. (2016, April 8). Angela Duckworth on passion, grit and success. *The New York Times*. Retrieved June 6, 2017, from https://www.nytimes.com/2016/04/10/education/edlife/passion-grit-success.html?_r=0

Schein, E. H. (1996). Three cultures of management: The key to organizational learning. *Sloan Management Review*, *38*(1), 9–20.

Schein, E. H. (1999). *The corporate culture survival guide*. San Francisco: Jossey-Bass.

Schein, E. H. (2010). *Organizational culture and leadership* (4th ed.). San Francisco, CA: Jossey-Bass.

Schmidt, W. H. & Posner, B. Z. (1982). *Managerial values and expectations: The silent power in personal and organizational life*. New York: AMA Membership Publications Division, American Management Associations.

Schölmerich, F., Schermuly, C. C., & Deller, J. (2016). How leader's diversity beliefs alter the impact of faultlines on team functioning. *Small Group Research*, *47*(2), 177–206.

Schön, D. A. (1984). *The reflective practitioner: How professionals think in action*. New York, NY: Basic Books.

Sendjaya, S. & Sarros, J. C. (2002). Servant leadership: Its origin, development, and application in organizations. *Journal of Leadership and Organization Studies*, *9*(2), 47–64.

Short, J. A., Williams, E., & Christie, B. (1976). *The social psychology of telecommunications*. New York: John Wiley & Sons.

Sinek, S. (2009). *Start with why: How great leaders inspire everyone to take action*. New York: Portfolio/Penguin.

Smircich, L. & Morgan, G. (1982). Leadership: The management of meaning. *The Journal of Applied Behavioral Science, 18*(3): 257–273.

Smith, Z. (2007). *Creating and testing the higher education leadership competencies (HELC) model: A study of athletics directors, senior student affairs officers, and chief academic officers* (Unpublished doctoral dissertation). University of Nevada, Reno.

Society for Human Resource Management (2015). *Developing and sustaining high performance work teams*. Retrieved February 22, 2017, from https://www.shrm.org/resourcesandtools/tools-and-samples/toolkits/pages/developingandsustaininghigh-performanceworkteams.aspx

Society of Professional Journalists. (2014). *Society of Professional Journalists code of ethics*. Retrieved August 6, 2017 from https://www.spj.org/ethicscode.asp

Spencer-Oatey, H. (2008). *Culturally speaking: Culture, communication, and politeness theory* (2nd ed.). New York: Continuum.

Spitzberg, B. H. & Cupach, W. R. (1984). *Interpersonal communication competence*. Beverly Hills, CA: Sage.

Stagl, K. C., Salas, E., & Burke, C. S. (2007). Best practices in team leadership. In J. Conger and R. Riggio (Eds.). *The practice of leadership* (pp. 172–197). San Francisco: Jossey-Bass.

Stogdill, R. (1974). *Handbook of leadership*. New York: The Free Press.

Stone, B. (2015). How I did it: Twitter's cofounder on creating opportunities. *Harvard Business Review, 93*(6), 39-42.

Sumner, W. G. (1906). *Folkways*. Boston: Ginn.

Tajfel, H., & Turner, J. C. (1979). An integrative theory of intergroup conflict. In W. G. Austin & S. Worchel (Eds.), *Psychology of intergroup relations* (pp. 33–47). Monterey, CA: Brooks/Cole.

Tajfel, H., & Turner, J. C. (1986). The social identity theory of inter-group behavior. In S. Worchel & L. W. Austin (Eds.), *Psychology of intergroup relations* (pp. 7–24). Chicago: Nelson-Hall.

Taylor, E. W. (2000). Analyzing research on transformative learning theory. In J. Mezirow & Associates (Eds.), *Learning as transformation: Critical perspectives on a theory in progress* (pp. 29–310). San Francisco, CA: Jossey-Bass.

Thayer, L. (1968). *Communication and communication systems*. Homewood, IL: Richard D. Irwin.

Thayer, L. (1988). Leadership/communication: A critical review and a modest proposal. In G. M. Goldhaber & G. A. Barnett (Eds.), *Handbook of organizational communication* (pp. 231–263). Norwood, NJ: Ablex.

Thayer, L. (2003). Communication: *Sine qua non* of the behavioral sciences. In R. W. Budd & B. D. Ruben (Eds.), *Approaches to human communication* (2nd ed., pp. 7–31). New York: Spartan-Hayden.

The Hofstede Centre. (2017). *Geert Hofstede*. Retrieved August 6, 2017 from https://geert-hofstede.com

The National Association of Colleges and Employers. (2016). *Employers identify four "must have" career readiness competencies for college graduates*. Retrieved February 10, 2017, from: http://www.naceweb.org/s04202016/four-career-readiness competencies.aspx#sthash.B7hK0YSD.dpuf

The Nature Conservancy. (2017) About us: Vision and mission. Retrieved July 6, 2017, from https://www.nature.org/about-us/vision-mission/index.htm

Thomassen, J. (2009). Democratic values. In R. J. Dalton & H.-D. Klingemann (Eds.), *The Oxford Handbook of Political Behavior*. Oxford: Oxford University Press.

Thompson, L. L. (2011). *Making the team: A guide for managers*. Saddle River: Pearson Education, Inc.

Thorton, L. F. (2013). *7 Lenses: Learning the principles and practices of ethical leadership*. Richmond, VA: Leading in Context LLC.

Tora, V. (2016). 12 Critical competencies for leadership in the future. *Critical Thinking*. Retrieved February 27, 2017, from http://qaspire.com/2016/01/06/leadership-skills-for-the-future/

Treem, J. W. & Leonardi, P. M. (2012). Social media use in organizations: Exploring the affordances of visibility, editability, persistence, and association. *Communication Yearbook, 36*(1), 143–189.

Treviño, L. K., Brown, M., & Hartman, L. P. (2003). A qualitative investigation of perceived executive ethical leadership: Perceptions from inside and outside the executive suite. *Human Relations, 56*(1), 5–37.

Treviño, L. K., Butterfield, K., & McCabe, D. (1998). The ethical context in organizations: Influences on employee attitudes and behaviors. *Business Ethics Quarterly, 8*(3), 447–476.

Treviño, L. K., Hartman, L. P., & Brown, M. (2000). Moral person and moral manager: How executives develop a reputation for ethical leadership. *California Management Review, 42*(4), 128–142.

Tromp, S. A. & Ruben, B. D. (2010). *Strategic planning in higher education: A guide for leaders* (2nd ed.). Washington, DC: NACUBO.

Tuckman, B. (1965). Developmental sequence in small groups. *Psychological Bulletin, 63(6), 384–399.*

Tuckman, B. & Jensen, M. (1977). Stages of small-group development revisited. *Group & Organization Management, 2*(4), 419–427.

Ubell, R. (Ed.). (2010). Mitigating conflict in online student teams. *Virtual teamwork: Mastering the art and practice of online learning and corporate collaboration* (pp. 65–90). New Jersey: Wiley Publishing.

United Nations. (2015). *244 million international migrants living abroad worldwide, new UN statistics reveal*. Retrieved August 6, 2017 from http://www.un.org/sustainabledevelopment/blog/2016/01/244-million-international-migrants-living-abroad-worldwide-new-un-statistics-reveal/

Useem, M. (1998). *The leadership moment*. New York: Random House.

Velsor, E. V., McCauley, C. D., & Ruderman, M. N. (2010). *The center for creative leadership handbook of leadership development*. San Francisco: Jossey-Bass.

Victor, B. & Cullen, J. B. (1988). The organizational bases of ethical work climates. *Administrative Science Quarterly, 33*(1), 101–125.

Walther, J. B. (1992). A longitudinal experiment on relational tone in computer-mediated and face-to-face interaction. In J. F. Nunamaker & R. H. Sprague (Eds.), Proceedings of the Hawaii International Conference on System Sciences (Vol. 4, pp. 220–231). Los Alamitos, CA: IEEE Computer Society Press.

Walther, J. B. (1994). Anticipated ongoing interaction versus channel effects on relational communication in computer-mediated interaction. *Human Communication Research*, *20*(4), 473–501.

Walther, J. B. & Burgoon, J. K. (1992). Relational communication in computer-mediated interaction. *Human Communication Research*, *19*(1), 50–88.

Walumbwa, F. O., Christensen, A. L., & Hailey, F. (2011). Authentic leadership and the knowledge economy. *Organizational Dynamics*, *40*(2), 110–118.

Wartzman, R. (2014, October 16). What Peter Drucker knew about 2020. *Harvard Business Review* (online). Retrieved August 6, 2017 from, from https://hbr.org/2014/10/what-peter-drucker-knew-about-2020

Waterman, R. H. (1990). *Adhocracy: The power to change*. Memphis, TN: Whittle Direct Books.

Watzlawick, P., Beavin, J. & Jackson, D. (1967). *Pragmatics of human communication: A study of interactional patterns, pathologies, and paradoxes*. New York: Norton.

Weick, K. E. (1979). *The social psychology of organizing*. Reading, MA: Addison-Wesley.

Weick, K. E. (1995). *Sensemaking in organizations*. Thousand Oaks, CA: Sage.

Weick, K. E., Sutcliffe, K. M., & Obstfeld, D. (2005). Organizing and the process of sensemaking. *Organization Science*, *16*(4), 409–421.

Weisburd, D., Mastrofski, S. D., Greenspan, R., & Willis, J. J. (2004, April). *The growth of Comstat in American policing. Police Foundation reports*. Retrieved August 6, 2017 from assets.lapdonline.org/assets/pdf/growthofcompstat.pdf

Weiss, J. & Hughes, J. (2005). Want collaboration?: Accept—and actively manage—conflict. *Harvard Business Review* (online). Retrieved February 27, 2017 from https://hbr.org/2005/03/want-collaboration-accept-and-actively-manage-conflict.

Wellman, B., Quan-Haase, A., Boase, J., Chen, W., Hampton, K., Díaz, I., & Miyata, K. (2003). The social affordances of the internet for networked individualism. *Journal of Computer Mediated Communication*, *8*(3) (online).

Wisniewski, M. A. (1999). Leadership competencies in continuing higher education: Implications for leadership education. *Continuing Higher Education*, *47*(1), 14–23.

Witherspoon, P. D. (1997). *Communicating leadership: An organizational perspective*. Boston: Allyn & Bacon.

Witt, D. (2015). *4 types of team conflict—And how to deal with each effectively*. Retrieved February 25, 2017, from: https://leaderchat.org/2015/07/16/4-types-of-team-conflict-and-how-to-deal-with-each-effectively/

World Health Organization. (2015). What do we mean by "sex" and "gender"? *World Health Organization*. Retrieved August 6, 2017 from https://web.archive.org/web/20150818074425/http://apps.who.int/gender/whatisgender/en/index.html

Yukl, G. (2001). *Leadership in organizations*. Upper Saddle River, NJ: Prentice Hall.

Yukl, G. (2010). Influence tactics for leaders. In E. Biech (Ed.), *The ASTD leadership handbook*. Alexandria, VA: ASTD Press.

Yukl, G. (2012). *Leadership in organizations* (8th ed.). Upper Saddle River, NJ: Prentice Hall.

Yukl, G., Seifert, C. F., & Chavez, C. (2008). Validation of the extended influence behavior questionnaire. *The Leadership Quarterly, 19*(5), 609–621.

Zaleznik, A. (1992). Managers and leaders: Are they different? *Harvard Business Review, (70)*2, 126–135.

Zumbrun, J. (2016, May 4). The rise of knowledge workers is accelerating despite the threat of automation. *The Wall Street Journal* (online). Retrieved August 6, 2017 from http://blogs.wsj.com/economics/2016/05/04/the-rise-of-knowledge-workers-is-accelerating-despite-the-threat-ofautomation/.

APPENDIX A

LEADERSHIP COMPETENCIES SCORECARD 2.0 (RUBEN, 2012)

> **Leadership Competencies Scorecard 2.0**
> **(LCS 2.0)**
>
> **Developed by**
>
> **Brent D. Ruben, Ph.D.**

The **LEADERSHIP COMPETENCIES SCORECARD 2.0** is the 2012 version of the **LCS**, first published in 2006 in *What Leaders Need to Know and Do.** The **Scorecard** provides a competency-based framework that identifies and integrates a diverse array of characteristics described in scholarly and professional writings as being important for effective leadership.

The **LCS** identifies five major competency themes, each of which includes a number of specific competencies. *Analytic Competencies* are associated with thoughtful reflection on one's own and others' behaviors, and careful consideration of the consequences of alternative leadership options and strategies. *Personal Competencies* refer to one's standards, character, and expression of values. *Communication Competencies* relate to the knowledge and skills necessary for effective interaction in interpersonal, group, organizational, and public settings. *Organizational Competencies* include administrative capabilities that are viewed as important for leading in organizations of varying purpose, function, and size. *Positional Competencies* include knowledge and skills related to the particular context, setting, field, or sector in which a leader is serving.

The **Scorecard** can be used to inventory and develop a profile of one's own or another person's leadership competencies, using 1-5 ratings for each of the 35 competencies. **LSC** ratings allow individuals to rate "understanding of the concept," and "effectiveness in practice." *Understanding* refers to theoretical knowledge that provides a foundation for anticipating and adapting to leadership needs of varying situations, organizations, cultures, or sectors. *Effectiveness* relates to skill in translating knowledge and applying it to practice. Both dimensions can be important to assessing and enhancing leadership capability. When using the **Scorecard** for self-assessment, rate both *understanding* and *effectiveness*. When using the **LCS** to assess others, the ratings should generally be limited to *effectiveness*. *Effectiveness* assessment is based on behavioral observation, and an individual's level of *understanding* or knowledge of particular competencies may not be apparent from his or her behavior. Scoring Instructions are provided on page 4.

*Brent D. Ruben, **What Leaders Need to Know and Do: A Leadership Competencies Scorecard.** Washington, DC: National Association of College and University Business Officers, 2006.

LCS 2.0

1 (low) ⟷ 5 (high)

Analytic Competencies		Understanding of the Concept	Effectiveness in Practice
1. SELF-ASSESSMENT	Analyzing one's own thoughts, emotions, and reactions	1 2 3 4 5	1 2 3 4 5
2. PROBLEM-DEFINITION	Identifying underlying issues, concerns, problems, and tasks that need to be addressed in a given situation	1 2 3 4 5	1 2 3 4 5
3. STAKEHOLDER ANALYSIS	Assessing perspectives of those likely to be affected by the decisions, policies, or practices of a leader or organization	1 2 3 4 5	1 2 3 4 5
4. SYSTEM, ORGANIZATIONAL, SITUATIONAL ANALYSIS	Focusing on "the big picture," including short- and long-term concerns and outcomes, for all those affected by leadership decisions, policies, or practices	1 2 3 4 5	1 2 3 4 5
5. ANALYSIS OF TECHNOLOGY TO SUPPORT LEADERSHIP	Assessing available technologies, and their potential strengths and weaknesses for supporting leadership efforts	1 2 3 4 5	1 2 3 4 5
6. PROBLEM-SOLVING	Analyzing a situation, identifying possible/appropriate leadership styles and courses of action; ensuring follow through	1 2 3 4 5	1 2 3 4 5
7. REVIEW AND ANALYSIS OF RESULTS	Debriefing and analyzing outcomes to derive "lessons learned" that can be applied in a future situation	1 2 3 4 5	1 2 3 4 5

Subtotals - Analytic Competencies _____ _____

Personal Competencies		Understanding of the Concept	Effectiveness in Practice
8. CHARACTER, PERSONAL VALUES, AND ETHICS	Maintaining personal and professional standards	1 2 3 4 5	1 2 3 4 5
9. COGNITIVE ABILITY AND CREATIVITY	Demonstrating insight and imagination	1 2 3 4 5	1 2 3 4 5
10. ENTHUSIASM	Maintaining a positive attitude	1 2 3 4 5	1 2 3 4 5
11. HIGH STANDARDS	Expecting excellent performance from oneself and others	1 2 3 4 5	1 2 3 4 5
12. PERSONAL CONVICTION AND PERSISTENCE	Being dedicated and persevering	1 2 3 4 5	1 2 3 4 5
13. SELF-DISCIPLINE AND SELF-CONFIDENCE	Having self-control, focus, and confidence in one's capabilities	1 2 3 4 5	1 2 3 4 5
14. ROLE MODELING	Enacting the values and behaviors that one advocates for others	1 2 3 4 5	1 2 3 4 5

Subtotals - Personal Competencies _____ _____

LCS 2.0

		1 (low) ⬄ 5 (high)	

Communication Competencies		Understanding of the Concept	Effectiveness of Practice
15. CREDIBILITY AND TRUST	Being admired, seen as magnetic, authoritative, honest, competent and trustworthy	1 2 3 4 5	1 2 3 4 5
16. INFLUENCE AND PERSUASION	Convincing others to adopt advocated ideas, points-of-view, or behaviors	1 2 3 4 5	1 2 3 4 5
17. INTERPERSONAL RELATIONS AND TEAM-BUILDING	Creating effective interpersonal relationships, groups, and teams	1 2 3 4 5	1 2 3 4 5
18. LISTENING, ATTENTION, QUESTION-ASKING AND LEARNING	Attending verbally and visually to the thoughts, behaviors and actions of others	1 2 3 4 5	1 2 3 4 5
19. WRITING AND PUBLIC SPEAKING	Conveying information, ideas, and opinions clearly through writing and oral presentations	1 2 3 4 5	1 2 3 4 5
20. DIVERSITY AND INTERCULTURAL RELATIONS	Valuing and working effectively with both men and women, and individuals of varying cultural, racial, ethnic, political or life-style orientations	1 2 3 4 5	1 2 3 4 5
21. FACILITATION, NEGOTIATION, AND CONFLICT RESOLUTION	Encouraging discussion and the expression of varying points of view, encouraging compromise, and effectively addressing tensions and conflicts	1 2 3 4 5	1 2 3 4 5

Subtotals - Communication Competencies   _____   _____

Organizational Competencies		Understanding of the Concept	Effectiveness of Practice
22. VISION-SETTING, STRATEGY DEVELOPMENT, AND GOAL ATTAINMENT	Motivating and providing a sense of purpose and direction, development approaches and goals, and ensuring follow through	1 2 3 4 5	1 2 3 4 5
23. MANAGEMENT AND SUPERVISION	Overseeing financial, physical, and human resources	1 2 3 4 5	1 2 3 4 5
24. INFO/KNOWLEDGE MANAGEMENT AND BOUNDARY SPANNING	Facilitating the flow and sharing of information within a group or organization, and across organizational boundaries	1 2 3 4 5	1 2 3 4 5
25. TECHNOLOGICAL CAPABILITY	Using appropriate communication technology and media to support leadership initiatives	1 2 3 4 5	1 2 3 4 5
26. COLLABORATIVE DECISION MAKING AND EMPOWERMENT	Effectively engaging others in decision making and other activities	1 2 3 4 5	1 2 3 4 5
27. TEACHING AND COACHING	Encouraging the development of leaders and leadership capacity	1 2 3 4 5	1 2 3 4 5
28. CHANGE, RISK AND CRISIS MANAGEMENT	Promoting and effectively guiding change and innovation, anticipating and managing risks, and coping effectively with unexpected and crisis situations	1 2 3 4 5	1 2 3 4 5

Subtotals - Organizational Competencies   _____   _____

LCS 2.0

1 (low) ⟷ 5 (high)

Positional Competencies		Understanding of the Concept	Effectiveness in Practice
29. EDUCATION	Having relevant formal education and/or training in sector-related competencies	1 2 3 4 5	1 2 3 4 5
30. EXPERIENCE	Having prior relevant experience in the sector—e.g., business, healthcare, government, or education	1 2 3 4 5	1 2 3 4 5
31. EXPERTISE	Having appropriate and/or required job competencies	1 2 3 4 5	1 2 3 4 5
32. KNOWLEDGE OF FIELD	Understanding of the field, its issues, challenges and opportunities—e.g., business, healthcare, government, or education	1 2 3 4 5	1 2 3 4 5
33. KNOWLEDGE OF ORGANIZATION	Understanding the particular organization, its issues, challenges, and opportunities	1 2 3 4 5	1 2 3 4 5
34. FAMILIARITY WITH WORK	Knowing about and being comfortable with tasks or work activities that are specific to the sector and organization	1 2 3 4 5	1 2 3 4 5
35. PROFESSIONAL INVOLVEMENT	Pursuing opportunities for personal and professional learning, growth, and advancement	1 2 3 4 5	1 2 3 4 5

Subtotals - Positional Competencies

Scoring Instructions

- Total the ratings for each competency category. If you used the LCS 2.0 for self-assessment and completed both understanding of the concept and effectiveness in practice, total your ratings for both dimensions. If you used the LSC 2.0 for assessing others, you may only have completed the effectiveness in practice ratings, and would only total the effectiveness columns.

- Transfer the sub-total scores to the blank bar graph below by drawing a horizontal line at the level which corresponds to your particular score. Then, color in the area below each score-line to create bar charts for each competency area.

- Note: Comparing totals across competencies highlights strengths and areas where improvement may be beneficial. Comparing understanding and effectiveness ratings highlights knowledge-skill alignment issues and identifies potential improvement targets.

SCALE	Analytic Competencies		Personal Competencies		Communication Competencies		Organizational Competencies		Positional Competencies	
35										
30										
25										
20										
15										
10										
5										
	Understanding	Effectiveness	Understanding	Effectiveness	Understanding	Effectiveness	Understanding	Effectiveness	Understanding	Effectiveness

APPENDIX B

This *Checklist**—like the Baldrige framework from which it takes its inspiration—covers seven dimensions of group and organizational functioning. Four statements are included for each of these categories. Each statement addresses one of the basic themes in the category. The *Checklist* is designed to provide a starting point for focused discussion of the areas of current strength and potential targets for improvement in any formal organization or group.

Instructions:

- Read each of the 28 statements in the following pages, and for each, circle the number that corresponds to your assessment.

- When you have completed the Checklist, turn to the last page for instructions on scoring and interpretation.

*Adapted from Brent D. Ruben, *Excellence in Higher Education*. Eighth Edition. Stylus Publishing, Sterling Virginia, 2017.

1.0 Leadership	Don't Know/ Never 1	Rarely 2	Sometimes 3	Often 4	Always 5
Our leaders clarify and build consensus on our direction, future aspirations, values, plans, and goals.	1	2	3	4	5
Leaders encourage and use feedback and performance reviews to improve their own leadership and leadership practices throughout the organization.	1	2	3	4	5
Our leaders are visibly committed to the advancement of our group or organization.	1	2	3	4	5
Our leaders are responsive to community and public concerns and contribute to our group or organization's efforts to help address them.	1	2	3	4	5
Subtotals					

Category 1.0 Total _____

2.0 Purposes and Plans	Don't Know/ Never 1	Rarely 2	Sometimes 3	Often 4	Always 5
Our group or organization has a formalized planning process.	1	2	3	4	5
We have a written plan that translates our mission, vision, and values into priorities, measurable goals, and action steps.	1	2	3	4	5
Members from our group or organization are appropriately engaged in developing and implementing our directions, plans, and goals.	1	2	3	4	5
Our group or organization's plans and goals are synchronized with those of the organization or institutions of which we are a part.	1	2	3	4	5
Subtotals					

Category 2.0 Total _____

3.0 Beneficiary and Constituency Relationships	Don't Know/ Never 1	Rarely 2	Sometimes 3	Often 4	Always 5
Our organization has a systematic approach to learning about the needs, expectations, and satisfaction levels of the groups for which we provide programs and services.	1	2	3	4	5
We are well informed about the needs, expectations, and priorities of those who benefit from our programs, services, and activities.	1	2	3	4	5
Mechanisms are in place to ensure regular two-way communication with our beneficiary and constituency groups.	1	2	3	4	5
Information about needs, expectations, satisfaction, and perceptions is well-organized, analyzed, shared, and used for improvement.	1	2	3	4	5
Subtotals					

Category 3.0 Total _____

4.0 Programs, Services, and Activities	Don't Know/ Never 1	Rarely 2	Sometimes 3	Often 4	Always 5
We maintain high standards in all of our mission-critical programs and services.	1	2	3	4	5
High standards are maintained in administrative and support services.	1	2	3	4	5
Our internal procedures are effective, efficient, well documented, and consistently followed.	1	2	3	4	5
We formally review our programs, services, and activities—and our internal procedures—on a regular basis.	1	2	3	4	5
Subtotals					

Category 4.0 Total _____

5.0 Members and Climate	Don't Know/ Never 1	Rarely 2	Sometimes 3	Often 4	Always 5
We help members develop their full potential, and make it possible for them to participate actively in the life of the organization.	1	2	3	4	5
Our group or organization encourages excellence, participation, appreciation of diversity, and professional development.	1	2	3	4	5
We have effective approaches for assessing and recognizing member contributions.	1	2	3	4	5
We have a system for regularly assessing our group or organizational climate and member satisfaction.	1	2	3	4	5
Subtotals					

Category 5.0 Total _____

6.0 Assessment and Information Use	Don't Know/ Never 1	Rarely 2	Sometimes 3	Often 4	Always 5
We have a clear and shared view as to what standards to use in assessing the effectiveness of our group or organization, and our programs, services, and activities.	1	2	3	4	5
We have effective approaches for gathering assessment information on effectiveness, and progress toward our short- and long-term goals.	1	2	3	4	5
Information is used throughout the unit to analyze, review, and improve the quality of all that we do.	1	2	3	4	5
We obtain and use information from peer and leading organizations to assess our current effectiveness and progress.	1	2	3	4	5
Subtotals					

Category 6.0 Total _____

7.0 Outcomes and Achievements	Don't Know/ Never 1	Rarely 2	Sometimes 3	Often 4	Always 5
We have objective documentation indicating that our group or organization is successful in achieving our mission, vision, plans, and goals.	1	2	3	4	5
The groups for which we provide programs, services, and activities perceive that we are effectively meeting their needs and expectations.	1	2	3	4	5
We have a positive climate within our group or organization, and our members are satisfied with their roles and participation opportunities.	1	2	3	4	5
Our record of achievement in all of the previous categories compares favorably with that of peers and leaders.	1	2	3	4	5
Subtotals					

Category 7.0 Total _____

TOTAL FOR ALL CATEGORIES _____

Scoring

1.   Add up the total points for each category.

2.   For each category, draw a marker line across the bars on the graph below to indicate the total score.

3.   Refer to the table (to the right) for score interpretation.

Interpretation

4-7   A priority area for improvement.

8-12   The beginning of a systematic approach with many improvement possibilities.

13-16 Many indicators of an effective, systematic approach to addressing this area.

	4	6	8	10	12	14	16	18	20
1. Leadership									
2. Purposes and Plans									
3. Beneficiaries and Constituencies									
4. Programs, Services, and Activities									
5. Members and Climate									
6. Assessment and Information Use									
7. Outcomes and Achievements									

INDEX

CPSIA information can be obtained
at www.ICGtesting.com
Printed in the USA
LVHW062250240620
658927LV00009B/1633

9 781524 942137